Larry

Jany 2014

GIVE 'EM HELL BOYS!

BOOKS BY LOCHLAINN SEABROOK

A Rebel Born: A Defense of Nathan Bedford Forrest - Confederate General, American Legend
(winner of the 2011 Jefferson Davis Historical Gold Medal)

Nathan Bedford Forrest: Southern Hero, American Patriot - Honoring a Confederate Icon and the
Old South

The Quotable Nathan Bedford Forrest: Selections From the Writings and Speeches of the
Confederacy's Most Brilliant Cavalryman

Give 'Em Hell Boys! The Complete Military Correspondence of Nathan Bedford Forrest

Everything You Were Taught About the Civil War is Wrong, Ask a Southerner! - Correcting the
Errors of Yankee "History"

Honest Jeff and Dishonest Abe: A Southern Children's Guide to the Civil War

Abraham Lincoln: The Southern View - Demythologizing America's Sixteenth President

The Unquotable Abraham Lincoln: The President's Quotes They Don't Want You To Know!

Lincolnology: The Real Abraham Lincoln Revealed in His Own Words - A Study of Lincoln's
Suppressed, Misinterpreted, and Forgotten Speeches and Writings

The Quotable Jefferson Davis: Selections From the Writings and Speeches of the Confederacy's First
President

The Quotable Alexander H. Stephens: Selections From the Writings and Speeches of the
Confederacy's First Vice President

The Quotable Robert E. Lee: Selections From the Writings and Speeches of the South's Most Beloved
Civil War General

The Old Rebel: Robert E. Lee As He Was Seen By His Contemporaries

The Constitution of the Confederate States of America: Explained

The Quotable Edward A. Pollard: Selections From the Writings of the Confederacy's Greatest
Defender

Encyclopedia of the Battle of Franklin - A Comprehensive Guide to the Conflict that Changed the
Civil War

Carnton Plantation Ghost Stories: True Tales of the Unexplained from Tennessee's Most Haunted
Civil War House!

The McGavocks of Carnton Plantation: A Southern History - Celebrating One of Dixie's Most Noble
Confederate Families and Their Tennessee Home

The Caudills: An Etymological, Ethnological, and Genealogical Study - Exploring the Name and
National Origins of a European-American Family

The Blakeneys: An Etymological, Ethnological, and Genealogical Study - Uncovering the Mysterious
Origins of the Blakeney Family and Name

Britannia Rules: Goddess-Worship in Ancient Anglo-Celtic Society - An Academic Look at the United
Kingdom's Matricentric Spiritual Past

UFOs and Aliens: The Complete Guidebook

Christmas Before Christianity: How the Birthday of the "Sun" Became the Birthday of the "Son"

The Book of Kelle: An Introduction to Goddess-Worship and the Great Celtic Mother-Goddess Kelle,
Original Blessed Lady of Ireland

The Goddess Dictionary of Words and Phrases: Introducing a New Core Vocabulary for the Women's
Spirituality Movement

Aphrodite's Trade: The Hidden History of Prostitution Unveiled

SEA RAVEN PRESS

Thought Provoking Books For Smart People
www.SeaRavenPress.com

GIVE 'EM HELL BOYS!

The Complete Military Correspondence
of Nathan Bedford Forrest

Collected and Edited, with an Introduction and Notes, by

LOCHLAINN SEABROOK

WINNER OF THE JEFFERSON DAVIS HISTORICAL GOLD MEDAL

SEA RAVEN PRESS, FRANKLIN, TENNESSEE, USA

GIVE 'EM HELL BOYS!

Published by
Sea Raven Press, P.O. Box 1054, Franklin, Tennessee 37065-1054 USA
www.searavenpress.com • searavenpress@nii.net

First Sea Raven Press Civil War Sesquicentennial Edition: January 2012
ISBN: 978-0-9838185-6-4
Library of Congress Catalog Number: 2011946072

The Quotable Nathan Bedford Forrest: Selections From the Writings and
Speeches of the Confederacy's Most Brilliant Cavalryman / collected and
edited, with an introduction and notes, by Lochlainn Seabrook. Includes
an Index and bibliographical references.

Front and back cover design, book design and layout, by Lochlainn Seabrook
Typography: Sea Raven Press Book Design
Front cover painting: "That Devil Forrest" © John Paul Strain
Sketch of the author on "Meet the Author" page © Tracy Latham
All images are from 19th-Century public domain sources, unless otherwise indicated
(Portions of this book have been adapted from the author's other works.)

The views on the American "Civil War" documented in this book *are* those of the publisher.

The paper used in this book is acid-free and lignin-free. It has been certified by the Sustainable Forestry
Initiative and the Forest Stewardship Council and meets all ANSI standards for archival quality paper.

PRINTED & MANUFACTURED IN OCCUPIED TENNESSEE, FORMER CONFEDERATE STATES OF AMERICA

Dedication

To the cause for which General Nathan
Bedford Forrest fought Lincoln and his
illicit invaders: Constitutional freedom.

Epigraph

"The magic name of Forrest will truly always be remembered with love, devotion, awe, and respect in all of the Southern states. For, like the immortal archetypal hero of ancient legend that he represents, Forrest will ride his warhorse through the pages of history for all eternity; ageless, timeless, glorious, invincible."[1]

Lochlainn Seabrook, *A Rebel Born* (2010)

CONTENTS

NOTES TO THE READER

🔫 In an effort to retain the true character and meaning of General Forrest's words, they have been printed here exactly as they appear in the original manuscripts, including typographical and grammatical peculiarities inherent to 19th-Century American writing and speaking. Forrest's words begin at the place marked with a traditional Victorian "hand" pointer. My chapter introductions are in normal font, my explanatory comments appear in italics above the writers' quotes, and my clarifications are in brackets within their quotes. (Note that in some instances bracketed words are those of the original 19th-Century U.S. editors.)

🔫 In any study of the "Civil War" it is vitally important to keep in mind that the two major political parties were then the opposite of what they are today. The Democrats of the mid 19th Century were conservatives, akin to the Republican Party of today, while the Republicans of the mid 19th Century were liberals, akin to the Democratic Party of today. Thus the Confederacy's Democratic president, Jefferson Davis, was a conservative (with libertarian leanings); the Union's Republican president, Abraham Lincoln, was a liberal (with socialistic leanings).

🔫 For those interested in the truth about the War for Southern Independence, see my books:

A Rebel Born: A Defense of Nathan Bedford Forrest
Nathan Bedford Forrest: Southern Hero, American Patriot - Honoring a Confederate Icon and the Old South
The Quotable Nathan Bedford Forrest: Selections From the Writings and Speeches of the Confederacy's Most Brilliant Cavalryman
Everything You Were Taught About the Civil War is Wrong, Ask a Southerner! - Correcting the Errors of Yankee "History"
Honest Jeff and Dishonest Abe: A Southern Children's Guide to the Civil War
The Quotable Jefferson Davis: Selections From the Writings & Speeches of the Confederacy's First President

The Quotable Robert E. Lee: Selections From the Writings and Speeches of the South's Most Beloved Civil War General

The Old Rebel: Robert E. Lee As He Was Seen By His Contemporaries

Abraham Lincoln: The Southern View - Demythologizing America's Sixteenth President

Lincolnology: The Real Abraham Lincoln Revealed in His Own Words - A Study of Lincoln's Suppressed, Misinterpreted, and Forgotten Speeches and Writings

The Unquotable Abraham Lincoln: The President's Quotes They Don't Want You to Know!

The Constitution of the Confederate States of America: Explained

Encyclopedia of the Battle of Franklin: A Comprehensive Guide to the Conflict that Changed the Civil War

The McGavocks of Carnton Plantation: A Southern History - Celebrating One of Dixie's Most Noble Confederate Families and Their Tennessee Home

Carnton Plantation Ghost Stories: True Tales of the Unexplained from Tennessee's Most Haunted Civil War House!

Forrest's handwritten dispatch to his superior, Confederate General Leonidas Polk, September 21, 1863, from "on the road." Forrest's well-known "git 'er done," no nonsense attitude and aggressiveness are evident.

INTRODUCTION

This book contains Forrest's complete *known* and *officially recognized* correspondence during Lincoln's War between the years 1861 and 1865. I emphasize "known" because, due to the many difficulties related to tracing and maintaining military records (from any war), not all of his words from this period were preserved. Thus, while no collection of this kind can be truly "complete," mine is as comprehensive as I have been able to make it.

I emphasize "official" because I have only included here those correspondences that are listed in the U.S. government's massive multi-volume work, *The War of the Rebellion: A Compilation of the Official Records of the Union and Confederate Armies*, known more commonly as the *Official Records of the Union and Confederate Armies*, or ORA. (There is also a multi-volume set devoted to the *Official Records of the Union and Confederate Navies*, or ORN.)

Forrest's monumental impact on Lincoln's War is reflected in his nearly ubiquitous presence throughout the ORA. In those volumes regarding the states where Forrest fought, the General is, of course, mentioned hundreds of times. What is truly informative, however, is that he is also mentioned hundreds of times in volumes regarding states that he never stepped foot in, by officers he never met, concerning battles he never fought in! Forrest devoted his military career to putting the "skeer" on the Yankees, a mission at which he succeeded most admirably, for, according to the ORA itself, the General's scare reverberated across the entire Union army for the entire duration of the War.

I took the title for this book, *Give 'Em Hell Boys!*, from one of General Forrest's favorite battle cries, and which was always so inspiring and loved by his troops. These pages contain some 300 of Forrest's reports, dispatches, orders, returns, letters, notes, communiques, and telegrams, written and sent by Forrest to a wide assortment of Civil War figures, from the president of the Confederacy (Jefferson Davis) and fellow Confederate officers to his many Yankee enemies on the field of action.

While Forrest created all (or nearly all) of his dispatches, he did not write each one by hand. Instead, many, if not most, he dictated to his aides, such as Major Charles W. Anderson. Still, Forrest did in fact pick up pen and paper and write out a number of his correspondences, some which have survived to this day.

When one reads the ORA one is struck by the manner in which Forrest's military writings stand out from those of his contemporaries. Ranging from a few terse words concerning mundane items, to dozens of powerfully poetic pages, in my opinion his reports are unique in their energy, vivacity, bluntness, forcefulness, quickness, pithiness, drama, dynamism, and emotional drive. In his thoughts, words, and actions he is revealed here as, without question, one of the most unique officers among the military brass on both sides.

The impulsive Tennessee frontiersman had difficulty, as he often admitted, controlling his feelings, which is readily apparent from many of his dispatches. When he lost patience with someone, even a superior officer, he could not hold it back. All formality was thrown out the window as he unleashed his anger upon his unsuspecting, and often innocent, recipient. While this was uncharacteristic of most militarily educated men, Forrest was, proudly, no West Point graduate (he had only six months of formal schooling as a young boy). To some degree his military correspondence reflects this limited education—as well as the stunning manner in which he transcended it—in a myriad of fascinating and enlightening ways.

Despite the tactless manner in which Forrest sometimes spoke to others in the Confederate army, the vast majority of his writings reveal a man who had tremendous respect for his fellow commanders, men such as General Richard Taylor.

Also revealed here is a man of incredible intelligence, amazing mental agility, and dazzling natural abilities, especially when it came to leading men into battle and spur-of-the-moment strategy and tactics. It was not for nothing that General Robert E. Lee, the commander-in-chief of all Confederate States armies, called Forrest a military genius who "accomplished more with fewer troops than any other officer on either side."[2] The two had never even met.

Indeed, Forrest was the only man, Rebel or Yankee, of the entire war to rise from the rank of private to lieutenant general.[3] Like everything else he accomplished in his short life—including becoming a multimillionaire by the time he was forty—this he did on his own merits, in his own way, on his own terms, and in his own time.

My cousin Nathan Bedford Forrest was a true force of nature, an individual who, had he been given charge of larger armies, would have certainly turned the tide of Lincoln's War in the South's favor—as even President Davis himself tragically admitted years later.

Let this record of Forrest's military correspondence stand as an eternal testament to all that is truly American, manly, heroic, patriotic, and righteous, all characteristics still highly valued here in Dixie, just as they were in 1861.

After reading the many engrossing military reports of the celebrated Confederate chieftain, I hope you will join with me in saying: Long live Forrest, long live the South!

Lochlainn Seabrook, Jefferson Davis Historical Gold Medal winner
Franklin, Williamson County, Tennessee, USA
January 2012, Civil War Sesquicentennial

HISTORICAL TIME LINE

Highlights of Forrest's Life & Military Career

(Excerpted from Seabrook's *A Rebel Born*)

July 13, 1821: Forrest born near what is now Chapel Hill, Bedford Co. (now Marshall Co.), TN.

1833: Forrest's father, William Forrest, moves his family to Tippah Co., MS (near what used to be the town of Salem).

Fall 1842: Forrest, now 21, leaves home permanently.

1842: Forrest moves to Hernando, DeSoto Co., MS, and begins working for his uncle, Jonathan Forrest.

December 28, 1843: In Marshall, MS, Forrest's mother Mariam remarries to Joseph Luxton, Sr.

1845: Forrest's twin sister, Fanny Forrest, dies.

Sometime after March 11, 1845: Forrest is made sheriff (constable) of the town of Hernando and Coroner of DeSoto Co., MS, by grateful citizens.

April 25, 1845: Forrest marries high society Southern belle, Mary Ann Montgomery (a relative of Sam Houston), at Hernando, MS.

September 26, 1846: Forrest's first of two children born: William Montgomery "Willie" Forrest (named after Forrest's father William).

1847: Forrest becomes a member of the Independent Order of Odd Fellows.

About 1848: Forrest opens a stage line connecting Hernando, MS, to Memphis, TN.

1849: Forrest's second of two children born: Frances Ann "Fanny" Forrest (named after Forrest's twin sister Fanny).

Early 1852: Forrest moves his family to Memphis, TN.

June 26, 1854: Forrest's daughter, Frances Ann "Fanny" Forrest, dies at six years of age of flux (dysentery).

1858: By this year Forrest is a multimillionaire.

June 27, 1858: Forrest is elected alderman of the city of Memphis for the first time. This was to be the only political office ever held by him.

October 16, 1858: Forrest buys 1,900 acres of cotton land in Coahoma, Co., MS.

Sometime in 1858: Forrest opens up a slave trading business in Vicksburg, MS.

Sometime in 1859: Forrest becomes a large-scale cotton planter at his plantation Green Grove, at Sunflower Landing, in Coahoma Co., MS.

June 1859: Forrest is renominated Memphis alderman.

By July 1, 1859: Reelected Memphis alderman.

About July 21, 1859: Resigns as Memphis alderman.

September 8, 1859: Forrest agrees to take up the office of alderman of Memphis once again.

Before the end of 1859: Forrest sells his last commercial slave and closes both his slave business and his real estate business.

Late June 1860: Forrest reelected third time as alderman of Memphis, TN.

Mid July 1860: Forrest resigns a second time as alderman of Memphis, TN.

August 14, 1860: Forrest appointed by the Shelby Co. (Memphis) Democratic Association to help with an enormous public meeting hosted by fiery Southern secessionist William L. Yancy.

November 6, 1860: Anti-South, big-government liberal, Abraham Lincoln, elected president of the U.S.

Close of 1860: Forrest's slave trading business comes to a complete and final end.

April 12-14, 1861: Lincoln tricks the Confederacy into firing the first shot at the Battle of Fort Sumter, intentionally launching the War for Southern Independence.

June 14, 1861: At Memphis, TN, Forrest enlists in the Confederate army as a private in White's Tennessee Mounted Rifles, and begins his stunning military career.

July 10, 1861: Forrest promoted to lieutenant colonel.

March 10, 1862: Forrest promoted to colonel.

July 21, 1862: Forrest promoted to brigadier general.

May 1, 1863: First vote of thanks (of four) given to Forrest by Confederate Congress.

Fall, 1863: Forrest attempts to resign his commission as a brigadier-general. Realizing he is too important to the Confederacy, President Jefferson Davis refuses to accept Forrest's resignation. He then invites Forrest to meet with him.

Sometime between October and November 1863: Forrest at Montgomery, AL, where he meets with President Davis. At the meeting, described as "a long and satisfactory conference," Forrest is transferred to North Mississippi.

December 4, 1863: Forrest promoted to major-general (some records say this occurred on December 13).

February 17, 1864: Second vote of thanks (of four) given to Forrest by Confederate Congress.

February 22, 1864: Forrest's brother, Brig. Gen. Jeffrey Forrest, killed at Battle of Okolona, MS.

April 13, 1864: Forrest's brother, Lt. Col. Aaron H. Forrest (CSA), dies of pneumonia.

May 23, 1864: Third vote of thanks (of four) given to Forrest by Confederate Congress.

November 6, 1864: Forrest is given command of all the cavalry of the Army of TN.

November 17, 1864: Forrest assumes command of all the cavalry of the Army of TN.

December 6, 1864: Fourth vote of thanks (of four) given to Forrest by Confederate Congress.

March 2, 1865: Forrest promoted to lieutenant general (second to the highest possible in the Confederate army). Some records say he attained this rank on February 25 or 28, 1865. He is now in charge of 10,000 men, covering three states.

May 3, 1865: Forrest officially (and finally) accepts the defeat of the Confederacy (his men were among the last to surrender in the Western theater).

May 4, 1865: Forrest at Meridian, MS; gives unofficial farewell speech to his troops.

About May 9, 1865: Forrest's official farewell speech handed out to troops as flyers.

May 25, 1865: Forrest returns to his plantation Green Grove, at Sunflower Landing, in Coahoma Co., MS.

1867: Forrest joins the Pale Faces, a Mason-like organization.

December 15, 1867: Forrest's mother, Mariam Beck, dies in Navasota, TX, after stepping on a rusty nail while disembarking from a buggy.

Early 1868: Forrest elected President of Memphis, Okolona, and Selma Railroad.

February 5, 1868: Forrest files for bankruptcy in Memphis, TN.

June 9, 1868: Forrest at Nashville, TN; he is elected and sent here as a Democratic delegate to the Nashville State Convention.

July 4, 1868: In New York City, delegate Forrest attends the first postwar Democratic National Convention, creating a sensation.

July 17, 1868: Forrest pardoned by President Andrew Johnson for "treason" against the U.S.

August 1, 1868: Forrest at Nashville, TN; he is elected chairman of the Council of Peace, a futile but valiant effort by Southerners to reduce the unnecessary brutality of so-called "Reconstruction."

November 9, 1868: Forrest elected President and Director of Memphis and Selma Railroad.

Sometime in 1869: Forrest disbands the original KKK locally in TN.

January 25, 1869: Forrest orders the KKK to "entirely abolish and destroy" its masks and costumes.

March 14, 1869: Forrest orders the entire national KKK organization to disband.

September 1869: Forrest forms a business partnership in Memphis with Edmund W. Rucker, who had led Rucker's Brigade during Hood's Nashville Campaign; Forrest and Rucker's partnership lasts until 1874.

1871: Forrest's brother, Captain William Hezekiah "Bill" Forrest (CSA), dies.

June 27, 1871: Forrest at Washington, D.C.; appears before U.S. governmental committee investigating the KKK, where he is rigorously grilled and exonerated.

In 1871, day unknown, Nathan Bedford Forrest II, the General's grandson, is born in Oxford, MS, to William Montgomery Forrest and Jane Taylor Cook.

1873: Forrest leases a double log cabin and 1,300 acres on President's Island (south of Memphis on the Mississippi River) and moves there with his wife Mary Ann.

About January 1874: Forrest volunteers to fight under Sherman (then in command of the U.S. Army) in an expected war with Spain (Sherman turns him down).

Late March 1874: Forrest resigns as president and director of Memphis and Selma Railroad.

1875: Forrest publically calls for equality for all blacks.

May 8, 1875: Forrest's five-year contract with Shelby County (TN) for the hire of prison laborers begins.

July 5, 1875: Forrest at Memphis, TN; invited by an all-black group to give a speech at their gathering.

August 1875: Forrest becomes a Christian in Memphis, TN.

1876: Forrest contracts diabetes.

1876: Forrest's brother, John Nathaniel Forrest, dies.

1876: Forrest elected chairman of the Democratic party's Shelby County Executive Committee.

September 1876: Forrest gives one of his last, perhaps his final, public speech (before the Seventh Tennessee Cavalry).

July 27, 1877: Forrest at Hurricane Springs, TN (for health rehabilitation). Here, on this day, was held the first reunion of Forrest's Escort and Staff. The group came to be called the Veterans Association.

Late October 1877: Forrest at Memphis, TN; deathly ill, he is taken to the home of his brother Jesse.

October 29, 1877, about 7:00 PM: Memphis, TN, at age fifty-six, Forrest dies at his brother Jesse Forrest's home due to complications from diabetes, an old war wound, and general exhaustion and debilitation brought on by Lincoln's War.

October 31 (Halloween), 1877: Forrest is buried at Elmwood Cemetery, Memphis, TN.

December 14, 1890: Forrest's brother, Jesse Anderson Forrest, dies.

January 22, 1893: Forrest's wife, Mary Ann, dies in Memphis, TN.

April 7, 1905: Nathan Bedford Forrest III, the General's great-grandson, born in Memphis, TN, to Nathan Bedford Forrest II, and Mattie Patton.

February 8, 1908: Forrest's only son, Captain William M. "Billie" Forrest, dies in Memphis, TN, while attending a play about the KKK called *The Clansman* (adapted from the novel by Thomas

Dixon, Jr.). He is said to have passed away at the exact moment an actor playing his famous father walked out onto the stage.

1921: The Tennessee legislature proclaims Forrest's birthday, July 13, a legal holiday. (As early as 1958 Forrest's birthday began to go unobserved in Tennessee, and the day is no longer recognized as an official holiday.)

March 13, 1931: Forrest's grandson, Nathan Bedford Forrest II (son of Forrest's son Willie), dies in FL (some say in Oxford, MS).

June 13, 1942: Forrest's great-grandson, Nathan Bedford Forrest III (son of Nathan Bedford Forrest II), dies while fighting in World War II, at Kiel, Germany, ending the Nathan Bedford Forrest line; Forrest III is buried at Arlington National Cemetery.[4]

GIVE 'EM HELL BOYS!

*The Complete Military Correspondence
of Nathan Bedford Forrest*

SECTION ONE

1861

1861

Forrest wrote the fewest military correspondences in 1861. This is because he did not join the Confederate army until midway through the year, on June 14, and he was a private for the first month. On July 10 he was promoted to lieutenant colonel. Several months later, after "fittin' up" his command that Fall, he sent out his first dispatch.

Forrest to Confederate Brigadier-General William W. Mackall, November 14, 1861:
☛ HOPKINSVILLE [KENTUCKY], NOVEMBER 14, 1861. W. W. MACKALL, ASSISTANT ADJUTANT-GENERAL:

I have been operating with my command of eight companies near Fort Henry and Fort Donelson, by order of [Union] General [Leonidas] Polk. Finding the country impracticable for cavalry, and with scant subsistence, I moved a part of my command to Canton, north side Cumberland River, leaving two companies at Dover. I am of no use south of Cumberland; desire my command united, and can do vast service with [Confederate] General [Lloyd] Tilghman. Will you so order?

N. B. Forrest, Commanding Tennessee Cavalry.[5]

Forrest to Confederate General Charles Clark, December 5, 1861:
☛ REPORT OF COL. N. B. FORREST, TENNESSEE CAVALRY (CONFEDERATE). REGIMENTAL HEADQUARTERS, HOPKINSVILLE, KY., DECEMBER 5, 1861. [TO: BRIG. GEN. CHARLES CLARK, COMMANDING AT HOPKINSVILLE]

Leaving Hopkinsville November 24 with 300 men and their officers, under orders from brigade headquarters, we went to Greenville, where we found some arms and equipments belonging to the enemy, as will be seen by a list herewith returned; also a [Yankee] soldier in full uniform, whom we made prisoner and returned to the commander of the post; from thence to Madisonville, where I sent Captain Overton, with 30 men, in the direction of Ashbysburg and Calhoun, who reported that all the troops had left the former place and gone to the latter (Calhoun). I then sent a scout to Henderson, dressed as a citizen, who reported that all the Federal forces had been sent from that town to Calhoun and their sick to Evansville.

I then visited Providence and Claysville and Morganfield, at all of which places the people met us with smiles and cheers, and fed and greeted us kindly.

I then went to Caseyville, on the Ohio River; then up the Tradewater 12 miles, where I crossed and went to Marion, in Crittenden County. When near that place a lady came from her door and begged in the name of her children for help, and representing that her husband (who was a citizen of standing and unconnected with the war) had been captured by Federal soldiers, led on and assisted by citizens of the neighborhood, whose names being given, I deemed it proper to arrest. William Akers was arrested, and when I approached the house of Jonathan Bells he shot the surgeon of my regiment from the door and escaped by a back opening in the house. A noble and brave man, and skillful surgeon, and high-toned gentleman was Dr. Van Wyck, and his loss was deeply felt by the whole regiment. Dispatching the body in care of Major Kelly [Kelley], with 100 men, to Hopkinsville. I remained in the vicinity of Marion another day, and my scouts arrested one Federal soldier and brought him as prisoner, and killed one Scott, the leader of the band, who had sworn to shoot Southern men from their horses and behind trees, he (Scott) attempting it by wounding three horses with a shot-gun. The scouts found with him three guns and a pistol, which are returned to the Ordnance Department; also two horses of the enemy.

From Marion I went to Dycusburg and Eddyville, where I learned that no boats or soldiers had been on the Cumberland for twelve days at those points. The people at the latter places treated us with the utmost liberality and kindness.

It is believed that the expedition has done great good in giving confidence to the Southern-rights men, destroying the distorted ideas of Union men, who expected every species of abuse at the hands of the Confederate soldiers, many of them expressing their agreeable disappointment and change of views in regard to our army, and not a few assured us that they would no longer use any influence against the cause of the South. Universal kindness was the policy of the officers in command. With me were Captains Overton, May, Fruitt [Trewhitt?], and Hambrick, in command of detachments of their own companies, and Lieutenant Sims, in command of a detachment of Captain Gould's company, and Lieutenant Gentry, in command of a detachment of Captain Logan's company, and as guide Lieutenant Wallace, of Captain G. A. Huwald's company.

A number of hogs and cattle were started from the counties between this and the river and along the river under the auspices of the expedition.

There are no Federal forces remaining on this side of the Ohio from the mouth of Green to the mouth of Cumberland, and with the exception of a few scouts none have been there for twelve days.

After I left Madisonville, Jackson's cavalry visited the place, about 400 in number, but he attempted no pursuit; he might have easily overtaken us. After we were at Caseyville 200 Federal troops came there and captured about eighty hogs, became intoxicated on stolen whisky, and left in a row [fight].

All of which is respectfully submitted.

N. B. Forrest, Colonel, Commanding Forrest Regiment Cavalry.[6]

Forrest to Confederate General Charles Clark, December 28, 1861, regarding his first major conflict, the Battle of Sacramento, Kentucky (fought December 28, 1861):
☞ REPORT OF COL. NATHAN B. FORREST, FORREST'S REGIMENT, C. S. ARMY. HOPKINSVILLE, KY., DECEMBER 30, 1861. [TO: GENERAL CHARLES CLARK, C.S.A.]

Under orders to reconnoiter to the front, especially in the direction of Rochester and Greenville, and if deemed best to continue our observations towards Ramsey, my command left camp Thursday, 26th instant, myself with detachments from Companies A, C, and D, First Lieutenant Crutcher, Captains May and Gould with a detachment of 25 men of Captain Meriwether's company, under his command, Major Kelly [Kelley] , with detachments from Companies E, F, and G, under Lieutenants Hampton, Kance, and Cowan, having been ordered to Greenville to await orders. Leaving the Greenville road 4 miles from Hopkinsville I moved in the direction of Rochester, until fully satisfied that there were no movements of the enemy in that direction.

The next day, on reaching the Russellville and Greenville road, I turned towards Greenville, and on Saturday morning formed a junction with a detachment of 40 cavalry from Russellville, under command of Lieutenant-Colonel Starnes and Captain McLemore, who, with Major Kelly, were awaiting my arrival at Greenville. Colonel Starnes had the day before been at South Carrollton, where he had engaged a party of the enemy, killing 3.

Hearing nothing still from the enemy, it was determined to extend our march to the vicinity of Rumsey. The command, about 300 strong, were moved forward in one column, with advance guard under Captain Meriwether and rear under Captain McLemore; the head of the column under my command; the center under Major Kelly, and the rear under Lieutenant-Colonel Starnes. We had moved 8 miles down the Rumsey road when information reached me that the enemy 500 strong had that morning crossed from Calhoun to Rumsey. My men were ordered to a rapid pace, and as the news of the proximity of the enemy ran down the column it was impossible to repress jubilant and defiant shouts, which reached the height of enthusiasm as the women from the houses waved us forward. A beautiful young lady, smiling, with untied tresses floating in the breeze, on horseback, met the column just before our advance guard came up with the rear of the enemy, infusing nerve into my arm and kindling knightly chivalry within my heart.

One mile this side the village of Sacramento our advance guard came up with their rear guard, who halted, seemingly in doubt whether we were friends or foes. Taking a Maynard rifle, I fired at them, when they rode off rapidly to their column. The column moved up the hill and formed just over its brow. I ordered up the head of my column, telling my men to hold their fire until within good range. The enemy commenced firing from the time we were within 200 yards of them. When we had moved 120 yards farther I ordered my men to fire. After three rounds I found that my men were not up in sufficient numbers to pursue them with success, and as they showed signs of fight, I ordered the advance to fall back. The enemy at once attempted to flank our left, and moved towards us and appeared greatly animated, supposing we were in retreat. They had moved down over 100 yards and seemed to be forming for a charge, when, the remainder of my men coming up, I dismounted a number of men with Sharp's carbines and Maynard rifles to act as sharpshooters; ordered a flank movement upon the part of Major Kelly and Colonel Starnes upon the right and left, and the detachments from the companies under my command, still mounted, were ordered to charge the enemy's center.

The men sprang to the charge with a shout, while the undergrowth so impeded the flankers that the enemy, broken by the charge and perceiving the movement on their flanks, broke in utter confusion, and, in spite of the efforts of a few officers, commenced a disorderly flight at full speed, in which the officers soon joined. We pressed closely on their rear, only getting an occasional shot, until we reached the village of Sacramento, when, the best mounted men of my companies coming up, there commenced a promiscuous saber slaughter of their rear, which was continued at almost full speed for 2 miles beyond the village, leaving their bleeding and wounded strewn along the whole route. At this point Captain Bacon, and but a little before Captain Burges, were run through with saber thrusts, and Captain Davis thrown from his horse and surrendered as my prisoner, his shoulder being dislocated by the fall. The enemy, without officers, threw down their arms and depended alone upon the speed of their horses. Those of my men whose horses were able to keep up found no difficulty in piercing through every one they came up with, but as my horses were almost run down while theirs were much fresher, I deemed it best to call off the chase, for such it had become, leaving many wounded men hanging to their saddles to prevent their falling from their horses. Returning, we found their dead and wounded in every direction. Those who were able to be moved we placed in wagons. Captains Bacon and Burges were made as comfortable as we could, and applied to the nearest farm house to take care of them.

There were killed on the field and mortally wounded, who have since died, about 65; wounded and taken prisoners, about 35, making their loss about 100. Among their killed were two captains and three lieutenants and several non-commissioned officers.

The fight occurred in the woods; the run was principally along lanes. I have the pleasure of stating that Colonel Starnes and Major Kelly acted in the most noble and chivalrous manner, and, indeed, I can say that Captain Gould, Captain May, Captain Meriwether (who unfortunately fell in front of the engagement), Lieutenant Crutcher, in command of Captain Overton's company; Lieutenant Nance left in command of Captain Hambrick's company; Lieutenant Cowan, in command of Captain Logan's company (he acting as surgeon at the time), and Lieutenant Hampton, in command of Captain Truett's [?] company, with the men under their respective commands are deserving praise for their conduct.

Our loss was Captain Meriwether and Private Terry, of Captain McLemore's company, killed, and 3 privates slightly wounded; 2 from Captain May's and the other from Captain Hambrick's.

We returned to Greenville the night of the fight (Saturday), and from thence started to camp, and arrived last night.

Before closing this report I most respectfully call your attention to the gallant conduct of Lieutenant Bailey, of Captain Gould's company; Private J. W. Ripley, of Captain May's company, and Private J. M. Luxton, also of Captain May's; and Private B. W. Johnson, of Captain Logan's company, and, indeed, many others, whose horses being not quite so fast, did not come immediately under my own observation. Capt. M. B. Logan (who was acting as surgeon on that occasion) deserves praise for his noble conduct throughout the engagement.

All of which is most respectfully submitted.

Respectfully, N. B. Forrest, Colonel, Commanding Forrest Regiment.[7]

SECTION TWO

1862

1862

Forrest's star continued to rise quickly in 1862: on March 10 he was promoted to colonel, and on July 21 he was promoted to brigadier general. With his newly assumed responsibilities his military correspondence also greatly increased.

What follows is Forrest's official report on the Battle of Fort Donelson (fought February 11-16, 1862), which he submitted to Confederate authorities in late February 1862:

☞ REPORTS OF COL. NATHAN B. FORREST, TENNESSEE CAVALRY. FEBRUARY —, 1862.

Having been ordered by [Confederate] Brigadier-General [Charles] Clark to Fort Donelson from Hopkinsville, I arrived at Fort Donelson on Monday evening, February 10, and finished crossing with my command on Tuesday morning.

On the same afternoon I was ordered, with 300 of my cavalry, to reconnoiter in the direction of Fort Henry. We met about 3 miles from Fort Donelson the enemy's cavalry, supposed to be about 600, and, after a short skirmish, pressing them hard about 6 miles, captured 1 prisoner and mortally wounded several others.

The following morning I was ordered out with my own regiment, three Kentucky companies, viz, Captains Williams, Wilcox, and Hewey's, and Lieutenant-Colonel Gantt's battalion of Tennessee cavalry (the commanding general having signified to me the night before his desire that I should take charge of all the cavalry at the post as brigadier of cavalry.)

I had gone about 2 miles on the road towards Fort Henry when we met the advance of the enemy. My advance guard engaged them, when I sent forward three rifle companies, and after a skirmish they retreated, leaving several dead and wounded. The enemy halted, and, after maneuvering for some time, commenced to move by a parallel road towards the fort. Receiving information of this change, I changed my position from the right to the extreme left of my line of battle, throwing two squadrons of cavalry across the road. As soon as the enemy's advance came in sight I again attacked them vigorously. The enemy were on an elevated ridge, thickly wooded, and, when the attack was made, little else than their cavalry could be seen.

My first squadron as skirmishers, having been dismounted, were hotly engaged with greatly superior numbers. To enable them to withdraw, the second squadron was ordered to charge, hearing which, Major Kelly, by my request, commanding the left (now center) of my line, ordered an advance of the three squadrons under his command. The enemy gave back at the point where the charge was made, and the cavalry wheeling out of the way on their flank opposite Major Kelly, the infantry rose from the ground and poured in at short range a terrific fire of musketry, accompanied by a volley of grape. I was now able to mount and draw off in good order my skirmishers, and, finding the enemy in large force, ordered my cavalry to fall back, no infantry being near to support me. In answer to my couriers from the fort, General Buckner (General G. J. Pillow absent at Cumberland City) now ordered me back within our intrenchments.

This skirmish was from about 9 a. m. to near 2 p. m. We killed during the day a hundred men and wounded several hundred more, which so delayed the advance of the enemy that they did not move to the attack that day, satisfying themselves with planting a few cannon and commencing at long range a slow cannonade.

In the afternoon General Floyd reached the fort, and the whole army, infantry and cavalry, were engaged during the night in throwing up intrenchments, crowning several hills surrounding Dover. The enemy planted their batteries during the night, and commenced a cannonade from their batteries and ten gunboats early on the morning of Thursday. Soon after, our intrenchments were vigorously attacked at all points, and for six hours there was scarcely a cessation of small-arms and artillery. The musketry ceased about 1 p. m., the cannonading continuing until after dark. The gunboats drew off early in the engagement, supposed to be crippled, returning occasionally. The cavalry were but little engaged, acting only as pickets and couriers.

On Friday I was ordered out with the infantry, passing our intrenchments on the left; but after maneuvering a short time and some sharp shooting between the cavalry and the enemy, I was ordered back into the intrenchments. A demand was then made on me for sharpshooters to dislodge the enemy, who were from heights and trees annoying our infantry in the intrenchments, which we accomplished in about two hours, returning to my command about the time the gunboat attack was made on the fort. Of this attack I was an eye-witness, and have never seen a description which did anything like justice to the attack or defense. More determination could not have been exhibited by the attacking party, while more coolness and bravery never was manifested than was seen in our artillerists. Never was there greater anxiety depicted in the face of brave men than during the terrific roar of cannon, relieved ever and anon by the slow but regular report of our one single 10-inch gun. Never were men more jubilant than when the victory crowned the steady bravery of our little fort; old men wept; shout after shout went up; the gunboats driven back; the army was in the best possible spirits, feeling that, relieved of their greatest terror, they could whip any land force that could be brought against them.

During the night I was called into council with the generals commanding, when it was determined to bring on the attack the next morning by again passing our intrenchments and attacking the enemy's right.

In the early gray of the morning I moved to the attack, the cavalry on the left and in the advance. I found the enemy prepared to receive us, and were again engaged with the sharpshooters till our infantry were formed for the attack, the first gun from the enemy killing a horse in my regiment. General B. H. Johnson commanded the left, which now moved to the front. An obstinate fight of two hours ended in the retreat of the enemy. The undergrowth was so thick that I could scarcely press my horses through it. Finding that the flank of the enemy in retreat was exposed across an open field to my front and left, I immediately led my cavalry to the field, but found the ground a marsh, and we were unable to pass it.

The enemy formed in the edge of a second field to our front and right, and flanking the left of our advancing line of infantry. We could not move to flank them, but by maneuvering to their front and right doubtless prevented their attempting a flank movement on our infantry. Finding that our advancing line of infantry would cut them off while the cavalry prevented their flanking us, they commenced a retreat, accompanied by their cavalry, which we could now see in the distance, but not participating during the day in the fight. Our infantry had now driven them near a mile, they doggedly disputing the whole ground, leaving dead and wounded scattered through the woods and fields up in the ravine. The enemy, leaving their third position for the first time, retreated in haste, advancing by a road through a ravine. I here passed our line of infantry with my command in moving to the center.

I charged the enemy's battery of six guns, which had kept several of our regiments in check for several hours, killing and slaughtering a great many of our men. I captured the battery, killing most of the men and horses. I then immediately moved on the flank of the enemy, obstinately maintaining their position. They finally gave way, our infantry and cavalry both charging them at the same time, committing great slaughter. Moving still farther to our right, I found a regiment of our infantry in confusion, which I relieved by charging the enemy to their front. Here 64 of the enemy were found in 40 yards square. General Pillow, coming up, ordered me to charge the enemy in a ravine. I charged by squadrons, filing the first company of each squadron to the right, and the second to the left, on reaching the ravine, firing and falling in the rear of the third squadron until the three squadrons had charged. We here completely routed the enemy, leaving some 200 dead in the hollow, accomplishing what three different regiments had failed to do. Seeing the enemy's battery to our right about to turn on us, I now ordered a charge on this battery, from which we drove the enemy, capturing two guns. Following down the ravine captured the third, which they were endeavoring to carry off, gunners and drivers retreating up the hill. In this charge I killed about 50 sharpshooters, who were supporting the guns. I ordered forward a number of scouts, who, returning, informed me that the enemy, with three guns and three regiments of infantry, were moving up by the road from Fort Henry. We had driven the enemy back without a reverse from the left of our intrenchments to the center, having opened three different roads by which we might have retired if the generals had, as was deemed best in the council the night before, ordered the retreat of the army. Informing General Pillow of the position the enemy had taken, he ordered two new regiments and one of the regiments in the field, with one piece of artillery, to attack the enemy.

The fight here ended about 2.30 p. m. without any change in our relative positions. We were employed the remainder of the evening in gathering up the arms, and assisting in getting off the wounded. I was three times over the battle-field, and late in the evening was 2 miles up the river on the road to the forge. There were none of the enemy in sight when dark came on. Saturday night our troops slept, flushed with victory, and confident they could drive the enemy back to the Tennessee River the next morning.

About 12 o'clock at night I was called in council with the generals, who had under discussion the surrender of the fort. They reported that the enemy had received 11,000 re-enforcements since the fight. They supposed the enemy had returned to the positions they had occupied the day before.

I returned to my quarters and sent out two men, who, going by a road up the bank of the river, returned without seeing any of the enemy, only fires, which I believed to be the old camp fires, and so stated to the generals; the wind, being very high, had fanned them into a blaze.

When I returned General Buckner declared that he could not hold his position. Generals Floyd and Pillow gave up the responsibility of the command to him, and I told them that I neither could nor would surrender my command. General Pillow then said I could cut my way out if I chose to do so, and he and General Floyd agreed to come out with me. I got my command ready and reported at headquarters. General Floyd informed me that General Pillow had left, and that he would go by boat.

I moved out by the road we had gone out the morning before. When about a mile out crossed a deep slough from the river, saddle-skirt deep, and filed into the road to Cumberland Iron Works. I ordered Major Kelly and Adjutant Schuyler to remain at the point where we entered this road with one company, where the enemy's cavalry would attack if they attempted to follow us. They remained until day was dawning. Over 500 cavalry had passed, a company of artillery horses had followed, and a number of men from different regiments, passing over hard-frozen ground. More than two hours had been occupied in passing. Not a gun had been fired at us. Not an enemy had been seen or heard.

The enemy could not have reinvested their former position without traveling a considerable distance and camped upon the dead and dying, as there had been great slaughter upon that portion of the field, and I am clearly of the opinion that two-thirds of our army could have marched out without loss, and that, had we continued the fight the next day, we should have gained a glorious victory, as our troops were in fine spirits, believing we had whipped them, and the roads through which we came were open [i.e., no Federal soldiers] as late as 8 o'clock Sunday morning [the 16th], as many of my men, who came out afterwards, report.

I made a slow march with my exhausted horses to Nashville, Tenn., where we arrived on Tuesday morning [the 18th], and reported myself to General Floyd, who placed me in command of the city on Thursday, at the time of his leaving. I remained in the city until Sunday evening, during which time I was busily engaged with my regiment restoring order to the city and removing public property.

My loss at the battle in killed, wounded, and taken prisoners amounted to between 300 and 400 men. Among the number was Capt. Charles May, who fell at the head of his company while leading a charge.

My regiment charged two batteries, taking nine pieces of artillery, which, with near 4,000 stands of arms, I had taken inside of our lines. I cannot speak too highly of the gallant manner in which my officers and men conducted themselves on that occasion, as well as others that came under my observation, with the exception of Lieutenant-Colonel Gantt, commanding a battalion of Tennessee Cavalry, who failed to fight on Saturday, and refused to bring his men out with my regiment on Sunday morning when ordered to do so.

Respectfully submitted.

N. B. Forrest, Colonel, Commanding Forrest's Regiment of Cavalry.[8]

On March 15, 1862, due to some debate as to the facts, Colonel Forrest made the following "sworn statement" to his superiors regarding the Battle of Fort Donelson:
☞ Between 1 and 2 o'clock on Sunday morning, February 16 [1862], being sent for, I arrived at General Pillow's headquarters, and found him, General Floyd, and General Buckner in conversation. General Pillow told me that they had received information that the enemy were

again occupying the same ground they had occupied the morning before. I told him I did not believe it, as I had left that part of the field, on our left, late the evening before. He told me he had sent out scouts, who reported a large force of the enemy moving around to our left. He instructed me to go immediately and send two reliable men to ascertain the condition of a road running near the river bank and between the enemy's right and the river, and also to ascertain the position of the enemy. I obeyed his instructions and awaited the return of the scouts. They stated that they saw no enemy, but could see their fires in the same place where they were Friday night; that from their examination and information obtained from a citizen living on the river road[,] the water was about to the saddle skirts, and the mud about half-leg deep in the bottom where it had been overflowed. The bottom was about a quarter of a mile wide and the water then about 100 yards wide.

During the conversation that then ensued among the general officers General Pillow was in favor of trying to cut our way out. General Buckner said that he could not hold his position over half an hour in the morning, and that if he attempted to take his force out it would be seen by the enemy (who held part of his intrenchments), and be followed and cut to pieces. I told him that I would take my cavalry around there and he could draw out under cover of them. He said that an attempt to cut our way out would involve the loss of three-fourths of the men. General Floyd said our force was so demoralized as to cause him to agree with General Buckner as to our probable loss in attempting to cut our way out. I said that I would agree to cut my way through the enemy's lines at any point the general might designate, and stated that I could keep back their cavalry, which General Buckner thought would greatly harass our infantry in retreat. General Buckner or General Floyd said that they (the enemy) would bring their artillery to bear on us. I went out of the room, and when I returned General Floyd said he could not and would not surrender himself. I then asked if they were going to surrender the command. General Buckner remarked that they were. I then stated that I had not come out for the purpose of surrendering my command, and would not do it if they would follow me out; that I intended to go out if I saved but one man; and then turning to General Pillow I asked him what I should do. He replied, 'Cut your way out.' I immediately left the house and sent for all the officers under my command, and stated to them the facts that had occurred and stated my determination to leave, and remarked that all who wanted to go could follow me, and those who wished to stay and take the consequences might remain in camp. All of my own regiment and Captain Williams, of Helm's Kentucky regiment, said they would go with me if the last man fell. Colonel Gantt was sent for and urged to get out his battalion as often as three times, but he and two Kentucky companies (Captains Wilcox and Huey) refused to come. I marched out the remainder of my command, with Captain Porter's artillery horses, and about 200 men of different commands up the river road and across the overflow, which I found to be about saddle-skirt deep. The weather was intensely cold; a great many of the men were already frost-bitten, and it was the opinion of the generals that the infantry could not have passed through the water and have survived it.

N. B. Forrest, Colonel, Commanding Forrest's Regiment of Cavalry.

(Sworn to and subscribed before me on the 15th day of March, 1862. Levi Sugars, Intendant of the Town of Decatur, Ala., and ex-officio Justice of the Peace.)[9]

The loss of Fort Donelson greatly upset the balance of military power in the region (in favor of the Yanks), spreading fear and panic throughout the Southern citizenry. One result was a riot in Nashville that lasted for several days, February 16-18, 1862. Forrest happened to be in the city at the time and masterfully quelled the disorder, peacefully evacuating most of the town. On March 22, 1862, Forrest gave the following "response" to "interrogatories of Committee of Confederate House of Representatives" concerning the situation:

☛ COL. NATHAN B. FORREST'S RESPONSES TO INTERROGATORIES OF COMMITTEE OF CONFEDERATE HOUSE OF REPRESENTATIVES:

Interrogatory 1st. I was not at the city of Nashville at the time of its surrender, but was there at the time the enemy made their entrance into that part of the city known as Edgefield, having left Fort Donelson, with my command, on the morning of its surrender, and reached Nashville on Tuesday, February 18, about 10 a.m. I remained in the city up to the Sunday evening following.

Interrogatory 2d. It would be impossible to state, from the data before me, the value of the stores either in the Quartermaster's or Commissary Departments, having no papers then nor any previous knowledge of the stores. The stores in the Quartermaster's Department consisted of all stores necessary to the department—clothing especially, in large amounts, shoes, harness, etc., with considerable unmanufactured material. The commissary stores were meat, flour, sugar, molasses, and coffee. There was a very large amount of meat in store and on the landing at my arrival, though large amounts had already been carried away by citizens.

Interrogatory 3d. A portion of these stores had been removed before the surrender. A considerable amount of meat on the landing, I was informed, was thrown into the river on Sunday before my arrival and carried off by the citizens. The doors of the commissary depot were thrown open, and the citizens in dense crowds were packing and hauling off the balance at the time of my arrival on Tuesday. The quartermaster's stores were also open, and the citizens were invited to come and help themselves, which they did in larger crowds, if possible, than at the other department.

Interrogatories 4th and 5th. On Tuesday morning I was ordered by General Floyd to take command of the city, and attempted to drive the mob from the doors of the departments, which mob was composed of straggling soldiers and citizens of all grades. The mob had taken possession of the city to that extent that every species of property was unsafe. Houses were closed, carriages and wagons were concealed to prevent the mob from taking possession of them. Houses were being seized everywhere. I had to call out my cavalry, and, after every other means failed, charge the mob before I could get it so dispersed as to get wagons to the doors of the departments to load up the stores for transportation. After the mob was partially dispersed and quiet restored a number of citizens furnished wagons and assisted in loading them. I was busily engaged in this work on Friday, Saturday, and Sunday. I transported 700 hundred large boxes of clothing to the Nashville and Chattanooga Railroad depot, several hundred bales of osnaburgs and other military goods from the Quartermaster's Department, most, if not all, of the shoes having been seized by the mob. I removed about 700 or 800 wagon loads of meat. The high water having destroyed the bridges so as to stop the transportation over the Nashville and Chattanooga

Railroad, I had large amounts of this meat taken over the Tennessee and Alabama Railroad. By examination on Sunday morning I found a large amount of fixed ammunition in the shape of cartridges and ammunition for light artillery in the magazine, which, with the assistance of General Harding, I conveyed over 7 miles on the Tennessee and Alabama Railroad in wagons, to the amount of 30 odd wagon loads, after the enemy had reached the river. A portion was sent on to Murfreesborough in wagons. The quartermaster's stores which had not already fallen into the hands of the mob were all removed, save a lot of rope, loose shoes, and a large number of tents. The mob had already possessed themselves of a large amount of these stores. A large quantity of meat was left in store and on the river bank and some at the Nashville and Chattanooga Railroad depot, on account of the break in the railroad. I cannot estimate the amount, as several store-houses had not been opened up to the time of my leaving. All stores left fell into the hands of the enemy, except forty pieces of light artillery, which were burned and spiked by order of General Floyd, as were the guns at Fort Zollicoffer. My proposition to remove these stores, made by telegraph to Murfreesborough, had the sanction of General A. S. Johnston.

Interrogatory 6th. No effort was made, save by the mob, who were endeavoring to possess themselves of these stores, to prevent their removal, and a very large amount was taken off before I was placed in command of the city.

Interrogatory 7th. It was eight days from the time the quartermaster left the city before the arrival of the enemy, commissaries and other persons connected with these departments leaving at the same time. With proper diligence on their part I have no doubt all the public stores might have been transported to places of safety.

Interrogatory 8th. Up to Saturday the railroads were open and might have been used to transport these stores. Saturday the bridges of the Nashville and Chattanooga Railroad gave way. Besides these modes of conveyance, a large number of wagons might have been obtained, had the quiet and the order of the city been maintained, and large additional amounts of stores might by these means have been transported to places of safety.

Interrogatories 9th and 10th. I saw no officer connected with the Quartermaster's or Commissary Departments except Mr. Patton, who left on Friday. I did not at any time meet or hear of Maj. V. K. Stevenson in the city during my stay there.

Interrogatories 11th, 12th, and 13th. From my personal knowledge I can say nothing of the manner in which Major Stevenson left the city. Common rumor and many reliable citizens informed me that Major Stevenson left by a special train Sunday evening, February 16, taking personal baggage, furniture, carriage, and carriage-horses, the train ordered by himself, as president of the railroad.

Interrogatory 14th. All the means of transportation were actually necessary for the transportation of Government stores and sick and wounded soldiers, many of whom fell into the hands of the enemy for want of it, and might have been saved by the proper use of the means at hand. The necessity for these means of transportation for stores will be seen by the above answers which I have given. I have been compelled to be as brief as possible in making the above answers, my whole time being engaged, as we seem to be upon the eve of another great battle. The city was in a much worse condition than I can convey an idea of on paper, and the loss of public stores must be estimated by millions of dollars. The panic was entirely useless and not at all justified by the circumstances. General Harding and the mayor of the city, with Mr. Williams, deserve special mention for assistance rendered in removing the public property. In my judgment, if the quartermaster and commissary had remained at their post and worked diligently with the means at their command, the Government stores might all have been saved between the time of the fall of Fort Donelson and the arrival of the enemy at Nashville.

Respectfully submitted.

N. B. Forrest, Colonel, Commanding Forrest's Brigade of Cavalry.[10]

On July 13, 1862, Forrest raided and successfully captured Murfreesboro, Tennessee. It was his forty-first birthday, so he had two reasons to celebrate that day. Here is his official report of the engagement. It appears to have been written to Confederate Major General Edmund Kirby Smith, and was forwarded to Major H. L. Clay, Adjutant-General, Army of East Tennessee:

☛ We left Chattanooga on July 9 with the Texan Rangers, under Colonel Wharton, and the Second Georgia Cavalry, under Colonel Lawton. We made a forced march of nearly 50 miles, reaching Altamont on the night of the 10th instant. After resting one night we passed on to McMinnville, where I was joined on the night of the 11th by Colonel Morrison with a portion of the First Georgia Cavalry, two companies of Colonel Spiller's battalion, under Major Smith, and two companies of Kentuckians, under Captains Taylor and Waltham. After this junction my whole force was about 1,400 men, and both men and horses were much jaded and worn by their long travel. After feeding and refreshing for a single day and being joined by some few volunteers I left on the 12th at 1 o'clock for Murfreesborough. It was over 50 miles to our destination, but there was no halt except for a short time to feed the men and horses.

We approached Murfreesborough about 4.30 A.M. and fortunately captured the pickets of the enemy without firing a gun. I then learned that there were two regiments in and near Murfreesborough, one the Ninth Michigan and the other the Third Minnesota, 200 Pennsylvania cavalry, 100 of the Eighth Kentucky, and Captain Hewett's battery of four guns, numbering in all 1,400 or 1,500 men, under the command of General Thomas Crittenden, of Indiana. There were said to be two camps, one in Murfreesborough of one infantry regiment and the cavalry, the other with the artillery about a mile distant, and a small force with the officers in the court-house and private houses around the public square. I decided immediately to attack the camp in town and the buildings, while the camp with the artillery should be held in check until the first was stormed and surrendered. Colonel Wharton with his Texan Rangers was ordered to charge the camp in town. He moved forward in gallant style at the head of his men, but owing to the urgent necessity of using a portion of the Rangers for the attack on the buildings he did not carry with him but two of his companies. This fact, however, did not abate his courage or that of his men. They charged over the tent ropes right into the camp. Colonel Wharton was soon severely wounded and the command of his Rangers devolved on Colonel Walker.

Colonel Morrison with a portion of the Second Georgia was ordered to storm the court-house while the balance of the Texan Rangers were attacking the private buildings. After two or three hours hard struggle the court-house was fired and surrendered to Colonel

Morrison. The private buildings were also cleared by the Rangers and General Crittenden and his staff surrendered.

Lieut. Col. [Arthur] Hood, of the Second Georgia, with a portion of his force was ordered to storm the jail, which he did, releasing many prisoners confined for political offenses; he also took the telegraph office, capturing the operator.

Colonel Lawton, with the First Georgia, the Tennesseeans and Kentuckians, was ordered to attack the second camp with the artillery, which he did with great efficiency for several hours. The Tennesseeans, under Major Smith, and Kentuckians, under Captains Taylor and Waltham, stood the fire of shot and shell like veterans. The Georgians, under Captain Dunlop and Major Harper, made a gallant charge almost to the mouths of the cannon. After fighting them in front two or three hours I took immediate command of this force and charged the rear of the enemy into their camps and burned their camps and stores, demoralizing their force and weakening their strength.

The force of Texan Rangers sent to attack the first camp was so small that, although they fought with desperate courage and great skill, they were gradually driven back.

After the court-house and private buildings were surrendered and the fight had lasted five or six hours I prepared my whole force to storm both camps and summoned them to surrender. After some parley Colonel Duffield surrendered the infantry and artillery.

My aide, Colonel Saunders, rendered me efficient aid until he was severely wounded by a ball from the court-house. Major Strange, my adjutant, also performed his whole duty. Lieutenant-Colonel Walker and Major Harrison, of the Rangers, acted with their usual daring and bravery. All the officers and men who acted bravely cannot be particularly mentioned, but they acted their part nobly.

After the action was over I detached Major Smith to burn a railroad bridge below Murfreesborough, which he executed well. I intended to burn a railroad bridge above Murfreesborough and gave orders for the purpose, but by mistake they were not executed. I had the telegraph wire cut and a large portion of the railroad track torn up. I found four car-loads of provisions on the railroad track and the depot house full of stores, all of which I burned.

There were between 1,100 and 1,200 privates and

non-commissioned officers captured and brought to McMinnville and paroled on condition not to serve until exchanged. The officers have been already sent to Knoxville, in charge of Colonel Wharton (and I trust have safely reached their destination), except one or two who were wounded and left at Murfreesborough, on condition to surrender when restored to health.

I captured four pieces of artillery—three brass pieces and one Parrott gun—which are still in my possession, with harness and ammunition. There were some 50 or 60 large road wagons with the mule teams, harness, etc., captured. I burnt some of the wagons, which could not be got away, and sent you the balance. There were a large number of cavalry horses, saddles, and small-arms, with the ammunition, captured, and such as I have not been compelled to use are also forwarded to you.

In consequence of our being compelled to leave Murfreesborough, and not having received reports of the killed from some of my command, it is impossible to report accurately my loss. My best information is that we had about 25 killed and from 40 to 60 wounded. Among those killed is Lieutenant Green, of the Tennessee Battalion. The reports of the officers under my command when furnished will show more definitely the loss.

The enemy lost about 75 killed and 125 wounded. The pecuniary loss to the enemy must be near half a million of dollars [about $12 million in today's currency].

Yours, respectfully,

N. B. Forrest, Brigadier- General, Commanding Brigade of Cavalry.[11]

Forrest to Union Lieutenant Colonel John G. Parkhurst, Ninth Michigan Infantry, during the Battle of Murfreesboro, July 13, 1862:

☞ TO: COL. J. G. PARKHURST, U.S. ARMY. MURFREESBOROUGH, JULY 13, 1862:

Colonel: I must demand an unconditional surrender of your force as prisoners of war or I will have every man put to the sword. You are aware of the overpowering force I have at my command, and this demand is made to prevent the effusion of blood.

I am, colonel, very respectfully, your obedient servant,

N. B. Forrest, Brigadier-General of Cavalry, C.S. Army.[12]

Forrest to Confederate General John P. McCown, July 17, 1862:
☞ TO: MAJOR GENERAL J. P. McCOWN, C.S. ARMY. CHATTANOOGA, TENN., JULY 17, 1862:
Attacked Murfreesborough 5 A.M. last Sunday morning; captured two brigadier-generals, staff and field officers, and 1,200 men; burnt $200,000 worth of stores; captured sufficient stores with those burned to amount to $500,000, and brigade of 60 wagons, 300 mules, 150 or 200 horses, and field battery of four pieces; destroyed the railroad and depot at Murfreesborough. Had to retreat to McMinnville, owing to large number of prisoners to be guarded. Our loss 16 or 18 killed; 25 or 30 wounded. Enemy's loss 200 or 300.

N. B. Forrest, Brigadier-General of Cavalry, C.S. Army.[13]

Forrest to Confederate General H. L. Clay, July 24, 1862:
☞ HEADQUARTERS SECOND CAVALRY BRIGADE, MCMINNVILLE, TENN., JULY 24, 1862. MAJ. H. L. CLAY, ASSISTANT ADJUTANT-GENERAL, KNOXVILLE, TENN.:
Sir: Yours of 20th ultimo is just received, requesting me to send my captured battery and other public property which I had taken back across the Tennessee River. In reply I would say that your order has been anticipated to some extent. I sent by Colonel Wharton, of the Eighth Texas Regiment, all the wagons and mules, with the exception of eight wagons and four mules to the wagon, which were necessary for my brigade. I also forwarded all the horses (after selecting the best to mount my men), replacing those I kept by others which were unfit at present for service. The battery I have still and should like much to retain it, as I have a competent captain who has organized a company, and with it I feel greater security. I will await your further orders in regard to the battery. I also retained 100 muskets, which were necessary the recruits that have joined my brigade. I will retain my present position unless I find I am pressed by the enemy. I have information that the enemy are falling back from Battle Creek. I have two [railroad] engines and all of their transportation between the break across Mill Creek and Murfreesborough. I am of the opinion that he will fall back with the most of his force to Murfreesborough. We have succeeded in drawing

10,000 from Athens, via Columbia, to Nashville and to Murfreesborough, and also causing them to move three times in the past five days between Nashville and Murfreesborough.

Yours, respectfully,

N. B. Forrest, Brigadier-General, Second Cavalry Brigade.[14]

Forrest to Confederate General H. L. Clay, July 24, 1862, concerning his movements and engagements around Nashville in late July:

☞ TO: MAJOR H. L. CLAY, ASSISTANT ADJUTANT-GENERAL, KNOXVILLE, TENN. REPORT OF BRIG. GEN. NATHAN B. FORREST, C. S. ARMY, INCLUDING OPERATIONS JULY 18-24 [1862]. HEADQUARTERS SECOND CAVALRY BRIGADE, McMINNVILLE, TENN., JULY 24, 1862:

Sir: I have the honor to report to you that on Friday, the 18th, at noon I left my camp on Mountain Creek, 10 miles from this place, with about 700 effective men of this brigade, in the direction of Nashville, for the purpose of making a reconnaissance. On my arrival at Alexandria with a portion of my command (the Texas Rangers) I was advised that during the day some 700 Federal cavalry had been sent from Nashville to Lebanon. I immediately ordered forward the balance of my command, being portions of the First and Second Georgia Cavalry and the Tennessee and Kentucky squadrons, and by a forced march reached Lebanon soon after sunrise. We dashed into the city in fine style, but found that the enemy, having notice of my approach, had retired about 12 o'clock, leaving me in the undisturbed possession of that place. I found the entire population true and loyal, with perhaps a single exception.

I remained at Lebanon until Monday morning, and moved then with my command toward Nashville. On reaching the vicinity of Nashville, say 5 or 6 miles, I captured 3 of the enemy's pickets. I moved then around the city, semicircling it and the Nashville and Chattanooga Railroad, passing within 3 miles of the city, and capturing on the way 2 additional pickets. I moved on the road for the purpose of destroying the bridges on the railroad near the city, and to my entire satisfaction accomplished the purpose, destroying three important railroad bridges over Mill Creek and cutting the telegraph wires. At each bridge I found heavy pickets, and had some considerable skirmishing at each, and also at Antioch Depot.

In the several skirmishes there were 10 killed and some 15 or 20 wounded, 97 prisoners (94 privates and 3 lieutenants), besides destroying a considerable amount of stores at Antioch Depot. Our forces were reported to be four times their number, so I afterward learned.

The necessity of rapid marching to secure the end desired having exhausted to a very considerable extent both men and horses, I found it necessary to fall back to this point, with a view of recruiting, which I did in good order, having the satisfaction to report that I did not lose a single man on the expedition, either in killed or wounded. I regret [that] the limited time allowed me in which to make this report will not permit me to enter minutely into the details of this exploit. I hope it will fully meet the approbation and expectation of the general.

Permit me to add that the entire, force, officers and men, under my command acquitted themselves with great credit, and bore the fatigue and risk of the expedition in a manner only to be borne by Confederate troops. My demonstration on Nashville, I am advised, created great excitement in that city, by which the greater portion of the force at Murfreesborough was ordered to that point. I regretted then, and now sincerely regret, that the limited force I had with me, which was all that I had which was available, did not permit me to make a more solid demonstration against that city. They were evidently frightened. A few thousand would then have placed that city in our possession.

On my return I sent a flag of truce to Murfreesborough and found the troops at that point in great confusion and evident fright. They are attempting to fortify the place and have partially blockaded the road between that city and this. I am credibly informed that the same state of confusion and terror pervaded their entire army at Wartrace and all other points within my reach. I regret that my force will not permit me to avail myself of this terror.

The officers and men of my entire command, flushed with victory and our past success, are anxious and ready to meet the enemy. I feel secure in my present position. Should events render this an insecure place I will fall back to a less exposed point.

I am, very respectfully, your obedient servant,

N. B. Forrest, Brigadier-General, Second Cavalry Brigade.[15]

Forrest to Confederate General G. G. Garner, August 6, 1862:

☛ HEADQUARTERS FIRST CAVALRY BRIGADE, LEBANON [TENN.], AUGUST 6, 1862. MAJ. G. G. GARNER, ASSISTANT ADJUTANT-GENERAL:

General: Having this morning learned that the enemy was in large force seven miles below this place, I moved forward the largest proportion of my command, leaving my wagons and such men as were unwell, or had useless horses, at camp near Liberty, under command of Colonel Lawton, Second Georgia Regiment, Cavalry. When within six miles of this place several citizens informed me that a force of 12,000 or 15,000 of the enemy had come in this morning. I immediately sent forward a reconnoitering force and ascertained that it was only an observation corps, which remained but a very few minutes. I arrived here with my command at 3.30 P.M., and shall immediately move forward toward Murfreesborough [Tenn.]. My information here is that the enemy has a force stationed at the cross-roads, where the Jefferson road crosses the turnpike from this place to Murfreesborough. The point designated is seven miles from Murfreesborough. I believe, from the information that I now have, that this force is stationed there for the purpose of protecting them in the movement of their trains from Murfreesborough. I learn from a reliable source that the enemy is diligently engaged in running his heavy siege guns and artillery across the river from Nashville. Owing to the broken condition of the road between Nashville and Franklin, Ky., transportation between those points is very difficult and almost impossible. Therefore I am of an opinion that an energetic movement forward by our force would certainly result in overtaking the Federals before they could escape from Tennessee.

N. B. Forrest, Brigadier-General, Commanding Brigade.[16]

Forrest to Confederate General G. G. Garner, September 8, 1862:

☛ HEADQUARTERS FIRST CAVALRY BRIGADE, BLACK'S SHOP, SEVEN MILES FROM MURFREESBOROUGH, SEPTEMBER 8, 1862. MAJ. G. G. GARNER, ASSISTANT ADJUTANT-GENERAL:

Major: I arrived at this place at 9.30 A.M. The Federal pickets left here this morning. Hazen with three regiments and a lengthy train left here yesterday at 3 P.M. They were on their way to Nashville.

McCook's division is now moving from Murfreesborough to Nashville, and will pass this place in an hour or two. [Union] General Crittenden, with 16,000, encamped from Tuesday until yesterday morning, 2 A.M., at this place, and then hastily decamped for Nashville. McCook's division is said to be the rear of their forces. There is a large amount of flour, from 1,500 to 2,000 barrels, at Liberty, Alexandria, and Lebanon. If you pass that way you can get it, or you can send down your wagons. It is good flour at $10 per barrel. Please inform me where I shall next communicate with you.

   Respectfully,
   N. B. Forrest, Brigadier-General, First Cavalry Brigade.
P.S. Kirby Smith won a glorious victory near Richmond, Ky. The abolition forces have fallen back to Covington. General Smith occupied Lexington without resistance, and his forces are reported within thirty-nine miles of Covington. The abolition papers of Cincinnati admit a loss of one-third their force in the Richmond (Ky.) fight. General Nelson was wounded, supposed mortally.

   N. B. F.[17]

Forrest to Confederate General G. G. Garner, September 11, 1862:
☞ HEADQUARTERS FIRST CAVALRY BRIGADE, EIGHTEEN MILES SOUTH OF FRANKLIN, KY.; NEAR FRANKLIN AND NASHVILLE PIKE, SEPTEMBER 11, 1862—1 P.M. MAJ. G. G. GARNER, ASSISTANT ADJUTANT-GENERAL:

   General: My pickets attacked the enemy's pickets this morning. We lost 1 man and killed 3 of the enemy. We left them shelling the woods, and they still continue to do so. That engagement took place near Tyree Springs. I have halted their whole command, and they still remain where we left them. I shall continue to annoy them on as far as Franklin. Will then move to the place you designated, and expect to arrive there on the day after to-morrow. We are moving along in good condition in advance of the enemy.

   Yours, respectfully,
   N. B. Forrest, Brigadier-General.[18]

Forrest to Confederate Major George Williamson, September 17, 1862:
☞ HEADQUARTERS FIRST CAVALRY BRIGADE, BACON CREEK

[KENTUCKY], SEPTEMBER 17, 1862—6 P.M. MAJOR WILLIAMSON, ASSISTANT ADJUTANT-GENERAL:

Major: I have just received the general's last note, and will return with my command immediately.

Respectfully,

N. B. Forrest, Brigadier-General, Commanding.[19]

Forrest to Confederate Major George Williamson, September 17, 1862:

☞ HEADQUARTERS FIRST CAVALRY BRIGADE, MUNFORDVILLE, KY., SEPTEMBER 17, 1862. MAJOR WILLIAMSON, ASSISTANT ADJUTANT- GENERAL:

Major: I have made a requisition for the cavalry horses captured to-day. Many of my men lost their horses at Murfreesborough and the Government owes them for those killed. I will have them valued and charged to their [account]. I have also made a requisition for all the arms, sabers, pistols, and equipments, and hope you will order them turned over to my brigade, as [my] men need them much. I leave Major Strange to attend to the getting of the requisitions which I have made, and will at once proceed as ordered and make every effort to carry out your wishes. Maj. [J. P.] Strange will also take charge of and bring to my brigade Captain Davis' new company of cavalry you spoke of assigning to me.

Yours, respectfully,

N. B. Forrest, Brigadier-General.[20]

Forrest to Confederate General Leonidas Polk, September 22, 1862:

☞ HEADQUARTERS FIRST CAVALRY BRIGADE, BARDSTOWN, KY., SEPTEMBER 22, 1862—7 A.M. [TO: GENERAL LEONIDAS POLK]:

General: I have just received your dispatch ordering me to make a demonstration on West Point, at the mouth of Salt River, and to break up the railroad. It will be impossible for me to carry out your orders on account of the condition that my horses are in. All the available men that I have with me are now on picket. I am threatened with the enemy; my pickets were fired on this morning 3 miles from town, on the Louisville pike. I am just in receipt of information that the enemy have again driven in my pickets. I shall do the best I can to defend the wagon train.

The majority of my brigade were ordered back on Saturday morning, and I, being disabled, came with the wagon train and unfit men and horses, which constitute my command.

Very respectfully,

N. B. Forrest, Brigadier-General.[21]

Forrest to Confederate General George Williamson, September 23, 1862:

☞ HEADQUARTERS FIRST CAVALRY BRIGADE, TWO MILES BEYOND COX'S CREEK, KY., SEPT. 23, 1862—10 P.M. MAJ. GEORGE WILLIAMSON, ASSISTANT ADJUTANT-GENERAL:

Major: I have not a full company in the command, having furnished several guards and pickets, but I will send from the different companies a sufficiency to report, as you ordered. From the best information I can obtain there are none of the enemy nearer than 10 miles.

Yours, respectfully,

N. B. Forrest, Brigadier-General.[22]

Forrest to Confederate General Sam Jones, October 16, 1862:

☞ [OCTOBER 16, 1862. TO MAJOR-GENERAL SAM JONES:]

Strong rumor of evacuation of Nashville. Pontoon bridge thrown over the river for that purpose. Have sent 1,500 cavalry and a section of artillery under Col. J. T. Morgan to reconnoiter and pursue if retreating. All reports from Kentucky still favorable. Nothing official from General Bragg.

[N. B. Forrest, Brigadier-General].[23]

Forrest to Confederate General George W. Randolph (a grandson of U.S. President Thomas Jefferson), October 20, 1862:

☞ MURFREESBOROUGH, TENN., OCTOBER 20, 1862. GEORGE W. RANDOLPH:

Sir: I am in urgent need of 5,000 stand of arms. The men only wait to receive them. If you can only send me 1,000 short arms and sabers for cavalry they will be invaluable.

N. B. Forrest, Brigadier-General, Commanding.[24]

Forrest to Colonel J. A. Buckner, November 6, 1862, describing a fight on the outskirts of Nashville, on the routes toward Murfreesboro, Nolensville, and LaVergne, Tennessee:

☞ REPORT OF BRIG. GEN. NATHAN B. FORREST, C. S. ARMY, COMMANDING CAVALRY. BRIGADE HEADQUARTERS, LA VERGNE, TENN., NOVEMBER 6, 1862. [TO: LIEUT. COL. J. A. BUCKNER, ASSISTANT ADJUTANT-GENERAL]:

General: Agreeably to orders received, I moved my commands on the night of the 4ᵗʰ instant in the direction of Nashville, distributing them as follows: Col. John T. Morgan's regiment [Fifty-first Alabama], of Partisan Rangers, and Capt. W. C. Bacot's battalion, Forrest's regiment, to the right of the Murfreesborough pike, with instructions to move forward on the Lebanon, Stone's River, and Chicken pikes, and to drive in the Abolitionists' pickets at daylight, which was done agreeably to orders and in gallant style, killing and wounding several, with the loss of 1 man killed and 2 horses wounded. Lieutenant-Colonel [A. A.] Russell Partisan Rangers, on Murfreesborough pike, followed by Colonels [J. B.] Palmer's and [R. W.] Hanson's brigades, with four batteries of artillery, commanded by Major [R. E.] Graves, after proceeding to Dogtown, 3.5 miles from Nashville, encountered the Abolitionists' pickets, at which place he (Colonel Russell) was ordered to dismount his command, press forward, and drive in the pickets. He succeeded in driving them to their first line of fortifications with considerable firing for 1.5 miles. I here found them in some force behind a brush and log fortification around a high hill on right of Pike. Here they made a stand, but after a short resistance [I] drove them from their position and gained the hill, at which place I planted my rifle battery of four pieces and opened fire on Jones' Hill, 1.5 miles distant. At this time the firing was heard from Colonel [John T.] Morgan, at Edgefield. About the same time Colonel [James W.] Starnes opened fire on the Nolensville pike, he having been ordered, with Colonel [G. G.] Dibrell's regiment, Major [D. C.] Douglass' battalion, Captains [S. L.] Freeman's and [Franklin] Roberts' batteries, to the left of Murfreesborough pike, down the Nolensville, Mill Creek, and Franklin pikes. The engagement now became general, Captains Freeman's amid Roberts' batteries having opened from Nolensville pike a vigorous fire on Saint Cloud's Hill. The firing was kept up until 10 o'clock, when I withdrew my forces.

Our loss in this action was 3 killed, 10 wounded, and 5 missing.

Loss of Abolitionists, 15 killed, 20 prisoners, and supposed 20 wounded, one shell from Nolensville pike killing 5 in fortifications.

I then moved Colonels Starnes' and Dibrell's regiments and Captain Freeman's and Roberts' batteries out on the Franklin pike 5 miles. The Abolitionists were in ambush with four regiments of infantry, twelve pieces of artillery, and a battalion of [William B.] Stokes' cavalry, commanded by Brigadier-General [James S.] Negley. They opened fire upon us from their position. I placed Freeman's and Roberts' batteries (four pieces each) on left of Franklin pike, between the Nolensville and Franklin pike, and returned their fire. After a spirited contest of an hour, they gave way, falling back down the Franklin pike toward Nashville. At this time I ordered my cavalry to charge, which order was quickly obeyed, their infantry and cavalry retreating down the pike toward Nashville. From this position my guns commanded the pike and played upon the Abolitionists with good effect, killing and wounding some 20 at one fire, which caused them to break and flee in disorder. I followed them up for a mile, when my artillery ammunition gave out and I withdrew my forces.

My loss in this action was 1 killed and 3 wounded. Loss of Abolitionists, 40 killed, 20 prisoners, and reported 60 wounded.

After this engagement I moved back to La Vergne [Tenn.].

Great credit is due Captain Freeman, of Freeman's battery, and Lieutenant [J. H.] Wiggins, commanding Roberts' battery, and their officers and men, for their coolness and discretion during this engagement. My officers and men acted well during the day, obeying with promptness each command.

All of which is respectfully submitted. N. B. Forrest, Brigadier-General.[25]

In the Fall of 1862, due to some disputation of the facts, Forrest was asked to give a statement regarding an important officers' meeting that had been held during the Battle of Fort Donelson. This he wrote out from his current headquarters in Murfreesboro, Tennessee, on November 7, 1862. Though not addressed to anyone specifically, his "statement" passed through the hands of Confederate States District Judge W. H. Humphreys (who compared this version to the original and attested to it as a "true copy") and Confederate General Gideon J. Pillow, one of Forrest's superiors at the battle:

☛ MURFREESBOROUGH, TENN., NOVEMBER 7, 1862.

Being informed by General Pillow that it is material for the purposes of justice and a proper understanding by the Government of the operations of the army at Donelson that I should make a statement of the result of the conference of general officers on the night of February 14, at which I was present by order of General Floyd, I make the following supplemental report:

On that day and the day before a large, fresh force, said to be 20,000 men, had reached the landing below us. At that time we were invested by a force which our information led us to estimate at 30,000. All the officers present felt the necessity of cutting our way out and resuming our communication with General Johnston. It was therefore resolved to give them battle in the open field the next morning.

I understood it to be the ultimate intention to retire from the place if we succeeded in opening our way, but nothing was said about our retreating from the field. No order was given to that effect and no preparation was made for that purpose; no suggestion was made of that character and no such determination arrived at.

On the day of the fight (15th) no artillery was taken from our intrenchments, except, perhaps, one piece late in the evening; no rations were prepared or taken on the field; blankets and knapsacks were left behind; no order of retreat was prescribed; no quartermaster, commissary, or ordnance stores were prepared to accompany a retreat; and, if a retreat had been attempted from the field of fight, it could not have been accomplished. The commands were scattered and mixed in fragments; very many of the men after the middle of the day had gone back into the town, and were around the fires and up and down the river bank. I had again and again during the day sent portions of my command into the intrenchments and had ammunition brought out on horseback.

The day itself was mainly occupied in the active operations of the fight. Soon after the fighting in the field was terminated fighting was begun on our right, in General Buckner's rifle pits, which lasted until about sundown.

In my opinion the pursuit of the enemy could not have been continued longer without coming in contact with a large, fresh force, which, in the scattered and exhausted condition of our troops, we could not have withstood.

The character of the country over which we would have had to retreat from Donelson to Charlotte was excessively poor and broken, and at that time covered with snow and sleet, and could not have furnished a half-day's ration for our force.

N. B. Forrest, Brigadier-General, Commanding Cavalry.[26]

Forrest to Confederate General Joseph Wheeler, November 20, 1862:
☞ TULLAHOMA [TENN.], NOVEMBER 20, 1862. [TO: GENERAL JOSEPH WHEELER]:

Can you spare my brigade? If so, order them up to Murfreesborough with the battery and all their transportation on Sunday. Answer.

N. B. Forrest, Brigadier-General.[27]

On December 3, 1862, a bristling Forrest sent off this harsh note to Confederate General Joseph Wheeler, warning him not to make any changes to his command:
☞ BRIGADE HEADQUARTERS, BRIGADIER-GENERAL WHEELER, COLUMBIA, TENN., DECEMBER 3, 1862. CHIEF OF CAVALRY:

General: I have received the report in person of Lieut. John W. Morton, jr., ordered to report to me by Colonel Hallonquist, and to take command of the horse artillery in my brigade. I have no objections to receiving Lieutenant Morton in my command, provided he is willing to come under command of Captain Freeman; but I am unwilling to exchange Captain Freeman (who has made a reputation at Shiloh and before Nashville, and proven himself a gallant and efficient officer) for any other officer. Rather than do so, I would prefer to return the battery. I hope the order has been made without your knowledge and consent, and that you will not permit any changes, but allow my command to go on as organized. You are well aware of the trouble and dissatisfaction caused by these changes, and I hope none will be made. In a few days I hope to have the organization complete, and move off in the direction indicated by General Bragg. General, I remain, your obedient servant, N. B. Forrest, Brigadier-General.[28]

Forrest to Confederate General Braxton Bragg, December 24, 1862:
☞ REPORTS OF BRIG. GEN. NATHAN B. FORREST, C.S. ARMY,

COMMANDING EXPEDITION OF OPERATIONS DECEMBER 11, 1862—JANUARY 3, 1863. BRIGADE HEADQUARTERS, NEAR UNION CITY, TENN., DECEMBER 24, 1862. [TO: GENERAL BRAXTON BRAGG, COMMANDING ARMY OF TENNESSEE]:

General: In accordance with your order I moved with my command from Columbia on the 11th instant, reached the river at Clifton on Sunday, the 13th, and after much difficulty, working night and day, finished crossing on the 15th, encamping that night 8 miles west of the river.

On the 16th [18th] we met the pickets of the enemy near Lexington and attacked their forces at Lexington, consisting of one section of artillery and 800 cavalry. We routed them completely, capturing the two guns and 148 prisoners, including Col. [R. G.] Ingersoll and Maj. [L. H.] Kerr, of the Eleventh Illinois Cavalry. We also captured about 70 horses, which were badly needed and immediately put in service in our batteries. The balance of the Federal cavalry fled in the direction of Trenton and Jackson. We pushed on rapidly to Jackson, and on the evening of the 18th drove in their pickets on all the roads leading out of Jackson. On the same night I sent Col. [G. G.] Dibrell on the right of Jackson to tear up the railroad track and destroy the telegraph wires. He captured at Webb's Station 101 Federals, destroying their stockade, and tore up the road, switch, &c., at the turn-out. At the same time that Dibrell was sent on the right Col. [A. A.] Russell, [Fourth Alabama Cavalry], and Maj. [N. N.] Cox, [Second Battalion Tennessee Cavalry], with their commands were sent out on the left to destroy bridges and culverts on the railroads from Jackson to Corinth and Bolivar.

The next morning [December 19] I advanced on Jackson with Colonel [T. G.] Woodward's two companies and Col. [J. B.] Biffle's battalion of about 400 men, with two pieces of artillery from Freeman's battery. About 4 miles from Jackson skirmishing began with the skirmishers, and the enemy was reported advancing with two regiments of infantry and a battalion of cavalry. We opened on them with the guns, and after a running fight of about an hour drove them into their fortifications. The enemy had heavily re-enforced at Jackson from Corinth, Bolivar, and La Grange, and numbered, from the best information I could obtain, about 9,000 men. I withdrew my forces that evening and moved rapidly on Trenton and Humboldt. Colonel Dibrell's command was sent to destroy the bridge over the Forked Deer River between Humboldt and Jackson. Col. [J. W.] Starnes was sent to attack Humboldt. Colonel Biffle was sent so as to get in the rear of Trenton, while with Major Cox's command and my body guard, commanded by Capt. [M.] Little, and [S. L.] Freeman's [Tennessee] battery, I dashed into town and attacked the enemy at Trenton. They were fortified at the depot, but were without artillery. After a short engagement between their sharpshooters and our cavalry our battery opened on them, and on the third fire from the battery they surrendered.

We lost 2 men killed and 7 wounded; the enemy[,] 2 killed and over 700 prisoners, with a large quantity of stores, arms, ammunition, and provisions, which for want of transportation we were compelled to destroy. We captured several hundred horses, but few of them were of any value; those that were of service we took, and the balance I handed over to the citizens, from whom many of them had been pressed or stolen. Colonel Russell, who was protecting our rear at Spring Creek, found the enemy advancing and following us with 3,000 infantry, two batteries, and several hundred cavalry. He skirmished with them during the evening and the next morning before daylight dismounted half of his command and succeeded in getting within 60 yards of their encampment. They discovered him and formed in line of battle. He delivered a volley as soon as their line was formed and the balance of the regiment charged on horseback. The enemy became panic-stricken and retreated hastily across Spring Creek, burning the bridge after them. We have heard nothing from them since in that direction.

Col. [James W.] Starnes took Humboldt, capturing over 100 prisoners. He destroyed the stockade, railroad depot, and burned up a trestle bridge near that point.

Colonel Dibrell's command failed to destroy the bridge over the Forked Deer River, as the enemy were strongly fortified and protected by two creeks on one side of the railroad and a wide, swampy bottom on the other, which rendered the approach of cavalry impossible. He dismounted his men, and while approaching their fort a train arrived from Jackson with a regiment of infantry. Lieutenant [John W., Jr.,] Morton with two guns opened on the train, when it retired, the troops on it gaining the stockade. Owing to the situation of the stockade and the density of the timber and the wet, miry condition of the bottom, the guns could not be brought to bear on it. Night coming on Colonel Dibrell withdrew and rejoined my command.

We remained in Trenton during the night of the 20th, paroling all the prisoners and selecting from the stores at the depot such as were needed by the command.

On the morning of the 21st I fired the depot, burning up the remaining supplies, with about 600 bales of cotton, 200 barrels of pork, and a large lot of tobacco in hogsheads, used by the enemy for breastworks. After seeing everything destroyed I moved on in the direction of Union City, capturing at Rutherford Station two companies of Federals and destroying the railroad from Trenton to Kenton Station, at which place we captured Col. [Thomas J.] Kinney, of the One hundred and twenty-second [One hundred and nineteenth] Illinois Regiment, and 22 men left sick in the hospital. I took a portion of the command and pushed ahead to Union City, capturing 106 Federals without firing a gun. I destroyed the railroad bridge over the bayou near Moscow and am completing the destruction of the bridges over the North and South Fork of Obion River, with nearly 4 miles of trestling in the bottom between them. We have made a clean sweep of the Federals and roads north of Jackson, and know of no Federals except at Fort Heiman, Paducah, and Columbus, north of Jackson and west of the Tennessee River. Reports that are reliable show that the Federals are rapidly sending up troops from Memphis. One hundred and twenty-five transports passed down a few days ago within ten hours, and daily they are passing up loaded with troops. [Yankee] General [Ulysses] Grant must either be in a very critical condition or else affairs in Kentucky require the movement.

In closing my report, general, allow me to say that great credit is due to the officers of my command. They have exhibited great zeal, energy, endurance, and gallantry. Colonel Russell and his command deserve especial notice for their gallantry in the fight at Lexington and Spring Creek.

Capt. [F. B.] Gurley, [Fourth Alabama Cavalry], with 12 men charged a gun at Lexington supported by over 100 Federal cavalry. He captured the gun, losing his orderly-sergeant by the fire of the gun when within 15 feet of its muzzle. My men have all behaved well in action, and as soon as rested a little you will hear from me in another quarter.

Our loss so far is 8 killed, 12 wounded, and 2 missing. The enemy's killed and wounded [total] over 100 men; prisoners over 1,200, including 4 colonels, 4 majors, 10 captains, and 23 lieutenants. We have been so busy and kept so constantly moving that we have not had time to make out a report of our strength, and ask to be excused until the next courier comes over. We send by courier a list of prisoners paroled.

General, I am, very respectfully, your most obedient servant,

N. B. Forrest, Brigadier-General, Commanding in West Tennessee.[29]

SECTION THREE

1863

1863

On May 1 Forrest receives his first vote of thanks (of four) from the Confederate Congress. In the Fall he is transferred to North Mississippi and given a new command, and on December 4 he is promoted to major-general. His correspondence nearly doubles this year.

Forrest to Confederate Lieutenant Colonel George W. Brent, January 3, 1863:
☛ TO: LIEUT. COL. GEORGE WILLIAM BRENT, ASSISTANT ADJUTANT-GENERAL. BRIGADE HEADQUARTERS, CLIFTON, TENN., JANUARY 3, 1863:

General: I forwarded you from Middleburg, per Lieutenant Martin, a detailed report of my operations up to the 25th ultimo, which I hope reached you safely.

I left Middleburg on the 25th, proceeding via the Northwestern Railroad to McKenzie's Station, destroying all the bridges and trestles on that road from Union City to McKenzie's Station. From McKenzie's Station we were compelled to move southward in the direction of Lexington, as the enemy in force occupied Trenton, Humboldt, Huntingdon, and Lexington. After my command left Trenton they commenced re-enforcing and moving to the points named with a view of cutting off my command and prevent us recrossing the Tennessee [River]. Understanding a force was moving on me from Trenton in the direction of Dresden, I sent Col. [J. B.] Biffle, [Nineteenth Tennessee Cavalry], in that direction to protect our movements toward Lexington, intending if possible to avoid the enemy and go on and attack the enemy at Bethel Station on the Mobile and Ohio road, south of Jackson.

We left McKenzie's Station on the morning of December 28, but in crossing the bottom had great difficulty in crossing our artillery and wagons; the bridges proved to be much decayed and gave way, forcing us to drag our artillery and wagons through the bottom and the creeks. It was with great difficulty we got through by working the entire night, and our men and horses were so much fatigued that I was compelled to encamp at Flake's Store, about 16 miles north of Lexington, when under ordinary circumstances and good roads we ought to have reached Lexington that night, which place had been evacuated by the enemy, believing that I would either cross the Tennessee at Huntingdon or else that I would move northward.

On the morning of the 31st we moved off in the direction of Lexington, but had not gone more than 4 miles before we met the skirmishers of the enemy. We engaged and fought six regiments for five hours, driving them back until 3 o'clock in the evening, [when] they took shelter in a grove of timber of about 60 acres inclosed by a fence and surrounded by open fields. I had sent four companies to Clarksburg to protect and advise me of any advance from Huntingdon, and finding that we were able to whip the enemy, dismounted a portion of my cavalry to support my artillery and attack in front while I could flank them on each side and get Col. [A. A.] Russell's regiment, [Fourth Alabama Cavalry], in their rear. We drove them through the woods with great slaughter and several white flags were raised in various portions of the woods and the killed and wounded were strewn over the ground. Thirty minutes more would have given us the day, when to my surprise and astonishment a fire was opened on us in our rear and the enemy in heavy force under General [J. C.] Sullivan advanced on us. Knowing that I had four companies at Clarksburg, 7 miles from us on the Huntingdon road, I could not believe that they were Federals until I rode up myself into their lines. The heavy fire of their infantry unexpected and unlooked for by all[,] caused a stampede of horses belonging to my dismounted men, who were following up and driving the enemy before them. They also killed and crippled many of the horses attached to our caissons and reserved guns.

I had sent back 2 miles for more ammunition. My men had been fighting for five hours, and both artillery and small-arm ammunition were well-nigh exhausted. We occupied the battle-field, were in possession of the enemy's dead and wounded and their three pieces of artillery, and had demanded a surrender of the brigade, which would doubtless have been forced or accepted in half an hour, the colonel commanding proposing to leave the field entirely and withdraw his force provided we would allow him to bury his dead; but believing I could force, and that in a short time, the demand, the fighting continued, the Federals scattering in every direction. The stampede of horses and horse-holders announced that help was at hand, and finding my command now exposed to fire from both front and rear I was compelled to withdraw, which I did in good order, leaving behind our dead and wounded. We were able to bring off six pieces of artillery and two caissons, the balance, with the three guns we captured, we were compelled to leave, as most of the horses were killed or crippled and the drivers in the same condition, which rendered it impossible to get them out under the heavy fire of the enemy from both front and rear. Our loss in artillery is three guns and eight caissons and one piece which burst during the action.

The enemy's loss was very heavy in killed and wounded, and as we had the field and saw them piled up and around the fences[,] had a good opportunity of judging their loss. We gave them grape and canister from our guns at 300 yards, and as they fell back through the timber their loss was terrible. The prisoners say that at least one-third of the command was killed or wounded. From all I could see and learn from my aides and officers they must have lost in killed and wounded from 800 to 1,000 men. The fire of our artillery for accuracy and rapidity was scarcely, if ever, excelled, and their position in the fence corners proved to the enemy, instead of a protection, a source of great loss, as our shot and shell scattered them to the winds, and many were killed by rails that were untouched by balls.

Captain Freeman and Lieut. [J. W.] Morton of our batteries, with all of their men, deserve special mention, keeping up, as they did, a constant fire from their pieces, notwithstanding the enemy made every effort at silencing their pieces by shooting down the artillerists at the guns. The whole command fought well. We had about 1,800 men in the engagement, and fought six regiments of infantry, with three pieces of artillery, which we charged and took, but were compelled to leave them, as the horses were all killed or crippled. We brought off 83 prisoners, and they report their respective regiments as badly cut up. They lost 3 colonels and many company officers.

We have on our side to deplore the death of Col. [T.] Alonzo Napier, [Tenth Tennessee Cavalry], who was killed while leading his men in a charge on foot. He was a gallant officer, and after he fell his command continued to drive the enemy from their position on the right bank, strewing their path with dead and wounded Federals.

I cannot speak in too high terms of all my commanding officers; and the men, considering they were mostly raw recruits, fought well. I have not been able as yet to ascertain our exact loss, but am of the opinion that 60 killed and wounded and 100 captured or missing will cover it.

I saved all my wagons except my ammunition wagons, which, by a mistake of orders, were driven right into the enemy's line. This is seriously to be regretted, as we had captured six wagon loads of it; and when I ordered up one wagon of ammunition and two ambulances the wagon-master and ordnance officer not knowing exactly what kind was wanted, or misunderstanding the order, brought up all the ammunition, and by the time he reached the point with them where the battle begun that portion of the ground was in possession of the enemy, and the guards, &c., were forced to abandon them.

We have always been short of shot-gun caps, and as we captured nothing but musket-caps, all the men using shot-guns were out, or nearly so, of caps after the action was over. Considering our want of ammunition for small-arms and artillery and the worn-down condition of our men and horses I determined at once to recross the Tennessee River and fit up for a return. Had we been entirely successful in the battle of the 31st I should have attacked Bethel Station on the 2d instant; had already sent a company to cut wires and bridges, and had forage prepared 12 miles south of Lexington for my entire command but after the fight, and knowing we were followed by Federals in heavy force from Trenton and Huntingdon, and that a force would also move on us from Jackson as soon as they learned I had pushed south of Lexington, I deemed it advisable to cross the Tennessee, which I accomplished yesterday and last night in safety.

Colonel Biffle, who I before mentioned as having been sent to Trenton, or in that direction, returned in time to take part in the battle at Parker's Cross-Roads. He captured and paroled 150 Federals within 6 miles of Trenton.

The captains of the four companies sent to Clarksburg have not yet reached here with their commands. Had they done their duty by advising me of the approach of the enemy I could have terminated the fight by making it short and decisive, when without such advice I was whipping them badly with my artillery, and unless absolutely necessary was not pressing them with my cavalry. I had them entirely surrounded and was driving them before me, and was taking it leisurely and trying as much as possible to save my men. The four companies on the approach of the enemy left for Tennessee River and have not yet reported here.

I do not design this, general, as a regular report, but will make one as soon as I can do so. We crossed the river at three points, and the brigade is not yet together, or reports from the different commands have not come in. We have worked, rode, and fought hard, and I hope accomplished to a considerable extent, if not entirely, the object of our campaign, as we drew from Corinth, Grand Junction, and La Grange about 20,000 Federals. Will send you an additional list of paroles, &c, by next courier.

I am, general, very respectfully, your most obedient servant,

N. B. Forrest, Brigadier-General, Commanding Brigade.[30]

Forrest to Union General Jefferson C. Davis, February 10, 1863:
☞ BRIGADE HEADQUARTERS, COLUMBIA, TENN., FEBRUARY 10, 1863. GENERAL J. C. DAVIS, COMMANDING U.S. FORCES.

General: I have recently captured forty-eight non-commissioned officers and privates belonging to the Federal Army which were paroled and sent into Fort Donelson. We have here six of your men captured a few days since which have not been paroled, also Captain Von Minden, of the Fifth Iowa Cavalry, and First Lieut. Samuel Mitchell, the latter captured at Fort Donelson on the 3d instant. At the earnest solicitation of Captain Von Minden I send a flag of truce in charge of Lieut. J. G. Clouston, of Major-General Wheeler's staff, for the purpose of exchanging him for Captain Rambaut, my commissary, who I am informed was captured by your forces a few days since. I am willing to exchange the six men here for an equal number of men of mine [now in your] possession, or any of my command you may have paroled and sent out of your lines. Lieutenant Clouston also has in his charge a list of the forty-eight prisoners sent into Fort Donelson, which list has not yet been forwarded to the War Department of the Confederate States, any of whom I will release from their paroles in exchange for any of my men who may have fallen into your hands. Lieutenant Clouston is fully authorized and empowered to receive any prisoners of my command you may have and erase from the list the names of an equal number of those captured by us and to give you official notification in writing of the release from parole of the men whose names are thus erased. He is also authorized, should it meet your approbation, to arrange time and place for the exchange of Captains Von Minden and Rambaut and the six men now here in our possession. Any arrangements made by Lieutenant Clouston will be ratified by me and carried out in good faith.

I am, general, very respectfully, yours,

N. B. Forrest, Brigadier-General.[31]

Forrest to Confederate General Joseph Wheeler, February 18, 1863:
☛ BRIGADE HEADQUARTERS, COLUMBIA, FEBRUARY 18, 1863. MAJ. GEN. JOSEPH WHEELER, CHIEF OF CAVALRY:

General: My scouts report the Federals still at Franklin [Tenn.]; have made no advance so far. I have reliable information that the [railroad] cars were run out to Franklin last night; therefore they have repaired the Tennessee and Alabama [rail] road to that point. I have been unable, however, to ascertain whether they have or are repairing the bridge over [the] Harpeth River, near Franklin. I also ascertain that there are a large number of wagons on the Franklin pike, near Nashville, loaded with sections of pontoon bridges, but, of course, cannot tell whether they are intended for use over streams in this direction or not. They were brought to Nashville on steamboats, loaded on wagons, and hauled out and left standing near town, on the pike leading to this place.

From the same party who gave me information in regard to the boats or bridges, I learn that the Federals have about 2,000 mules quartered near the race-track below town; that they are lightly guarded, and only one regiment encamped in that direction. A feint on Franklin might enable a few hundred men to bring them out.

It is reported that [Confederate] General [Earl] Van Dorn will be here to-day. Some of his men on leave have arrived here, with orders to rejoin their commands at this place on the 25th. Presume his command will all be here by that time.

I am, general, very respectfully, your obedient servant,

N. B. Forrest, Brigadier-General.[32]

Forrest to Confederate General Joseph Wheeler, February 18, 1863:

☞ BRIGADE HEADQUARTERS, COLUMBIA, FEBRUARY 18, 1863:

General: I am in receipt of yours of the 17th, yesterday. For the helmet, please accept my thanks. Will furnish Major Nicholson with any details he may require.

Since I sent you dispatch at 5 o'clock this evening, I have received a dispatch of the advance of 300 Yankee cavalry toward Spring Hill. Colonel [T. G.] Woodward, with 160 men, dismounted and whipped them back, and, when the courier left, was chasing them toward Franklin.

Send forward the companies as quickly as possible, as it is important I should get my command organized before I go into the field again. Have ordered dress parade twice per week; all general orders to be read by the adjutant at dress parade, and by orderlies every morning at roll-call for one week after they are received at regimental head-quarters.

If I get the nine companies, and they are anything like full, I find it will give me about 3,000 troops. I am getting my men now here in very good condition.

I am, general, very respectfully, your obedient servant,

N. B. Forrest, Brigadier-General.[33]

Forrest to Confederate Major E. S. Burford, February 19, 1863:

☞ COLUMBIA [TENN.], FEBRUARY 19, 1863. MAJ. E. S. BURFORD, ASSISTANT ADJUTANT-GENERAL, CAVALRY:

Major: I have received information to-day that two regiments of cavalry have reached Franklin, making about 2,000 Federal cavalry at that place, and 4,000 infantry. They are evidently preparing to move on this way, as they are repairing the bridge at Franklin, over [the] Harpeth [River], and are putting the telegraph in order. If they should move out this way, I think, with General [Earl] Van Dorn's command and mine to move from here, Colonel [Philip D.] Roddey from Chapel Hill, and General Wharton in toward Brentwood, the command can be captured or cut to pieces. I only make these suggestions for your consideration.

I am much in need of some guns. My ordnance officer is now absent. We need 500 or 600, at least, and would be glad, if you know of any that we can get, if you would secure them for me, as I fear my ordnance officer may fail to obtain them.

General Van Dorn's command will commence reaching here tomorrow, having been detained one day by high water. I am anxiously awaiting the arrival of Douglass' battalion to complete the organization of a regiment, as I am desirous of completing the organizations and having quartermasters and commissaries appointed and bonded before leaving here.

I am, general, very respectfully, your obedient servant,

N. B. Forrest, Brigadier-General.[34]

What follows is Forrest's official report regarding the Battle of Thompson's Station (fought March 5, 1863). Although it is not addressed, it appears to be for General Braxton Bragg:

☞ REPORT OF BRIG. GEN. NATHAN B. FORREST, C.S. ARMY, COMMANDING CAVALRY BRIGADE. BRIGADE HEADQUARTERS, NEAR SPRING HILL, [TENN.,] MARCH —, [1863]:

General: On the morning of the 5th instant, I was ordered to place my brigade in line of battle on the right of General Jackson's division, which I did, dismounting and placing Colonel [J. H.] Edmondson on the left of my line and Colonel [J. W.] Starnes on the right, parallel with the line of battle already formed by forces under General Jackson. I also caused the regiments of Colonels [J. B.] Biffle and [N. N.] Cox to form upon my extreme right near the Lewisburg pike, with ample pickets and vedettes upon that pike, to give timely notice of the approach of the enemy from that quarter. By the time this disposition of my force was made, the firing began from the enemy's artillery, and, finding I had no position bearing upon the enemy with my artillery, I ordered Captain [S. L.] Freeman forward with his battery to a high hill, which placed it advantageously for operating on the enemy's left flank. As it was full half a mile in advance of my first position, I ordered up all the regiments of my brigade on foot to a line parallel with that hill and nearly at right angles with the pike. I found two regiments of infantry and a regiment of the Federal cavalry posted behind a stone fence to the left of their artillery. A few shells from my guns drove them from their position to the right of their battery and into the pike. I then ordered a fire opened upon their battery, and, after about 20 rounds, drove it from its position, retreating by the pike toward Franklin [Tenn]. At this time I was ordered to move forward, and, if possible, get in the rear of the enemy. This was done with as little delay as possible, but the two regiments of Biffle and Cox (the latter commanded by Lieutenant-Colonel [E. B.] Trezevant) were ordered up, but did not arrive as soon as desired, from the fact that they were 2 miles off, and dismounted, and a half a mile in advance of their horses. Pending this movement, Colonels Edmondson and Starnes were ordered to move forward, which they did in gallant style, driving the enemy from the cedar hill, and attacking them across the railroad in conjunction with Generals Armstrong's and Whitfield's brigades. The engagement there lasted for about an hour, which gave time for Biffle's and Cox's regiments to get up. They attacked vigorously, and dispersed that portion of the enemy's force moving on the pike, and formed in the field beyond King's house, on the right of the pike. The main force of the enemy was posted on the hill in front of Thompson's Station and to the left of the pike, and had driven back several times the forces under Generals Armstrong and Whitfield and my two regiments under Colonels Starnes and Edmondson. I moved Biffle's and Cox's regiments rapidly across the pike in the rear of the enemy; found they had fallen back from the first hill on the left of the pike, where they had successfully resisted the advance of our forces, and had taken a strong position, and were ready to receive us. As soon as the two regiments were formed, I ordered a charge, which was gallantly led by Colonel Biffle and Lieutenant-Colonel Trezevant, commanding Cox's regiment. The enemy opened a heavy fire upon us, the first volley mortally wounding Lieutenant-Colonel Trezevant and Capt. Montgomery Little, who commanded my escort. The men seeing those officers fall, raised a shout, and continued the charge to within 20 feet of the Federal line of battle. The enemy then threw down their arms and surrendered.

The two regiments, with my escort, numbered about 650 men; balance of effective strength holding horses. They captured from 1,200 to 1,500 Federal officers and privates, with their colors, &c.

No one can regret more than I do the loss of Lieutenant-Colonel Trezevant, commanding Cox's regiment of cavalry, Capt. M. Little, of my escort, and Captain [A. A.] Dysart, of the Third Tennessee Cavalry.

They were gallant men, and fell with their faces to the foe. I cannot speak in too high terms of the conduct of my whole command. The colonels commanding led their regiments in person, and it affords me much pleasure to say that officers and men performed their duty well. I discerned no straggling or shirking from duty on the field. Every order was promptly obeyed, and the bravery of the troops alike creditable to them and gratifying to their commanders.

I herewith forward you a statement of my loss, which shows 9 killed, 58 wounded, and 2 missing. I also beg leave to transmit you herewith the reports of regimental commanders of this action.

All of which is very respectively submitted.

N. B. Forrest, Brigadier-General.[35]

Forrest to Confederate Major General Earl Van Dorn, March 7, 1863:
☛ WEBB'S, MARCH 7, 1863. MAJOR-GENERAL VAN DORN, COMMANDING CAVALRY CORPS:

General: I am at Dr. Webb's, half mile from the river, and half mile from College Grove [Tenn.]. My forces are encamped at College Grove.

General Sheridan (Federal), with force from Murfreesborough (not known). They joined General Steedman, who has four regiments of infantry and one of cavalry, and both forces are said to be encamped about 3 miles from the river. I have sent out men to-night to ascertain where they are encamped, and to get any other possible information as to numbers and position.

They are encamped on the north side of the river, between this place and Nolensville, about 3 miles from the river. Will advise you, and give any information I may get.

I have sent men on all roads in this direction, and especially on the pike toward Shelbyville. Will establish my headquarters here to-night.

Very respectfully, your obedient servant,

N. B. Forrest, Brigadier-General.[36]

Forrest to an unidentified "Major," April 1, 1863, regarding the Battle of Brentwood, Tennessee (fought March 25, 1863):
☛ REPORT OF BRIG. GEN. NATHAN B. FORREST, C. S. ARMY,

COMMANDING FIRST DIVISION, FIRST CAVALRY CORPS.
HDQRS. FIRST DIVISION, FIRST CAVALRY CORPS, APRIL 1, 1863.

Major: I respectfully submit the following report of expedition to Brentwood [Tennessee]:

On the 24th ultimo I ordered Colonel [J. W.] Starnes, commanding Second Brigade, to proceed with his command in the direction of Brentwood, leaving Franklin on the left and crossing Harpeth River at Half-Acre Mill, 6 miles east of Franklin, and to pass through fields and byroads thence to Brentwood, ordering him to throw out a squadron on the pike and railroad between Brentwood and Franklin, cutting the telegraph wires, and tearing up the track of the railroad, sending two regiments forward to attack the stockade, and posting the balance of the Third [Fourth] Tennessee Regiment so as to cut off any retreat of the enemy toward Nashville and Triune. He was ordered to bring on the attack at daylight on the 25th, at which time I was to join him with General Armstrong's brigade, with the Tenth Tennessee Cavalry, temporarily attached to his brigade, which marched on Brentwood via Hillsborough and the Hillsborough pike. I failed to reach Brentwood with General Armstrong's command at the appointed hour, owing to delay in getting the artillery across Harpeth River. I arrived there, however, at 7 o'clock in the morning, sending one squadron of the Tenth Regiment down the Hillsborough pike to protect my rear, and another to the left and rear of Brentwood to prevent any retreat of the enemy toward Nashville, and give me timely information of any re-enforcements from Nashville. With the other six companies of the Tenth Tennessee and my escort, I moved to the right of the road running from Hillsborough pike to Brentwood, ordering General Armstrong, with his brigade and a section of Freeman's artillery, to move to the left of that, and attack the Federals at Brentwood.

After disposing of my troops as stated, I moved rapidly on with my escort to the Franklin pike, capturing a courier with a dispatch to the commander of the Federal forces at Franklin, asking for help. I found the enemy had thrown out his skirmishers on the pike and on the surrounding hills. A flag of truce was sent in, demanding an immediate and unconditional surrender. The colonel commanding replied that we must come and take him. By this time the other six companies of the Tenth Tennessee, commanded by Major [William E.] De Moss, had arrived at the pike. He was ordered to dismount his men and attack in front, while messengers were sent to General Armstrong to move up and open upon them with his artillery in the left and rear. Major De Moss promptly attacked them. As soon as this was done, with my escort I moved rapidly to the right of the pike, and, gaining a high position, found the enemy were preparing to make their escape toward Nashville. My escort was ordered to advance to the pike and engage them. By this time the firing in front between the enemy and Major De Moss became general. The enemy had been driven inside of their works, and I ordered my escort to charge them. Just as this order was given, and General Armstrong had taken position on the left, the enemy hoisted a white flag, and surrendered, with all their arms, wagons, baggage, and equipments.

I ordered General Armstrong to send off the prisoners, arms, wagons, &c., as quickly as possible to the Hillsborough pike, and to destroy by fire all the tents, camp equipage, &c., that could not be transported. With the Fourth Mississippi Cavalry and, the Tenth Tennessee and the pieces of artillery, I moved on the stockade at the bridge across Harpeth River, about 2 miles south of Brentwood. After getting position and firing one gun, they surrendered. We captured there 275 prisoners, 11 wagons, 3 ambulances, with all their arms and equipments.

We moved off as soon as possible to the Hillsborough pike, after destroying the railroad bridge and all the tents and supplies which could not be removed.

Before leaving Brentwood to attack the stockade, I ordered Colonel [J. H.] Lewis, of the First [Sixth] Tennessee Cavalry, to dash down the pike with his command toward Nashville. He ran their pickets in at Brown's Creek, capturing some negroes and a sutler's wagon within 3 miles of the city. He there turned to the left with his regiment, making a circuit around Nashville from the Franklin to the Charlotte pike.

Before the rear of my command reached the Hillsborough pike, they were attacked by a force of Federal cavalry. They succeeded in getting possession of several of the wagons captured at the stockade, and cut out and stampeded the mules.

As soon as the lines were formed, the enemy were repulsed and driven back to Brentwood; but having no harness or mules for them, several of the wagons were burned, and not knowing what forces might be marching on us, I deemed it expedient to move off with the prisoners as rapidly as possible.

I will here remark that Colonel Starnes reached the stockade at daylight; but, not knowing the force of the enemy, and being without artillery, and ignorant of the whereabouts of my portion of the command, moved over to the Hillsborough pike, where he remained until after the capture was made.

I refer you to official report of killed and wounded on our side, which is very small indeed. The enemy lost about 15 killed and 30 wounded and 800 prisoners. We captured and brought away 3 ambulances and harness, 9 six-horse wagons and harness, 2 two-horse wagons and harness, 60 mules, and 6 horses, which were placed in charge of Major [N. C.] Jones, assistant quartermaster First Brigade, who was ordered to turn them over to quartermaster at Columbia. Many of the men in the command who were unarmed got guns on the field, and many who had inferior guns, muskets, shot-guns, &c., exchanged them on the field, placing (or, at any rate, so ordered) their old guns in the wagons in lieu of them.

I ordered Colonel [J. H.] Edmondson's regiment and [E. J.] Sanders' battalion to take charge of the prisoners and wagons, and proceed direct to Columbia, via Williamsport. With the balance of the division I moved toward Spring Hill, regulating my march so as to keep on the flank of the commands with the prisoners, so as to meet promptly any attempt at recapture by the enemy's forces at Franklin.

Respectfully submitted.

N. B. Forrest, Brigadier-General.[37]

Forrest to Confederate General Braxton Bragg, June 1, 1863:

☛ SPRING HILL [TENN.], JUNE 1, 1863—9 P.M. [TO: CONFEDERATE GENERAL BRAXTON BRAGG]

General Bragg: My scouts report the enemy's cavalry all moved to the front of Murfreesborough. [Union General William S.] Rosecrans' headquarters are at Nashville. All the streets are being blockaded; [we are] cutting ditches and placing sand-bags. They [the Yanks] intend to move either forward or backward.

N. B. Forrest, Brigadier-General, Commanding.[38]

Forrest to Confederate General Braxton Bragg, June 1, 1863:

☛ SPRING HILL [TENN.], JUNE 1, 1863—10 P.M. [TO: CONFEDERATE GENERAL BRAXTON BRAGG]

General Bragg: My scouts have just returned from Franklin, and report the enemy have released all the citizen prisoners and are under marching orders. I will move up in the morning as near Franklin as possible, and remain as near the enemy as prudent, and would like the balance of the cavalry to move up, if you think it advisable.

N. B. Forrest, Brigadier-General, Commanding.[39]

Forrest to Confederate Captain Victor Von Sheliha, July 30, 1863:

☛ [FROM KINGSTON, TENN., JULY 30, 1863. TO: V. SHELIHA, CHIEF OF STAFF, HEADQUARTERS DEPARTMENT OF EAST TENNESSEE:]

I have arrived here and assumed command. My forces are on picket from this place to Chattanooga. No news from the front. Can you send me a map of the country from Pikeville in this direction? Give me the position of your pickets to your right.

[N. B. Forrest, Brigadier-General, Commanding.][40]

On August 9, 1863, Forrest, anticipating problems with his nemesis and superior, the cranky Braxton Bragg, wrote a letter to Confederate General Samuel Cooper at Richmond, asking for an independent command in West Tennessee or Mississippi. Included in Forrest's missive was a proposal for what was certainly the most outstanding plan by a Confederate officer during the entire conflict: prolong the War—thus exhausting the North—by closing down the Yankees' major supply routes, the Mississippi and Tennessee Rivers.[41] By this time most of the Union forces, including those under Grant, were relying strictly on these two waterways for provisions. Had Forrest's proposition (already backed by other important Confederate leaders, such as General Joseph E. Johnston) been taken seriously and implemented, it is clear that the outcome of Lincoln's War would have been very different.[42] Forrest's original letter to Cooper, which, unfortunately, was to pass through Bragg's hands,[43] reads:

☛ HEADQUARTERS FIRST DIVISION CAVALRY, KINGSTON, TENN., AUGUST 9, 1863. GENERAL S. COOPER, ADJUTANT-GENERAL, RICHMOND, VA.:

General,—Prompted by the repeated solicitations of numerous

friends and acquaintances resident in west Tennessee and northern Mississippi, also by a desire to serve my country to the best of my ability, and wherever those services can be rendered most available and effective, I respectfully lay before you a proposition which, if approved, will seriously, if not entirely, obstruct the navigation of the Mississippi River, and in sixty days procure a large force now inside the enemy's lines, which without this, or a similar move, cannot be obtained.

The proposition is this: Give me the command of the forces from Vicksburg to Cairo, or, in other words, all the forces I may collect together and organize between those points—say in northern Mississippi, west Tennessee, and those that may join me from Arkansas, Mississippi, and southern Kentucky. I desire to take with me only about four hundred men from my present command—viz., my escort, sixty; McDonald's battalion, one hundred and fifty; the Second Kentucky Cavalry, two hundred and fifty—selected entirely on account of their knowledge of the country in which I propose to operate. In all, say, men and outfit, four hundred men, with long-range guns (Enfield), four three-inch Dahlgren or Parrott guns, with eight number one horses to each gun and caisson, two wagons for the battery, one pack-mule to every ten men, and two hundred rounds of ammunition for small arms and artillery.

I would like to have Captain (W. W.) Carnes, now at Chattanooga, in some portion of General Bragg's army, to command the battery, and, in case he was detached for the expedition, that he be allowed to select his cannoneers, etc. I have resided on the Mississippi for over twenty years, was for many years engaged in buying and selling negroes, and know the country perfectly well between Memphis and Vicksburg, and also am well acquainted with all the prominent planters in that region, as well as above Memphis. I also have officers in my command and on my staff who have rafted timber out of the bottoms, and know every foot of the ground between Commerce and Vicksburg. With the force proposed, and my knowledge of the river- bottoms, as well as the knowledge my men have of the country from Vicksburg up, I am confident we could so move and harass and destroy boats on the river that only boats heavily protected by gunboats would be able to make the passage.

I ask also authority to organize all troops that can be obtained, and that I be promised long-range guns for them as soon as organizations are reported. There are many half-organized regiments, battalions, and companies in northern Mississippi and west Tennessee, but they are without arms and have no way of getting out, and it only requires a little time and a nucleus around which they can form, to organize and put them in the field. I believe that in sixty days I can raise from five to ten thousand men between Vicksburg and Cairo, well mounted and ready for service as soon as provided with guns and ammunition.

In making this proposition, I desire to state that I do so entirely for the good of the service. I believe that I can accomplish all that I propose to do. I have never asked for position, have taken position and performed the duties assigned me, and have never yet suffered my command to be surprised or defeated. I should leave this department with many regrets, as I am well pleased with the officers in my command and with the division serving under me. I shall especially regret parting with my old brigade. It was organized by me, and a record of its past services and present condition will compare favorably with any cavalry command in the service, and nothing but a desire to destroy the enemy's transports and property, and increase the strength of our army, could for a moment induce me voluntarily to part with them. There are thousands of men where I propose to go that I am satisfied will join me, and that rapidly (otherwise they will remain where they are), until all the country bordering on the Mississippi from Cairo down is taken and permanently occupied by our forces.

I am, general, very respectfully, your obedient servant,
N. B. Forrest, Brigadier-General.[44]

Assuming that General Bragg would intercept his letter to General Cooper and prevent it from being delivered, Forrest went right to the top, writing the following to Confederate President Jefferson Davis, August 19, 1863:

☞ HEADQUARTERS FIRST CAVALRY DIVISION, KINGSTON, TENN., AUGUST 19, 1863. HON. JEFFERSON DAVIS, PRESIDENT CONFEDERATE STATES OF AMERICA:

I have the honor respectfully to inclose herewith copy of a communication addressed to [Confederate] General [Samuel] Cooper, Adjutant and Inspector General, and sent by a friend to General Bragg, to be forwarded through the proper channel to General Cooper.

Having understood that it was likely it would not be forwarded by the general commanding department, and believing the matter of sufficient importance to merit the consideration of your excellency, I have taken the liberty of sending a copy direct. If, however, General Bragg has forwarded the original or duplicate, I shall regret troubling you with this. While I believe the general commanding is unwilling for me to leave his department, still I hope to be permitted to go where (as I believe) I can serve my country best, especially so as an experienced and competent officer, Brigadier-General Armstrong, would be left in command of my division.

I am, sir, with great respect, your most obedient servant,

N. B. Forrest, Brigadier-General, Commanding.[45]

Forrest to Confederate General Joseph Wheeler, September 6, 1863:
☞ HEADQUARTERS FIRST CAVALRY DIVISION, ON THE ROAD NEAR RINGGOLD, GA., SEPTEMBER 6, 1863. MAJOR-GENERAL WHEELER:

General: The First Brigade of my division left Ringgold for Rome this morning at 8 o'clock; the Second Brigade, General Armstrong, will leave there this evening at 2 o'clock. I shall move on the left-hand road from Ringgold to Rome, leaving La Fayette about 5 miles to my right, and proceeding down the west bank of Oostenaula River.

I send 2 couriers with orders to proceed to your headquarters. Should you need any assistance write me. Would be glad to know by return couriers of any movement of the enemy. I have ten pieces of artillery with me.

I am, respectfully, your obedient servant,

N. B. Forrest, Brigadier-General.[46]

Forrest to Confederate General Joseph Wheeler, September 8, 1863:
☞ HEADQUARTERS FIRST CAVALRY DIVISION, GOWER'S, SEPTEMBER 8, 1863—8 A.M. MAJOR-GENERAL WHEELER:

General: I have arrived here with one of my brigades and six pieces of artillery; the other brigade will be up by 12 m[idnight]. Please let me know what is going on in front. I am instructed by General Bragg to impede their advance on Rome as much as possible. If I hear nothing of the enemy to-day I shall cross the mountains and get in their front. What is the chance for forage along where you are? If you are telegraphing to General Bragg to-day let him know where I am. If the enemy does not advance we must move on them.

> Respectfully, your obedient servant,
> N. B. Forrest, Brigadier-General.[47]

Forrest to Confederate General Leonidas Polk, September 21, 1863:
☞ MISSIONARY RIDGE, ON THE POINT OPPOSITE, SOUTH OF ROSSVILLE, SEPTEMBER 21, 1863—11.30 A.M. LIEUTENANT-GENERAL POLK:

> General: I am on the point as designated, where I can observe the whole of the valley. They [the Yanks] are evidently fortifying, as I can distinctly hear the sound of axes in great numbers. The appearance is still as in last dispatch, that he is hurrying on toward Chattanooga. He is cutting timber on the point of this ridge. I have just captured a captain and 2 privates who were acting as a part of a corps of observers. He (the captain) reports that a number of forces passed up the road toward Chattanooga, but does not know who, or what their numbers. They passed up about 5 P.M. yesterday.

> N. B. Forrest, Brigadier-General, Commanding.[48]

Forrest to Confederate General Leonidas Polk, September 21, 1863:
☞ ON THE ROAD, SEPTEMBER 21, 1863. LIEUT. GEN. L. POLK:

> General: We are within a mile of Rossville. Have been on the point of Missionary Ridge. Can see Chattanooga and everything around. The enemy's trains are leaving, going around the point of Lookout Mountain. The prisoners captured report two pontoons thrown across for the purpose of retreating. I think they are evacuating as hard as they can go. They are cutting timber down to obstruct our passing. I think we ought to press forward as rapidly as possible.

> Respectfully, &c.,
> N. B. Forrest, Brigadier-General.
> Please forward to General [Braxton] Bragg.[49]

Forrest to Confederate General Joseph Wheeler, September 28, 1863:
☞ HEADQUARTERS FORREST'S CAVALRY, ATHENS,

SEPTEMBER 28, 1863—9 A.M. MAJOR-GENERAL WHEELER, COMMANDING:

General: My last advices from the front report the enemy advancing on us with a column of infantry, also cavalry. Would it not be well to have the fortifications at Charleston repaired and artillery placed in position there in order to defend the crossing if necessary? My command is falling back, and there may be more force advancing than we know of, as they can run trains from Knoxville to Loudon, and [Union General Ambrose Everett] Burnside may be moving in this direction.

Respectfully, your obedient servant,

N. B. Forrest, Brigadier-General, Commanding.[50]

Forrest to Confederate General Joseph Wheeler, September 28, 1863:
☞ HEADQUARTERS FIRST CAVALRY BRIGADE, FIVE MILES FROM CHARLESTON, SEPTEMBER 28, 1863. [TO: GENERAL J. WHEELER:]

General: When my command started out we were only ordered to Harrison, to meet and develop Burnside's forces reported there. I brought with me only 40 rounds of ammunition to the man, four pieces of artillery, with what ammunition I had left after the battle of Chickamauga. I cannot, therefore, send you artillery or ammunition. Have ordered General Davidson and General Armstrong to you, and to accompany Major Burford to where you are. Have retained Dibrell's and Pegram's brigades. They are all without rations, as we did not expect to be absent from our trains but a day or two, and unless they can be supplied they will be in no condition to cross the mountains. Major Burford will meet the commands at Athens to-night. Will forward a copy of your letter to Major Burford immediately, but am satisfied that neither men nor horses are in condition for the expedition. We have had no opportunity of shoeing the horses since the battle of Chickamauga commenced.

Respectfully, your obedient servant,

N. B. Forrest, Brigadier-General, Commanding.[51]

Forrest to Confederate General John H. Winder, October 22, 1863:
☞ HEADQUARTERS FORREST'S CAVALRY, DALTON, GA., OCTOBER 22, 1863. BRIG. GEN. JOHN H. WINDER:

General: Yours of September 15, inclosing copy of Colonel Streight's letter dated July 4 last, together with copy of yours of July 6, in relation to the articles of capitulation, and $850, is received.

It was agreed that private property would be protected and that the side-arms of the officers (so far as I was concerned) would also until their arrival at Richmond. Colonel Streight is correct in his statement in regard to the money in his possession.

My quartermaster purchased the horses of the surgeons and paid for them in Confederate money, and at the time that I made the exchange with Colonel Streight was of the impression that the money was the property of the surgeons. I exchanged about $800 with Colonel Streight, giving him U.S. greenback notes, mostly in $1 and $2 bills.

Colonel Streight's command had done but little damage to property, having destroyed only one furnace and one stable. Many of the residences by the roadside had been pillaged before I began to press them, when they began to cast aside such articles as they had taken. There was quite a number of negroes with the command when I first overtook Streight. Most of them escaped and returned to their masters. I found none of the negroes in arms. Indeed, very few (not exceeding fifteen) were with Colonel Streight's command at the time of the surrender.

Your letter would have been answered, but owing [to] my absence did not receive it until last evening.

Yours, most respectfully,

N. B. Forrest, Brigadier-General.[52]

Forrest to Confederate Colonel George W. Brent, October 22, 1863, concerning the Battle of Chickamauga (fought September 18-20, 1863):
☞ REPORT OF BRIG. GEN. NATHAN B. FORREST, C. S. ARMY, COMMANDING CAVALRY CORPS. HEADQUARTERS FORREST'S CAVALRY COMMAND, DALTON, GA., OCTOBER 22, 1863. [TO: LIEUT. COL. GEORGE WILLIAM BRENT, ASSISTANT ADJUTANT-GENERAL, ARMY OF TENNESSEE.]

Colonel: I have the honor to forward the following report of the operations of my command during the action at Chickamauga Creek on the [September] 19th and 20th ultimo; also a brief statement of its movements and engagements prior and subsequent to the battle of

Chickamauga, accompanying it with the reports of Brigadier-General Pegram, commanding division, and Col. J. S. Scott, commanding brigade. No report from Brigadier-General Armstrong, commanding First Division of the corps, has been received. A report is also due from Brigadier-General Davidson, who commanded a brigade of General Pegram's division during the battle of Chickamauga. The reports of both officers would no doubt have been furnished but for movements in East Tennessee, and afterward under General Wheeler in Middle Tennessee, which gave no time or opportunity to make them out.

On the 9th ultimo, I was ordered to establish my headquarters at Dalton and my command was located and disposed of as follows: Colonel Hodge's brigade was sent on the Cleveland and Dalton road to meet the enemy, then reported at Athens, Tenn., and advancing; Colonel Scott's brigade was ordered to Ringgold, Ga., to watch the enemy on the road from Chattanooga to that point; General Pegram was left at or near Pea Vine Church, and Brigadier-General Armstrong's division was located in front of General Cheatham's infantry division on the Chattanooga and La Fayette road. I retained with me at Dalton about 240 men of General Morgan's cavalry.

The reports of General Pegram and Colonel Scott sufficiently detail their operations prior to the battle of Chickamauga, and require no further comments here.

On Thursday (17th ultimo), I moved from Dalton, and Friday morning from Ringgold, toward Pea Vine Creek, having with me Morgan's men, under Lieutenant-Colonel Martin, and my escort, and met the enemy's cavalry (Minty's brigade) at Pea Vine Creek. Dismounting Lieutenant-Colonel Martin's command, and assisted by Brig. Gen. B. R. Johnson's command, the enemy were driven across the Chickamauga at Reed's Bridge, at which point I was joined by General Pegram's division. Crossing the creek at a ford above the bridge, the country was scoured for a mile west of the bridge. General Hood's command of infantry also crossed the Chickamauga and formed in line of battle, my command bivouacking on the field in the rear of his line near Alexander's Bridge.

On the morning of the 19th, I was ordered to move with my command down the road toward Reed's Bridge and develop the enemy which was promptly done, and their advance was soon engaged at the steam saw-mill near that point. Finding the enemy too strong for General Pegram's force, I dispatched a staff officer to Lieutenant-General Polk's quarters for General Armstrong's division. He could only spare Colonel Dibrell's brigade, which arrived shortly after we engaged the enemy; was speedily dismounted and formed, and, with General Pegram's division, were able to hold position until infantry re-enforcements arrived, the first brigade of which, under Colonel Wilson, formed on my left, advanced in gallant style, driving the enemy back and capturing a battery of artillery, my dismounted cavalry advancing with them. The superior force of the enemy compelled us to give back until re-enforced by General Ector's brigade, when the enemy was again driven back. From statements of prisoners captured, the enemy's force engaged was four brigades of infantry and one of cavalry; but when driven back the second time, with the loss of another battery, their full strength was developed, and, being met and overpowered by vastly superior numbers, we were compelled to fall back to our first position. A cavalry charge was made to protect the infantry as they retired, which they did in good order, but with loss. We captured many prisoners, but were unable for want of horses to bring off the guns captured from the enemy.

Until the arrival of Major-General Walker (being the senior officer present) I assumed temporary command of the infantry, and I must say that the fighting and the gallant charges of the two brigades just referred to excited my admiration. They broke the enemy's lines, and could not be halted or withdrawn until nearly surrounded. We fell back, fighting and contesting the ground, to our original position near the mill on the Reed's Bridge road. General Cheatham's division coming up and engaging the enemy drove them for some distance, but was in turn compelled to fall back. Seeing General Maney's brigade hard pressed and retiring before the enemy, I hastened to his relief with Freeman's battery of six pieces, dismounting Colonel Dibrell's brigade to support it.

The conduct of Maj. John Rawle, chief of artillery, and the officers and men of this battery on this occasion deserves special mention. They kept up a constant and destructive fire upon the enemy until they were within 50 yards of the guns, getting off the field with all their pieces, notwithstanding the loss of horses. They were gallantly protected by Colonel Dibrell in retiring, who fell back with the line of infantry. We had no further engagement with the enemy during the evening. General Armstrong, having been relieved by General Polk, arrived with his brigade and took command of his division, forming it, and, with Pegram's division, holding the road to Reed's Bridge, which had been repaired during the day.

On Sunday morning, the 20th, I received orders to move up and keep in line with General Breckinridge's division, which I did, dismounting all of General Armstrong's division, except the First Tennessee Regiment and McDonald's battalion, holding General Pegram's division in reserve on my right. The two commands of General Armstrong's division which were mounted took possession of the La Fayette road, capturing the enemy's hospitals and quite a number of prisoners. They were compelled to fall back, as the enemy's reserves, under General Granger, advanced on that road. Colonel Dibrell fought on foot with the infantry during the day. As General Granger approached, by shelling his command and maneuvering my troops, he was detained nearly two hours, and prevented from joining the main force until late in the evening, and then at double-quick, under a heavy fire from Freeman's battery and a section of Napoleon guns borrowed from General Breckinridge.

After Granger's column had vacated the road in front of me, I moved my dismounted men rapidly forward and took possession of the road from the Federal hospital to the woods on the left, through which infantry was advancing and fighting. My artillery was ordered forward, but before it could reach the road and be placed in position a charge was made by the enemy, the infantry line retreating in confusion and leaving me without support, but held the ground long enough to get my artillery back to the position from which we had shelled Granger's column, and opened upon the advancing column with fourteen pieces of artillery, driving them back, and terminating on the right flank the battle of Chickamauga. This fire was at short range, in open ground, and was to the enemy very destructive, killing 2 colonels and many other officers and privates.

It is with pride and pleasure that I mention the gallant conduct of the officers and men of my command. General Armstrong's division fought almost entirely on foot, always up and frequently in advance of the infantry.

My command was kept on the field during the night of the 20th, and men and horses suffered greatly for want of water. The men were without rations, and the horses had only received a partial feed once during the two days engagement.

On Monday morning, I moved forward on the La Fayette road toward Chattanooga, capturing many prisoners and arms. The latter were collected as far as practicable and sent to the rear, using for that purpose several wagons and ambulances captured from the retreating enemy or abandoned and left by them. On taking possession of Mission Ridge, 1 mile or thereabouts from Rossville, we found the enemy fortifying the gap; dismounted Colonel Dibrell's regiment, under command of Captain McGinnis, and attacked them, but found the force too large to dislodge them. On the arrival of my artillery, opened on and fought them for several hours, but could not move them.

We held possession of the ridge during the night, and on Tuesday moved down from Mission Ridge into the Chattanooga Valley, driving the enemy into their works, and on the La Fayette road advancing beyond Watkins' farm, and holding position there until the arrival of Kershaw's brigade. My command was kept in line of battle during the night, my left, under Colonel Dibrell, resting at the base of Lookout Mountain, and my right at Silvey's Ford, on the Tennessee River.

On Wednesday (23d), with McDonald's battalion, I gained the point of Lookout Mountain. My command, being gradually relieved by infantry, was ordered to the rear, and went into camp at and near Bird's Mill, with orders issued to cook up rations and shoe the horses as rapidly as possible.

On Friday morning (the 25th), I received orders to move with my entire command to meet the forces of Burnside, reported at or near Harrison, which order was immediately obeyed. Having proceeded as far as Chickamauga Station, a second courier overtook me with an order to proceed, via Cleveland, to Charleston, and disperse the enemy at that place, and, if necessary, to cross the Hiwassee River. I reached Cleveland that night and went on to Charleston the next morning; found the enemy on the opposite side of the river. Moved up my artillery, and after a sharp cannonading drove them off and threw my cavalry across the river. From prisoners captured we found the force opposite to

Charleston and retreating was a brigade of mounted infantry commanded by Colonel Byrd.

Learning also that Wolford's Federal cavalry was encamped at Cedar Springs, 3 miles from Athens, it was deemed necessary to follow, which was done rapidly, fighting them repeatedly, and driving them before us. Their last stand was made at Philadelphia, where Wolford's brigade was put to flight by the advance of Armstrong's division under Colonel Dibrell. Receiving orders to return at once, I withdrew my command back to Charleston, ordering General Davidson, with his division, and General Armstrong, with his brigade, to report to General Wheeler, at Cotton Port Ferry.

Our loss in the expedition to East Tennessee was 4 men wounded and 2 captured. We killed and wounded about 20 of the enemy and sent 120 prisoners to Dalton.

In closing this report, I desire to pay a just tribute to my officers and men for their gallantry and uncomplaining endurance of all the fatigues and dangers incident to the movements and engagements set forth in this report. The charges made by Armstrong's division (while fighting on foot) in the battle of Chickamauga would be creditable to the best drilled infantry.

The officers of my staff have, as on many previous occasions, discharged all duties with promptness and fidelity.

I am, colonel, very respectfully, your obedient servant,

N. B. Forrest, Brigadier-General, Commanding.

P.S. As soon as official reports can be obtained from General Armstrong's and General Davidson's divisions, they will be forwarded. At present our losses cannot be ascertained.[53]

Forrest to Confederate General Samuel Cooper, November 7, 1863:
☞ HEADQUARTERS FORREST'S CAVALRY COMMAND, ATLANTA [GEORGIA], NOVEMBER 7, 1863. GENERAL S. COOPER, ADJUTANT AND INSPECTOR GENERAL:

General: I inclose you a report [inclosure below] of the troops and battery which have been ordered to accompany me to West Tennessee.

In my application for a transfer to the Department of Mississippi for the purpose of raising troops in North Mississippi and West

Tennessee to operate on the Mississippi River, I asked for Woodward's battalion, McDonald's battalion, and one battery.

I had Major McDonald's battalion—who has since been killed at Farmington—and [my brother] Col. J. E. Forrest's regiment assigned me. Colonel Forrest was, so I have just learned, killed last week near Tuscumbia, Ala., and as the regiment lately commanded by Colonel Forrest was composed of Alabama troops, he being killed, it is my impression they will be unwilling to go, and if so I will allow them to remain in General Bragg's department.

Major McDonald's battalion, my escort company, and the battery will comprise my entire command, which is wholly inadequate to the undertaking; yet I will use all the energy I possess to accomplish the object that I have proposed.

Yours, most respectfully,

N. B. Forrest, Brigadier-General, Commanding.

[INCLOSURE ATTACHED TO PREVIOUS LETTER]
☞ Troops ordered to West Tennessee, commanded by Brig. Gen. Nathan B. Forrest, C.S. Army (compiled from original report): Command:

    Field and staff: 8 aggregate; 8 present and absent, aggregate.

    Escort: 65 present effective total; 67 aggregate; 67 present and absent, aggregate.

    McDonald's Battalion: 139 present effective total; 164 aggregate; 260 present and absent, aggregate.

    Morton's Battery: 67 present effective total; 71 aggregate; 71 present and absent, aggregate.

Total: 271 present effective total; 310 aggregate; 406 present and absent, aggregate.[54]

Forrest to Confederate Colonel Benjamin Stoddert Ewell, November 21, 1863:
☞ HEADQUARTERS FORREST'S CAVALRY, OKOLONA, MISS., NOVEMBER 21, 1863.   COL. B. S. EWELL, ASSISTANT ADJUTANT-GENERAL:

I have the honor respectfully to forward herewith reports and communications from Col. R. V. Richardson [commanding Northeast Mississippi]. I have been unable to ascertain or get a report from him of his force in camps. He states that he has about 300 men, but from other sources I think 250 men will be about the number. Colonel Richardson, from his communication, expects to remain in command or desires the command of a brigade, but as I shall only have about 1,000 men with which to cross the line of the Memphis and Charleston Railroad, shall take direct and immediate command myself.

I am, colonel, very respectfully, your obedient servant,

N. B. Forrest, Brigadier-General, Commanding.[55]

Forrest to Confederate Colonel Benjamin Stoddert Ewell, November 25, 1863:
☛ HEADQUARTERS FORREST'S CAVALRY, OKOLONA, NOVEMBER 25, 1863. COL. B. S. EWELL, ASSISTANT ADJUTANT-GENERAL:

Colonel: I send you herewith some newspapers. I hope to leave here to-morrow morning. Will do so if I can get horses to pull my artillery. General Lee has promised me 40 horses, and I hope they will get here to-day. Only 150 men of Colonel Forrest's regiment have reported, and a number of them are without arms, and so far I have been unable to get arms for them. I had hoped to get arms for all I had here, and to have carried guns with me for troops now in West Tennessee, as it would be rash to go into West Tennessee with only a few hundred men and they poorly armed. Requisitions have been made, and I trust the arms will be sent forward. Nothing new in front.

I am, colonel, very respectfully, your obedient servant,

N. B. Forrest, Brigadier-General, Commanding.[56]

Forrest to Confederate General Joseph Eggleston Johnston, December 6, 1863:
☛ HEADQUARTERS DEPARTMENT OF WEST TENNESSEE, JACKSON [TENN.], DECEMBER 6, 1863. GENERAL JOSEPH E. JOHNSTON, COMMANDING DEPARTMENT:

General: I have the honor to report the safe arrival of my command at this place; also to state that I am highly pleased with the prospect before me. I have never seen a more healthy spirit manifested anywhere than is shown by the people here. I have already about 5,000 men, and if I am unmolested until the 1st day of January will, I think, have 8,000 effective troops in the field.

The Federals are and have been conscripting in Southern

Kentucky, and of 130 conscripted at Columbus over 100 have escaped and joined my command. They are coming in daily at the rate of 50 to 100 per day, and as soon as it becomes known that my command is here large numbers will leave the Federal lines to join us.

The enemy is strengthening his works and increasing his force at Fort Pillow, Hickman, Paducah, and Columbus, and report says preparing for a raid in this direction, but if General Lee will keep engaged the attention of the force guarding the Memphis and Charleston Railroad, I think we can whip any force they can send from above. I hope therefore that General [S. D.] Lee may be kept operating on that road and keep the enemy from moving on me from that direction, as it is of the utmost importance that the country be held until arms can be procured and organization of troops completed.

I am exceedingly anxious to get the arms, &c., promised me by the President, and for which requisitions have been made. I also venture a suggestion which will no doubt meet the approval of General Lee and yourself, provided there are no movements on the part of the enemy to prevent it. It is this: That General Lee, with all the cavalry that can be spared, move up into West Tennessee, bringing with him all the arms and ammunition for my command, and returning with my force to assist him, and the co-operation of General [Philip D.] Roddey east of Corinth, we could effectually destroy the Memphis and Charleston Railroad and drive out from here from 4,000 to 6,000 head of good beef-cattle for the use of the army.

Provisions and army supplies are abundant, except where railroad and other thoroughfares have been in continual use or occupancy by the enemy or by our own troops. If General Lee should come, and will advise me, I will build a pontoon bridge across the Hatchie [River] and send out men to gather up the cattle, and make every other arrangement to co-operate. I would be glad also that he would bring with him the section of artillery and all the transportation I have in camp near Okolona and in charge of my quartermaster, Maj. C. S. Severson.

To enable me to succeed in raising troops, getting out absentees and deserters from the army, and army supplies and provisions for the army, two articles are indispensably necessary—they are arms and money; and I hope, general, that you will be able to supply me with both. I have had to advance to my quartermaster and commissary

$20,000 [about $400,000 in today's currency] of my private funds to subsist the command thus far; have written to Major Severson to make an estimate for $100,000 quartermaster funds and at least $150,000 [about $2 million in today's currency] pay funds. I am compelled to have the former for the purchase of transportation, artillery horses, forage, &c.; the latter is needed to pay off the troops, many of whom have received nothing for a long time, and if we could pay them the bounty (all entitled to it) they could get along for a few months.

I have a small battery at Selma which, when repaired, will be sent to Meridian, with 200 rounds of ammunition to the piece; if it can be done, would be glad if General Lee could bring them. I am satisfied that I can procure horses for them if the guns can be gotten here.

I send a duplicate of this across the railroad and this through via Tuscumbia, with strict instructions to effectually destroy where there is the least probability of capture.

I am, general, very respectfully, your obedient servant,

N. B. Forrest, Brigadier-General, Commanding.[57]

Forrest to Confederate General Braxton Bragg, December 8, 1863:
☞ HEADQUARTERS DEPARTMENT OF WEST TENNESSEE, JACKSON, TENN., DECEMBER 8, 1868. GENERAL BRAXTON BRAGG, COMMANDING ARMY OF TENNESSEE:

General: I herewith respectfully unclose you copy of a letter addressed to General Joseph E. Johnston, which fully states the condition of affairs in West Tennessee. I have succeeded thus far beyond my most sanguine expectations; troops and men are flocking to me from all quarters, and I hope soon to have a large effective force in the field. I am satisfied that there are from 5,000 to 6,000 men belonging to your army in this and Middle Tennessee that can be gotten out, and I only require arms and money, with the aid and co-operation of the troops south of this, to effect my purposes. A simultaneous movement on the part of General Roddey and General [S. D.] Lee, with a brigade of infantry from the Army of Mississippi thrown on the Memphis and Charleston Railroad would so destroy it that the enemy would be forced to content themselves within their fortifications at Memphis and Corinth. With open and uninterrupted communication with General Johnston's army the old soldiers could be easily sent out and forwarded to you. I am confident, also, that many thousand head of cattle can be driven out and still leave enough for the subsistence of the troops necessary to hold or occupy this country. There is also a large quantity of leather and bacon, and I know of no other region as accessible as this and which can be occupied, and all in it made available to the Confederacy, with as little cost. Commissary purchasers from your army are here, and I shall aid them and do all in my power to send you supplies; at the same time the want of arms prevents me from being able to give safe escort across the line southward, and nothing short of the destruction of the Memphis and Charleston Railroad from Memphis to Corinth will make the transit safe and reliable. I have given the people the opportunity of volunteering until 1st of January—after that all to be conscripted and sent to fill up infantry regiments; and suggest that after the 1st of January General Pillow be ordered in this department for that purpose. There being no general officer here but myself, another is greatly needed to aid me in organizing and commanding the troops, and I respectfully ask that Brig. Gen. F. C. Armstrong be ordered to report to me for duty. With his assistance and experience, I am confident that I shall have in a short time 8,000 effective men in the field, besides some thousand belonging to infantry command, all of whom will be sent back at the earliest possible moment. I am not only willing, but desirous, general, of rendering the country all the service possible in the occupancy and defense of West Tennessee; also to get out from here all the supplies I can for the subsistence of your army. If you can aid me in the services of a general officer or the procurement of arms I shall be thankful, and in turn use every exertion to send to you the absentees from your ranks and supplies, &c., for your troops.

I am, general, very respectfully, your obedient servant,

N. B. Forrest, Brigadier-General, Commanding.[58]

Forrest to Confederate General Samuel Cooper, December 8, 1863:

☞ HEADQUARTERS DEPARTMENT OF WEST TENNESSEE, JACKSON, TENN., DECEMBER 8, 1863. GENERAL S. COOPER, ADJUTANT AND INSPECTOR GENERAL, RICHMOND, VA.:

General: I have the honor herewith to transmit, by the hands of Maj. M. C. Galloway, copies of letters addressed by me to Generals Johnston and Bragg, which letters fully explain the condition of affairs in

West Tennessee.

I am highly gratified with my success so far and with the prospects before me.

Major Galloway fully understands my wants, and if they can be supplied, is fully authorized to make requisitions and receipt for what is obtainable. Am greatly in need of arms and money, and have sent Major G. to Richmond on purpose to represent more fully than can be done on paper the details necessary to a proper appreciation of the necessity of holding this country and the available supplies in it; also to send rapidly forward all the arms, &c., that can be spared me.

The destruction of the Memphis and Charleston Railroad, and the blockading of the Tennessee River, gives us West Tennessee. The former appears to me to be of easy accomplishment, and transports or boats navigating the Tennessee River can be so destroyed or harassed as to render transportation on it of troops or stores exceedingly unsafe and hazardous. With the means asked for, I am satisfied we can hold the country and secure for the army a vast amount of provisions and supplies not to be obtained in like quantity and at so little cost anywhere else.

I beg to assure you, general, that everything in the power of myself and command that can possibly be done shall be done in driving the enemy from the country and in feeding and clothing the army and swelling its numbers.

Hoping, therefore, to secure at an early date the supply of arms and money indispensably necessary to the accomplishment of these purposes,

I am, general, very respectfully, your obedient servant,

N. B. Forrest, Brigadier-General, Commanding.[59]

Forrest to Confederate General Stephen Dill Lee, December 9, 1863:
☞ HEADQUARTERS DEPARTMENT OF WEST TENNESSEE, JACKSON [TENN.], DECEMBER 9, 1863. [GENERAL LEE:]

General: I have the opportunity of sending you a few lines by Dr. Johnson, of General W. H. Jackson's staff.

I have succeeded so far beyond my most sanguine expectations. The news we have from your operations on the Memphis and Charleston Railroad I am in hopes may be confirmed.

I inclose you copy of letter to General Johnston fully explaining the condition of affairs here. Anything and everything I can do shall be done to render the defense of this country and its occupancy permanent.

I would be glad to open a line of communication with you, and if you will send me a courier with statement of courier-line established to the railroad, I will establish a line from this to the railroad to connect.

The enemy are reported as re-enforcing and fortifying at Union City. Therefore apprehend no danger of any advance from that quarter. If, however, they should do so and it becomes necessary to have re-enforcements, I respectfully ask that you will bring with you all the arms, &c., for my command.

I am, very respectfully, your obedient servant,

N. B. Forrest, Brigadier-General, Commanding.[60]

Forrest to Union General Stephen Augustus Hurlbut, December 12, 1863:
☛ HEADQUARTERS DEPARTMENT OF WEST TENNESSEE, IN THE FIELD, DECEMBER 12, 1863. MAJ. GEN. S. A. HURLBUT, COMMANDING FEDERAL FORCES, MEMPHIS, TENN.:

General: I have the honor respectfully to state that information has just reached me that [Confederate] Capt. Frank B. Gurley is on trial in Nashville for the so-called murder of General McCook, and that further time has [been] granted him for the purpose of procuring evidence. As I was his commanding officer at the time of the occurrence I feel it my duty to forward you under flag of truce, and by the hands of my adjutant-general, Maj. J. P. Strange, the following statement of facts to show that Captain Gurley was then, and is yet, a Confederate soldier and officer, and that he should be treated and regarded as such: Captain Gurley was regularly mustered into the C.S. Army as a member of the Kelley Troopers, in July, 1861, which company formed a portion of my old regiment known as Forrest's regiment.

After the fall of Fort Donelson (from which place I escaped with my command) Captain Gurley was left sick at Huntsville, Ala., with orders from me to gather up all the men of my command; also with power and authority to raise [a] company of cavalry. This he did, and reported to me with his company in July, 1862. It was inspected and mustered into the service at Chattanooga, by my inspector-general and by my order, in the month just named. Hence Captain Gurley has been regularly in the service from July, 1861, to the time of his capture.

In November last his company with three others from my old regiment (all from Alabama) were consolidated with Russell's battalion, and formed what is known as Russell's or the Fourth Alabama Cavalry, which regiment served under me until the 21st of February, 1863, when it was transferred from my command to General Wheeler. These, general, are facts, and, when known, I confidently rely upon his being treated as a prisoner of war, and not as a guerrilla or robber.

My desire is to show the court, through you, that Captain Gurley has been from the beginning a soldier in the Confederate service, and I claim for him the treatment due to a prisoner of war. What may have been attributed to him by the press of the country, North and South, is one thing, but actual facts and the muster-rolls in the Department at Richmond is quite another. Major Strange, the bearer of this, has been with me in the service (as my adjutant) from the organization of my old regiment to the present time, and can, if you think proper to receive it, add his testimony to the facts as stated.

While communicating with you, general, on this subject, allow me to say that it is my purpose to drive guerrillas from the country. They must join the service regularly, on the one side or the other, otherwise be disbanded and driven off; and while I deplore the existence of such men and their lawless conduct, I desire respectfully to call your attention to facts self evident and undenied. The charred walls of many dwellings have met my eyes. The naked chimneys and devastated premises of the now houseless and homeless is not calculated to soften the feelings of those engaged in this struggle, the merits of which, in its beginning, continuance, or end, the women and children of the country are in no wise responsible. It has ever been my desire to see this war conducted according to the rules of civilized warfare, and so far as I am concerned will so conduct it. At the same time I am determined to execute on the spot every house-burner and robber that may fall into my hands, whether he claims to be a Federal or a Confederate.

Hoping, general, that you view these matters as I do, I trust you will issue such orders and when disobeyed inflict such punishment as will prevent the destruction of houses and property of non-combatants. Whatever may be necessary for the use of troops, military necessity and military law authorizes to be appropriated, but the wanton destruction of the houses and dwellings of the people ought to be discontinued and severely punished by every civilized or Christian commander. Major Strange, with his escort of twenty men, is instructed to wait your pleasure and bear any message or communication you may think proper to make.

Hoping that you will forward, without delay, to the proper authorities at Nashville the facts in regard to Captain Gurley, also that you will receive this communication in the spirit in which it is sent,

I am, general, very respectfully, your obedient servant,

N. B. Forrest, Brigadier-General, Commanding.[61]

Forrest to Confederate Colonel Benjamin Stoddert Ewell on December 13, 1863:
☞ HEADQUARTERS DEPARTMENT OF WEST TENNESSEE, JACKSON [TENN.], DECEMBER 13, 1863. COL. B. S. EWELL:

I send out this morning the unarmed men of my Command here for the purpose of getting arms. I have directed Col. R. M. Russell, in command of one of the new regiments, to report himself at Meridian, for the purpose of going before an examining board; from what I can learn he is deemed qualified to command a regiment of cavalry, and when examined, if pronounced qualified, I desire to place him in a like committee to examine officers who are candidates for field and company positions. I respectfully ask that the opportunity be given him for an examination, and a certificate given him if found competent.

I am, very respectfully, your obedient servant,

N. B. Forrest, Brigadier-General, Commanding.[62]

Forrest to Confederate General Joseph Eggleston Johnston, December 18, 1863:
☞ HEADQUARTERS DEPARTMENT OF WEST TENNESSEE, JACKSON [TENN.], DECEMBER 18, 1863. GENERAL JOSEPH E. JOHNSTON, COMMANDING ARMY OF THE MISSISSIPPI, BRANDON, MISS.:

General: From the movements of the enemy I am of opinion they are preparing to move against me, and that they will do so by the 25th instant or soon thereafter. I shall have at least 1,000 head of beef-cattle ready to move south by that time, and I write to ask that General Ferguson's and General Chalmers' brigades be sent up without delay to aid in taking the cattle out and meeting any expedition of the enemy against me.

I can collect together in two or three days at least 100,000 pounds of bacon, and if wagons are sent over with the troops asked for, will load them out with bacon. If you can help me, general, for thirty days I shall organize 7,000 troops, beside getting out a great number of absentees and deserters from the army. General [Philip D.] Roddey has written me that he would move in from Tuscumbia at any time to my assistance. Have dispatched him to-day to come at once. With his brigade and the two above asked for can secure the cattle and bacon and hold possession against any raid they may send, and if dispatched without delay, that Generals Ferguson and Chalmers with their commands will come, I will have boats prepared for crossing the Hatchie [River] at Estenaula, and will have forage gotten up and ready for them.

If they cannot be sent in here, I ask that General [S. D.] Lee harass the enemy as much as possible along the line of the Memphis and Charleston Railroad west of Corinth. Think I am able to protect myself against any move from Union City, but should they move from Fort Pillow also, shall have more than I can manage with the raw and unarmed troops I have, and especially so should they move from below at the same time.

If these suggestions or those made in my letter of 5th instant are adopted and approved and carried out, we can largely increase the army. I have reliable information to-day that they are pressing every horse in Memphis to mount infantry, and that nearly all the enemy's force at La Grange has been sent down to Memphis and from thence up the river on boats. Their reported destination is Fort Pillow, from which point a raid under [Union General Benjamin H.] Grierson is to move on me. The troops which were at Eastport, and a number of boats loaded with supplies, have passed down the Tennessee [River] and been taken to Paducah and Columbus, and they are moving up from Memphis to Fort Pillow and Columbus.

They are evidently preparing for a move from that quarter—north—or are fixing to establish a line of communication from Columbus to Tennessee River, and from Reynoldsburg, on Tennessee River, to Nashville; they have a large force completing the Northwestern Railroad from Nashville to Reynoldsburg.

My great desire is to get out the troops and hold the country, if possible; also the provisions necessary for the use of the army. If it can be done without detriment to the service, I hope, general, that you will send all the cavalry you can spare, and at the earliest possible moment, and with them any arms that can be obtained. Have not heard as yet from the troops sent out for arms, but hope they got them and are now on the way back.

There are several West Tennessee regiments of infantry in General Bragg's army whose numbers range from 150 to 250 men for duty. If it were possible to get them ordered to you, am satisfied they could soon be filled up from this section. I am gathering up as rapidly as possible all the absentees and deserters from these commands, and will use them until they can be returned to their proper commands.

I am, general, very respectfully, your obedient servant,

N. B. Forrest, Brigadier-General, Commanding.[63]

Forrest to Confederate General Stephen Dill Lee, December 18, 1863:
☛ HEADQUARTERS DEPARTMENT OF WEST TENNESSEE, JACKSON, TENN., DECEMBER 18, 1863. MAJ. GEN. STEPHEN D. LEE, OXFORD, MISS.:

General: I have written to-day to General [Joseph E.] Johnston, and desire also to address you in regard to the state of affairs here, and urge the importance of sending, if they can be spared, at least two brigades of cavalry up here without delay. I have reliable information that every man that can be spared from Memphis and from the Memphis and Charleston road is being sent up the river to Fort Pillow or to Columbus. Two brigades that were at Eastport, Miss., have gone down the Tennessee to Paducah and around to Columbus, and from thence to Union City. Northern papers of the 9th report a rebel force, from 5,000 to 10,000 strong, as moving on Mayfield and Paducah. Every horse in Memphis has been seized and sent up the river on boats to mount infantry, and a raid is preparing under [Union General Benjamin H.] Grierson to move on me. From present indications Fort Pillow and Union City will be starting-points.

I will have collected here by the 25th at least 1,000 head of cattle, and if wagons are sent can send out 100,000 pounds of bacon. If you come or send the troops advise me at once, and I will arrange for your crossing the Hatchie [River] at Estenaula, and will have forage provided for the troops and the cattle, and bacon ready to be moved out. My scouts report yesterday the [Federal] force on the Memphis and Charleston Railroad as follows:

At Corinth two [Union] regiments cavalry (500 men), one regiment infantry (white), and two regiments of negroes. At Chewalla three companies of cavalry. At Pocahontas two regiments of infantry and one regiment cavalry. At Middleton 400 cavalry and about 400 infantry. Troops from La Grange have gone to Memphis by railroad, except 300 or 400 men.

Forces at other points not known exactly, but are reported as small.

I regard it as of the utmost importance to hold this country. Think if I can have assistance that I shall have 7,000 organized troops in less than thirty days.

The supplies and provisions so much needed by our army are abundant, and ought to be secured.

I hope, general, that circumstances will allow the aid asked for to be sent me without delay. At any rate keep the forces on the Memphis and Charleston Railroad so engaged that they cannot move on me from that quarter.

I am, general, very respectfully, your obedient servant,

N. B. Forrest, Brigadier-General, Commanding.[64]

Forrest to Confederate General Stephen Dill Lee, December 22, 1863:

☞ HEADQUARTERS DEPARTMENT OF WEST TENNESSEE, JACKSON [TENN.], DECEMBER 22, 1863. MAJ. GEN. S. D. LEE, COMMANDING CAVALRY, ARMY OF MISSISSIPPI:

General: I am perfectly satisfied that the enemy will move on me with a large force in a few days. I do not think it will be more than three days before they will begin their programme, which is not yet fully developed.

My opinion is (from all reports) that they are concentrating at Corinth and La Grange, on the railroad, and at Fort Pillow and Union City. I write, therefore, to ask you to be prepared to aid me at short notice, and when they move on me, to have you move on them on the railroad. I will move round them and join you in the destruction of the road, and will drive out cattle sufficient for our use. I have only about 3,000 armed men, and they, in gathering up the balance of commands, are much scattered. I will gather up everything possible and be prepared for the moment.

I have 1,200 men now out in Mississippi after arms. I hope they have gotten them and that they will be here in a day or two. I have arranged to send communications to you through Captain Higgs, commanding my scouts. Would be glad to know when you can make a stand of couriers so that I can communicate with you promptly. I suggest some point at or in the neighborhood of Salem.

In view of the present condition of affairs, I respectfully suggest that you be prepared to move at once or as soon as you are advised of any movement from the railroad in this direction, if you have not already done so, in accordance with my previous requests.

I have been anxiously expecting a letter from yourself or from General [Joseph E.] Johnston for some days, and ask that you will write me by return courier, so that I can know exactly what to depend on. I still think that if you and Roddey would move in here, we can whip anything they may send against us, and I hope that you will come; at any rate, I shall confidently rely upon your co-operation against the Memphis and Charleston Railroad.

Will dispatch General Roddey again; have already done so, and rely upon his joining me.

I have instructed the courier if he finds any of your command, to forward this dispatch and remain at Salem for an answer. If he finds none, he will go with it to your headquarters. I will order a guide for your courier to Salem, to remain there for your answer, and suggest that you duplicate your dispatches, sending them by different men, so as to insure my getting one of them.

Have ordered Captain Higgs to send one of his best scouts to Salem, to remain there for your reply. If you can possibly come and aid me in breaking up this move of the enemy, it will give us 10,000 men, infantry and cavalry, by the 1st of April. You are aware that with my force of raw, undrilled, and undisciplined troops it will not do for me to risk a general engagement with a superior force. I have been gathering up the cattle and will, I fear, have to abandon them unless I can get your assistance.

Very respectfully, your obedient servant,
N. B. Forrest Brigadier-General, Commanding.

[P.S.] One courier will deliver this; another will be at Salem to receive a reply. I suggest that your answer be duplicated, one of which send by the bearer of this, and the other forward by your own courier to the man waiting at Salem. Between the two we shall be certain of a reply.

Respectfully,

N. B. Forrest, Brigadier-General.[65]

Forrest to Confederate General James Ronald Chalmers, December 23, 1863:

☞ HEADQUARTERS, JACKSON, TENN., DECEMBER 23, 1863.
BRIGADIER-GENERAL CHALMERS:

I am moving this morning southward. I find that I have so many unarmed men that I take them south.

I therefore write to ask that you will make demonstration on the railroad, but not cross it. It will give me an opportunity of crossing. Have written to Russell, in command of the unarmed men, not to move at all, but to keep his men together and locate where he can get forage, &c., for his command.

I hope, therefore, that you will engage the attention of the enemy until I effect the crossing.

N. B. Forrest, Brigadier-General.[66]

Forrest to Confederate General James Ronald Chalmers, December 28, 1863:

☞ HEADQUARTERS, HOLLY SPRINGS, DECEMBER 28, 1863.
BRIGADIER-GENERAL CHALMERS:

General: From one of your couriers I learn you are moving on Collierville, expecting to join me there. The inclosed note, written before I learned of [from] your courier your movements, fully explains why I abandoned the attack. I desire to see you if possible here, as I am unwell and much fatigued. I suggest that you move your command to some place in the neighborhood of Taylor's or Pipkins' to-night, and come in. I will be at Squire Fennell's.

Very respectfully,

N. B. Forrest, Major-General.[67]

Forrest to Confederate General Stephen Dill Lee, December 29, 1863:

☞ [TO: GENERAL S. D. LEE, COMMANDING CAVALRY IN

MISSISSIPPI.] REPORTS OF MAJ. GEN. NATHAN B. FORREST, C. S. ARMY. HEADQUARTERS DEPARTMENT OF WEST TENNESSEE, HOLLY SPRINGS, DECEMBER 29, 1863:

General: I arrived with the greater portion of my troops in this vicinity this morning, regretting very much that I had to leave West Tennessee so early. The concentration of a heavy force compelled me to move on the 24th from Jackson. The Corinth force of the enemy reached Jack's Creek, within 25 miles of Jackson, on the 23d. I sent out a force to meet and develop their strength and retard their progress. They were found to consist of three regiments of cavalry, a brigade of infantry, and four pieces of artillery. We drove the cavalry back to the infantry and then retired. I moved my forces to Estenaula, on the Hatchie [River], crossing it by the night of 25th. Met a cavalry regiment and routed them. Fought the enemy again on the 26th, at Somerville, killing and wounding 8 or 10 and capturing about 35 prisoners. I then moved a part of my force, under Colonel Faulkner, to Raleigh, and with the balance moved square to the left to La Fayette Bridge, on Wolf River.

On the morning of the 27th, my advance reached the bridge and attacked the bridge guard; drove them back and put to flight the force at La Fayette Station, killing several and capturing 4 or 5 prisoners. Cavalry advanced on me from Collierville, which we met and drove back. The enemy also sent re-enforcements by trains from Moscow, which we held in check until all my wagon train was safely across the river and on the road in the rear of my advance on Collierville. We closed the fight at Collierville about 8 o'clock at night, driving the enemy into their fortifications.

Not being able to hear anything of General Chalmers, and my men being worn out, I felt it to be prudent to retire, which I did, and my command is encamped about 7 miles west of this place. Another difficulty in the matter was that all my men armed with Austrian rifles were out of ammunition, having had the misfortune to lose my Austrian ammunition by the upsetting of a wagon at Forked Deer River.

I have brought out about 2,500 men. Colonel Faulkner, who is to cross at Raleigh, has with him about 800 more. I hope to hear that they have gotten out safely by to-morrow. If I could have staid there 10 days longer, could have almost doubled that number. I brought out my wagon train and artillery safely, although I have never experienced such weather and roads. My stock [horses], however, is much jaded and requires rest.

I have a lot of prisoners, and General Tuttle has signified his willingness to exchange man for man. Would I be justified in doing so?

I think of moving my headquarters to Oxford, and will encamp my command in Panola in order to organize it, and arm and equip it. The locality is a good one for forage, unless my command can be supplied with forage from the railroad. If so, I would prefer to be south of the Tallahatchie [River] to organize. I will advise you positively of my location as soon as made.

I am, general, very respectfully, your obedient servant,

N. B. Forrest, Major-General, Commanding.[68]

Forrest to Confederate General Leonidas Polk, December 29, 1863:
☞ [TO: LIEUT. GEN. L. POLK.] HEADQUARTERS DEPARTMENT OF WEST TENNESSEE, HOLLY SPRINGS, DECEMBER 29, 1863:

General: I have succeeded in getting out with about 2,500 men. Fought the enemy in heavy force at Jack's Creek, 25 miles east of Jackson, and drove them back. Commenced moving from Jackson on the next day (24th). Fought them on 25th at Estenaula, putting them to flight. Met Seventh Illinois Regiment at Somerville. Succeeded in getting in their rear and cut them up badly, capturing their wagons, a good many arms and horses, and 45 prisoners, and killed and wounded quite a number. We moved by La Fayette Bridge, on Wolf River. Found a heavy guard at the bridge, which my advance drove off; also scattered the force at La Fayette Station, and succeeded in crossing all my unarmed men, wagons, artillery, and beef cattle. The enemy advanced on me from Collierville and Moscow. We held the Moscow force in check and drove the troops from Collierville back to that place and into their fortifications. Fighting ceased at 8 o'clock at night. I then withdrew to this place. I will move into Panola County, or to Oxford, for the purpose of organizing the men I brought out. Owing to my having to leave Jackson so soon there are about 3,000 men left that I could not get together in time. If arrangements can be made to go back again, can bring out at least 3,000 men.

I am, in haste, general, your obedient servant,
N. B. Forrest, Major-General, Commanding.[69]

Forrest to Union General Stephen Augustus Hurlbut, December 30, 1863:
☞ HEADQUARTERS DEPARTMENT OF WESTERN TENNESSEE,
IN THE FIELD, DECEMBER 30, 1863. MAJ. GEN. S. A. HURLBUT,
COMMANDING U.S. FORCES, MEMPHIS:

General: I have in my hands forty-five or fifty Federal prisoners,
among them two captains and three lieutenants.

I suppose that I have lost some men also, and, owing to the
fatigue and exposure necessary to send your men to Richmond, I write
to propose exchanges. The desire, also, to get my own men prompts me
to make the proposition to exchange with you for them or for any
Confederate soldiers you may have in your hands.

I have asked permission to make the exchanges, provided you
consent to do so. I should be pleased to make such an arrangement, with
the understanding that I exchange, first, for my own troops, afterward
for any other belonging regularly to the C.S. Army. Should you consent
to do so, you will please forward by the flag a list of men now in your
hands, and I will exchange for them as far as I have men, and at any point
you may designate on the railroad between La Grange and Memphis.

I am, general, very respectfully, your obedient servant,
N. B. Forrest, Major-General, Commanding.[70]

SECTION FOUR

1864

1864

This year starts out with Forrest's second vote of thanks, on February 17, from the Confederate Congress. This is soon followed, on May 23, by a third vote of thanks, and on November 6 he is given command of all the cavalry of the Army of Tennessee. On December 6 the Confederate Congress bestows its fourth and final vote of thanks on Forrest.

His many glorious victories in 1864, however, are tempered by the loss of two of his brothers: Brigadier General Jeffrey Forrest, killed at the Battle of Okolona on February 22, and Lieutenant Colonel Aaron Forrest, who dies of pneumonia on April 13.

As Lincoln's War escalates into its fourth year, the volume of Major General Forrest's military correspondences nearly quadruples.

Forrest to Confederate General Samuel Cooper, January 2, 1864:
☞ HEADQUARTERS, COMO, MISS., JANUARY 2, 1864. GENERAL S. COOPER, ADJUTANT AND INSPECTOR GENERAL, RICHMOND, VA.:

General: I have the honor to state that I have succeeded in getting out of West Tennessee with about 3,000 troops, parts of sixteen different commands, with companies composed of 15 to 35 men each. I learn that muster-rolls have been forwarded by Colonel Richardson and others, and it is my duty to say to the Department that none of those rolls of new regiments from West Tennessee are legal. There are no regiments except upon paper, having (in order to fill up companies) illegally conscripted and sworn into the service men who are not now and never have been with their commands, and, until forcibly brought out and placed in infantry, never will be in the service. I can see no way of making these troops effective or organizing them, except by an order from the War Department annulling all authorities previously given to raise troops, accompanied with an order to consolidate into full companies and full regiments all the troops that can be gotten together in West Tennessee and North Mississippi.

By adopting this method I can get six full regiments of cavalry, or about 4,000 men; the balance will have to be conscripted. It is my opinion that as soon as the cavalry can be equipped and organized that I can get out at least 10,000 conscripts and place them in the service; at any rate, there are in West Tennessee alone more than that number subject to military duty. There are hundreds of officers in West Tennessee with an authority from various colonels, pretending to be raising companies for various regiments; they have collected together or mustered into the service squads of 15 or 20 men; they have no desire to complete a company and never expect to do so, but are using the authority to recruit as a means of keeping out of the service. For the good of the service I respectfully ask that all authorities given to raise troops in West Tennessee and North Mississippi be revoked, and that I be ordered to consolidate into full companies and full regiments all the troops that I may be able to get together; also, that, if approved and granted, the revocation of authorities and orders to consolidate be forwarded to me as early as practicable, having given those who have been raising troops until the 26th instant to complete their companies and regiments, desiring to have organizations complete by the 1st of February. In case it should not meet the views of the Department to revoke those authorities, a general order for all parties having such authorities to report to me without delay with what men they have for consolidation and organization will answer the purpose. Without a withdrawal or limitation to such recruiting the troops never will be organized or made available.

I am, general, very respectfully, your obedient servant,

N. B. Forrest, Major-General.[71]

Forrest to Confederate General William Wing Loring, January 4, 1864:
☞ [COMO, VIA SENATOBIA, MISS., JANUARY 4, 1864. TO: MAJOR-GENERAL W. W. LORING.]

Send back the Federal prisoners if they have reached Canton under Captain Goodwin. I have effected an exchange with [Union] General [S. A.] Hurlbut at Memphis for our troops. Answer immediately.

N. B. Forrest, Major-General.[72]

Forrest to Union General Stephen Augustus Hurlbut, January 4, 1864:
☛ HDQRS. CAVALRY of WEST TENN. AND NORTH MISS., PANOLA, JANUARY 4, 1864. MAJ. GEN. S. A. HURLBUT, U.S. ARMY, COMMANDING SIXTEENTH ARMY CORPS, MEMPHIS, TENN.:

Sir: I have the honor to acknowledge receipt of your favor of 31st ultimo, and respectfully forward you herewith a list of Federal prisoners now in my camps; have telegraphed to Grenada for the balance to be sent to my headquarters with as little delay as possible. Will forward a list of them as soon as they arrive.

If not objectionable to yourself it would be more expeditious and less fatiguing to the prisoners now in my possession to make the exchange at some point on the Mississippi and Tennessee Railroad, say at Hernando or at Farrar's, ten miles south of Memphis; also that you will set a time for the exchange several days hence in order that the balance of the prisoners now at Grenada may be exchanged also.

George M. Robertson, who is reported in your list of officers as second lieutenant Company B, McDonald's battalion, is not and never was an officer. He is a private, a deserter and a thief. In order to get him will give a man for him. He has represented himself falsely, as also have others on the same list belonging to Twelfth Tennessee Cavalry. They were men sent out to gather up absentees from the army and from their commands, but never were commissioned officers.

I respectfully inclose [a] list of those desired in exchange for your prisoners now in my camp. The balance I have will more than cover your entire list of privates. Am willing, however, when they arrive for exchange to turn you over any excess, with the understanding and assurance that you will release and send to me an equal number of my men when captured.

I am, general, very respectfully, your obedient servant,
N. B. Forrest, Major-General, Commanding.[73]

From Forrest to Confederate General Leonidas Polk, January 20, 1864:
☛ [COMO, MISS., JANUARY 20, 1864. TO: LIEUT. GEN. L. POLK:]

My scouts report 5,000 cavalry and 4,000 infantry at La Grange, preparing to move on Grenada.

N. B. Forrest, Major-General.[74]

After being assigned the command of the Department of Mississippi and East Louisiana, Forrest issued his first general order to his men on January 26, 1864:
☛ GENERAL ORDERS, NO. 1, HDQRS. FORREST'S CAVALRY DEPT., COMO [MISS.], JANUARY 26, 1864.

In obedience to orders from Lieutenant-General Polk, commanding Department of Mississippi and East Louisiana, I hereby assume command of the Northern Cavalry Department, which consists of all cavalry commands in West Tennessee and North Mississippi, as far south as the southern boundaries of the counties of Monroe, Calhoun, Chickasaw, Yalobusha, Tallahatchie, and that part of Sunflower and Bolivar lying north of a line drawn from the southwest corner of Tallahatchie County to the town of Prentiss, on the Mississippi River, to be known and designated as "Forrest's Cavalry Department." All cavalry commanders north of this line will at once report to these headquarters the strength and condition of their commands. The strength of the enemy in our front, and their merciless ravages on this portion of the country during the past two years, should furnish a sufficient appeal to men to rally at once for the defense of their homes. I come to you with a full supply of arms, ammunition, and accouterments, and there are men enough in the department, if properly organized, to drive the enemy from our soil. Let us then be prompt in our organizations and ready for the spring campaign.

N. B. Forrest, Major-General.[75]

Forrest to Confederate General Leonidas Polk, January 31, 1864:
☛ COMO [MISS.], JANUARY 31, 1864.

A gentleman just from Memphis says the enemy design moving a large force from Vicksburg on Jackson and contemplate rebuilding the railroad between those points moving from Jackson on Mobile and Meridian. He thinks the source from which his information is derived is reliable, and that they are anxious to draw our troops from the Army of Tennessee.

N. B. Forrest, Major-General.[76]

Forrest to Confederate Colonel Thomas M. Jack, February 1, 1864:

☞ PANOLA, MISS., FEBRUARY 1, 1864.

Col. T. M. Jack: My headquarters will be to-morrow at Oxford. Please send all papers there.

N. B. Forrest, Major-General.[77]

Forrest to Confederate General James Ronald Chalmers, February 4, 1864:

☞ OXFORD [MISS.], FEBRUARY 4, 1864:

Brigadier-General Chalmers: Keep your scouts well out. If there is not more than a brigade of the enemy, and they attempt to cross at month of Coldwater, let them do so, secreting your force and attacking them in the bottom between the river and the hills. Leaving a regiment at Panola to guard, keep your command well in hand ready to move at a moment's notice, keeping four days' cooked rations on hand. Send all your extra baggage, tents, and surplus arms by railroad to Grenada. Have 40 rounds in cartridge-boxes and 40 in wagons if you can get it. Have ordered McGuirk back to you. If he has not reported send for him. Withdraw all your forces south of Tallahatchie except small scouts.

N. B. Forrest, Major-General.[78]

Forrest to General Leonidas Polk, February 5, 1864:

☞ TUPELO [MISS.], FEBRUARY 5, 1864:

Lieutenant-General Polk: Have telegraphed General [S. D.] Lee to come up. Desire greatly that you meet him here. If matters are not arranged to my satisfaction I shall quit the service.

N. B. Forrest, Major-General.[79]

Forrest to General James Ronald Chalmers, February 5, 1864:

☞ OXFORD [MISS.], FEBRUARY 5, 1864:

Brigadier-General Chalmers: McGuirk is here. Send all his transportation with Colonel Forrest to Grenada.

N. B. Forrest, Major-General.[80]

Forrest to General James Ronald Chalmers, February 5, 1864:

☞ OXFORD [MISS.], FEBRUARY 5, 1864:

Send Colonel Forrest's brigade, with all their wagons, &c., to Grenada immediately. Give them all the arms required. If accouterments were not sent to Panola[,] will send them back from here for his command.

N. B. Forrest, Major-General.[81]

Forrest to Confederate President Jefferson Davis, February 5, 1864:
☛ HDQRS. CAVALRY DEPT. OF W. TENN. AND N. MISS., OXFORD, MISS., FEBRUARY 5, 1864. [TO: HON. JEFFERSON DAVIS, PRESIDENT, RICHMOND VA.:]

Dear Sir: I take the liberty of addressing you, believing a communication relative to the state of affairs in this department would prove interesting and perhaps of importance. I succeeded in bringing out of West Tennessee 3,100 troops, and have since received several hundred more. I regret, however, to state that the difficulties attending organizing regiments by consolidating the odds and ends of paper commands into full regiments have caused quite a number of disaffected officers and men to run away. Having also to leave West Tennessee at very short notice, and unexpectedly to many of the men, they were illy [i.e., poorly] supplied with clothing and blankets, which has contributed in some measure to cause desertion. I have, nevertheless, 3,000 new troops, and hope soon to do good service with them.

The enemy have evacuated Corinth and the Memphis and Charleston Railroad as far west as Germantown, and I have ordered the destruction of the road from Corinth to La Grange. The advance of the enemy on Jackson, Miss., and up [the] Yazoo River rendered it necessary to withdraw my command south of the Tallahatchie River in order to co-operate with Major-General [S. D.] Lee, should it be necessary; otherwise the destruction of that road would have been continued farther west. This step, whenever it can be accomplished, is necessary in order to prevent its reoccupation by the enemy, and to keep open communication with West Tennessee, in which there are at this time provisions sufficient to subsist an army of 20,000 men for six months. The people of West Tennessee generally are loyal to the South, and whenever circumstances will admit of it I expect to re-enter it, and am confident I shall be able to raise and organize at least four more full regiments of troops. I regret, however, to state that the people of North Mississippi and the counties adjacent to the Mississippi River are much demoralized by the cotton trade carried on with the enemy. Have endeavored as far as possible to break up all communication with the enemy, seizing all the cotton found *in transitu*, confiscating wagons and teams, and placing the parties under heavy penal bonds not to repeat the offense or hold any communication with the enemy or traffic with citizens inside of their military lines. As soon as the roads through the bottoms will permit the moving of troops and artillery, I hope to operate successfully against the boats navigating the Mississippi River. At present it is impracticable.

You are no doubt fully posted as to the movements of the enemy from Vicksburg and the Yazoo River against Jackson. My scouts, who have been on the river ever since the movement began, report that up to the 3d instant thirty-four transports loaded with troops have passed Friar's Point, going down. Estimated strength, 12,000. They have evacuated Fort Pillow and Columbus, and, except around Memphis, West Tennessee is almost entirely clear of Federal troops.

With an earnest desire to place in the service every available man in the department assigned me, and to secure as far as in my power the subsistence now in West Tennessee so much needed by the army,

I am, Mr. President, very respectfully, your obedient servant,

N. B. Forrest, Major-General, Commanding.[82]

Forrest to Confederate General James Ronald Chalmers, February 6, 1864:
☞ OXFORD [MISS.], FEBRUARY 6, 1864:

Brigadier-General Chalmers: Scouts report a force of the enemy moving from Collierville toward Holly Springs. Keep scouts well to the front. Stop Colonel Forrest at Oakland. Order him to keep five days rations on hand. Send all extra baggage to Grenada.

N. B. Forrest, Major-General.[83]

Forrest to Confederate General James Ronald Chalmers, February 6, 1864:
☞ OXFORD, FEBRUARY 6, 1864:

Brigadier-General Chalmers: Halt Colonel Forrest's command at Oakland, with instructions to remain there until further notice. If you have not already a sufficient scout, send 20 reliable men well to your front to watch the enemy should he attempt to move.

N. B. Forrest, Major-General.[84]

Forrest to Confederate General James Ronald Chalmers, February 7, 1864:
☞ OXFORD [MISS.], FEBRUARY 7, 1864.

Brigadier-General Chalmers: Colonel [Jeffrey E.] Forrest reports himself at Grenada with his command. Allow him to remain there.

N. B. Forrest, Major-General.[85]

Forrest to Confederate General James Ronald Chalmers, February 7, 1864:
☞ OXFORD, FEBRUARY 7, 1864.

Brigadier-General Chalmers: If you find the enemy moving south of Coldwater telegraph me upon what road. Have all the ferries above Panola to Hamburg guarded. Will move a brigade to Toba Tubby Ferry should the enemy move in that direction. Be certain to ascertain their movements. Have 30 men of McGuirk's north of the river in the direction of Holly Springs. No movement of the enemy in that direction reported as yet.

N. B. Forrest, Major-General.[86]

Forrest to Confederate General James Ronald Chalmers, February 7, 1864:
☞ OXFORD, FEBRUARY 7, 1864—8 p. m.

Brigadier-General Chalmers: If you find a force moving on Panola from Hernando you will move out a regiment to skirmish with them until a force can be got to Panola. Have all the corn possible brought to Panola by railroad.

N. B. Forrest, Major-General.[87]

Forrest to Confederate General Samuel Jameson Gholson, February 8, 1864:
☞ HDQRS. CAVALRY, DEPT. OF WEST TENN. AND MISS., OXFORD [MISS.], FEBRUARY 8, 1864. MAJOR-GENERAL GHOLSON:

General: My scouts report the enemy crossing Coldwater on the Hernando road 3,000 strong. Twelve regiments of cavalry are at Germantown and Collierville preparing to move south. Smith's (Federal) brigade, estimated at 4,000 strong, from Columbus, Ky., are crossing Hatchie near Bolivar, Tenn. Indications are that they will move in two columns—one by Panola to Grenada, the other by Salem, New Albany, and Pontotoc toward Okolona. If General [Philip D.] Roddey's command is in your front, in the neighborhood of Corinth, I think it will be advisable for you to move your command out to Red Land, in the direction of Houston, or even to the right of that, where you can get forage and be in striking distance in case I have to fall back, establishing to my headquarters a line of couriers. If I should leave here myself and go to Panola or Grenada, your dispatches can be telegraphed from this place. I shall rely upon you to watch the force now at Bolivar, and keep me advised of all the movements and protect my flank. I have written to General Roddey, if consistent with his orders, to move his command down in the neighborhood of Tupelo and establish communication with your headquarters, and through you to this place. I am of the opinion that they will endeavor to move toward Columbus, and if the Bolivar force should move, Roddey and yourself combined could either whip or greatly harass them, and retard their progress and prevent them from gaining my rear.

I am, general, very respectfully, your obedient servant,

N. B. Forrest, Major-General.[88]

Forrest to Confederate General James Ronald Chalmers, February 8, 1864:
☛ OXFORD, FEBRUARY 8, 1864.

Brigadier-General Chalmers: Have McCulloch's brigade moved to Panola at once. Will send Richardson's brigade to Toba Tubby and Wyatt. Bell's brigade will move toward Panola this morning. McGuirk is at Abbeville. Put Bell at Belmont and the railroad bridge. Have ordered Thrall's battery to Oakland; if you find the enemy advancing send for it. I will come down by Toba Tubby and Belmont. Keep a small picket at the mouth of Coldwater.

N. B. Forrest, Major-General.[89]

Forrest to Confederate General James Ronald Chalmers, February 9, 1864:
☛ OXFORD [MISS.], FEBRUARY 9, 1864.

General Chalmers, [at] Panola: Dispatch received. Have twice given orders in regard to transportation of First Mississippi Partisans. Obey the orders previously given or turn over your command to McCulloch and report to me for orders.

N. B. Forrest, Major-General.[90]

Forrest to Confederate General James Ronald Chalmers, February 9, 1864:

☞ OXFORD, FEBRUARY 9, 1864—5.40 p.m.

General Chalmers, [at] Panola: I will not come over to-morrow. Get Thrall's battery up and keep sharp lookout. I am of opinion the real move is in direction of Okolona and Meridian. Keep your force well in hand, so as to move at once if necessary. Watch at Belmont with your battery. Send pickets to Burlingham [Mississippi]. Your explanation is satisfactory.

N. B. Forrest, Major-General.[91]

Forrest to Confederate General James Ronald Chalmers, February 9, 1864:
☞ OXFORD, FEBRUARY 9, 1864.

General Chalmers, [at] Panola: Do not allow your command to engage a superior force. Fall back to the river and defend the crossings.

N. B. Forrest, Major-General.[92]

Forrest to Confederate General James Ronald Chalmers, February 10, 1864:
☞ OXFORD, FEBRUARY 10, 1864.

General Chalmers, [at] Panola: Place scouts in their rear and ascertain what is behind them. Let them come to the bayou if they choose to do so. Show no artillery unless compelled, but defend the crossings. If they attempt to lay a pontoon I think it will be at Belmont or the railroad bridge.

N. B. Forrest, Major-General.[93]

Forrest to Confederate General James Ronald Chalmers, February 10, 1864:
☞ OXFORD, FEBRUARY 10, 1864.

General Chalmers, [at] Panola: If Thrall's battery has arrived order the section of Morton's battery to this place. Order men belonging to McLendon's battery to report to that battery at Grenada.

N. B. Forrest, Major-General.[94]

Forrest to Confederate General Leonidas Polk, February 10, 1864:
☞ OXFORD [MISS.], FEBRUARY 10, 1864—1 P.M. [TO: LIEUT. GEN. POLK:]

Fifteen hundred infantry and 300 cavalry came out as far as Senatobia. Colonel McCulloch met and drove them back to Hickahale. I think this only a feint. Their real move is to go from Collierville to

Pontotoc and strike the Prairies and Mobile and Ohio Road. Am preparing to meet that move as best I can. They have about 10,000 cavalry and mounted infantry. Smith's Dutch brigade from Columbus passed Somerville on the 7th, going in direction of Memphis; mounted recently in West Tennessee.

      N. B. Forrest, Major-General.[95]

Forrest to Confederate General James Ronald Chalmers, February 11, 1864:
☞ OXFORD, FEBRUARY 11, 1864.

      General Chalmers, [at] Panola: Move everything here except Colonel Chalmer's battalion and his transportation.

      N. B. Forrest, Major-General.[96]

Forrest to Confederate General Leonidas Polk, February 11, 1864:
☞ OXFORD, MISS., FEBRUARY 11, 1864—10 P.M. [TO: LIEUTENANT-GENERAL POLK, MERIDIAN (CARE LIEUTENANT OTEY):]

      My scouts report a large force of cavalry and mounted infantry crossing Coldwater and moving toward Holly Springs from Byhalia.

      N. B. Forrest, Major-General.[97]

Forrest to Confederate General Leonidas Polk, February 11, 1864:
☞ OXFORD [MISS.], FEBRUARY 11, 1864. [TO: LIEUTENANT-GENERAL POLK:]

      Letters per Lieutenant Otey received. Enemy 5 miles from Byhalia, moving east. I am concentrating all my force at this place except Forrest's brigade, at Grenada, and two regiments left to guard the Tallahatchie from Abbeville to Panola. Another column of the enemy will no doubt move from Collierville via Salem and Ripley, their destination said to [be the] Prairies and junction with Sherman. Their force is twelve regiments of cavalry and mounted infantry.

      On the 4th, the Second Brigade, of the Twelfth Army Corps, passed down the river, reporting the whole corps on the way from Chattanooga for Vicksburg. Two hundred pack-mules were sent from Memphis to Germantown on the 7th. My force will be ready to move from here to-morrow morning.

      N. B. Forrest, Major-General.[98]

Forrest to Confederate General Leonidas Polk, February 12, 1864:
☞ OXFORD, MISS., FEBRUARY 12, 1864. [TO: LIEUTENANT-GENERAL POLK (CARE LIEUTENANT OTEY):]

Yazoo [River] too low for gun-boats to get up far. About 12,000 cavalry and mounted infantry in my front. Expect they will attempt crossing Tallahatchie [River] to-morrow. If I find they do not make a move toward Okolona and I cannot prevent their crossing, will fall back to Grenada.

N. B. Forrest, Major-General.[99]

Forrest to Confederate General James Ronald Chalmers, February 14, 1864:
☞ GRENADA [MISS.], FEBRUARY 14, 1864.

General Chalmers, [at] Oxford: Move with the force you have at once to Houston, leaving those below to follow on, taking McGuirk's [regiment] and Wheeler's battery with you. Answer when received.

N. B. Forrest, Major-General.[100]

Forrest to General Leonidas Polk, February 14, 1864:
☞ HEADQUARTERS, GRENADA, MISS., FEBRUARY 14, 1864—2 P.M. [TO: LIEUTENANT-GENERAL POLK:]

I am to-day falling back from Oxford and the line of the Tallahatchie River to this place. I have skirmished with the enemy from Panola to mouth of Tippah River. Their forces are moving to my right, crossing Tippah to-day 10 miles above its mouth on the road to New Albany. I am of opinion the larger portion of their forces will move via Pontotoc to Houston or Okolona and thence southward. Their forces are variously estimated at twenty-seven to thirty-one regiments cavalry and one brigade of infantry, thirteen pieces of artillery. From the best information I can get from scouts and other sources, I think they have 10,000 to 12,000 cavalry. Colonel Forrest's and General Chalmers' brigades move this evening to Houston. I have ordered all the balance of my forces to concentrate here, and will follow to West Point with all my forces to-morrow. Watch your right wing closely, and have General [S. D.] Lee's forces in position to co-operate with me. In the event the enemy proves too strong for me I shall fall back in the enemy's front toward Meridian, in case I am forced to fall back at all.

Yours, N. B. Forrest, Major-General.[101]

Forrest to General Leonidas Polk, February 14, 1864:

☞ HEADQUARTERS, GRENADA, MISS., FEBRUARY 14, 1864—8 P. M. [TO: LIEUTENANT-GENERAL POLK, MERIDIAN, MISS.:]

General Smith, with 10,000 mounted infantry and cavalry and thirty-one pieces artillery, passed Holly Springs on the evening of the 12th, going in direction of Beck's Spring and New Albany. Colonel Forrest's brigade, with battery, left here at 2 P.M. for West Point. Brigadier-General Chalmers, with Colonel McCulloch's brigade and battery of mountain howitzers, left Oxford at 4 o'clock this evening, moving in same direction. Richardson's and Bell's brigades, with two batteries, will leave here to-morrow evening at 4 o'clock, following Colonel Forrest. Lieut. Col. A. H. Forrest is on the Yazoo River with one regiment fighting gun-boats and transports. Gun-boats checked; transports moving down river. I will leave a force at this place. Look out for enemy. They may get ahead of me and attempt to gain your rear and cut railroad. Send force up the road to meet them if they can be spared. Think I can make West Point by morning of 19th.

N. B. Forrest, Major-General.[102]

Forrest to Confederate General Charles Clark, February 15, 1864:

☞ OXFORD, MISS., FEBRUARY 15, 1864 (VIA MACON, 18TH). [MISSISSIPPI] GOVERNOR CHARLES CLARK:

The enemy, 10,000 strong, with thirty pieces artillery, crossed at New Albany on the 13th and 14th. Have not learned the route taken by them. You have no doubt learned by this time. Will leave here to-morrow morning with two brigades and two batteries; will move in the direction of Macon.

N. B. Forrest, Major-General.[103]

Forrest to General Leonidas Polk, February 15, 1864:

☞ GRENADA [MISS.], FEBRUARY 15, 1864. (VIA MACON, 10 P.M., 17TH.) [TO: LIEUTENANT-GENERAL POLK (CARE MAJ. A. M. PAXTON):]

My scouts report the enemy, 10,000 strong, crossing at New Albany on 13th and 14th with thirty pieces of artillery. I fear they are ahead of me. General Chalmers' brigade is moving to Houston from Oxford. Colonel Forrest's brigade left here yesterday, and I think will reach West Point by 8 A.M. to-morrow. I move from here with Bell's and Richardson's brigades at 4 o'clock in the morning, and will endeavor to fall in about Starkville.

N. B. Forrest, Major-General.[104]

Forrest to Confederate General James Ronald Chalmers, February 17, 1864:
☞ HEADQUARTERS, NEAR BELLEFONTAINE [MISS.], FEBRUARY 17, 1864. BRIG. GEN. J. R. CHALMERS:

General: You will carry out the above order and impress horses and mules to fit up your division and your trains and artillery, in all cases giving the citizens broken-down stock for that impressed, so as to leave the farmer something to plow and make a crop with in raising crops. You will detail men expressly for that purpose, under proper officers, who will keep a strict account and make a proper return of all impressments made, and give a receipt to the parties for stock taken. You will send into the Prairie country and impress for artillery (and reserve them for that purpose) 100 good horses; also all the good mules you can get for transportation. Take all carriage and saddle horses that can be spared first; also require all stock for cavalry to be passed through the hands of your quartermaster, that when issued to the men they can be charged with the valuation or difference between their broken-down horses and those impressed. Men who have no horses will, as far as they have money or pay due them, be required to pay for their horses and be charged with the balance on muster-rolls. Owing to broken-down condition of the horses this command will not be able to reach Starkville to-morrow night, but will be in that vicinity on the road from this place.

Respectfully, N. B. Forrest, Major-General.[105]

Forrest to Confederate General Stephen Dill Lee, February 18, 1864:
☞ HDQRS. STARKVILLE, FEBRUARY 18, 1864—4 P.M. [TO: MAJOR-GENERAL LEE:]

I have just arrived here. Have not more than 40 rounds of ammunition to the man. All my artillery will be here to-night, but the horses have been pulled through the mud and are in a broken-down condition. If possible, send me some small-arms ammunition, caliber .54. The enemy is reported moving from Houston in this direction, but I am of opinion if they find out we are here that they will move by

Greensborough. At any rate, if they are not too strong will meet and fight them. Have offered them battle two or three times, and they are evidently trying to dodge around. If I find them too strong will fall back in the direction of Macon, advising you of the fact. Have three brigades here, with all my artillery. McCulloch's brigade is 25 miles north of this. I think the enemy are fully posted of our movements, as several men [who had] been questioned by our scouts have run off and no doubt fully posted the enemy of our position, force, &c. I am ready to obey any orders you may give, and would like to be kept fully advised of your position, &c., and if the enemy is too strong will so move as to be enabled, with the assistance you may give, to meet and fight them. Have just learned that General Clark, or Governor Clark, has some ammunition, caliber . 54. Cannot some of it—say 50,000 rounds—be sent up on hand-cars to Artesia? I can get along with that amount, having plenty for all other arms except the Austrian rifles and Sharps rifles. The ammunition, I understand, is at Macon or Columbus. Have an operator with me, and think it would be well to open telegraphic communication with you. Will send my operator to Artesia to-night to fit up an office at that place. If you can establish an office it will greatly facilitate communication.

And I am, general, very respectfully, your obedient servant,

N. B. Forrest, Major-General.[106]

Forrest to Confederate Colonel Isham Harrison, February 19, 1864:

☛ HEADQUARTERS FORREST'S CAVALRY DEPARTMENT, STARKVILLE [MISS.], FEBRUARY 19, 1864—4 A.M. COL. I. HARRISON:

Colonel: I have ordered Col. J. E. Forrest's brigade to proceed at once to Aberdeen. You will co-operate with him, and should you find that the enemy is moving upon Aberdeen you will notify him at once. He will move by way of West Point. You will press them hard and delay their progress as much as possible.

Respectfully,

N. B. Forrest, Major-General, Commanding.[107]

Forrest to Confederate General Stephen Dill Lee, February 19, 1864:

☛ HEADQUARTERS, STARKVILLE [MISS.], FEBRUARY 19, 1864.

GENERAL S. D. LEE, [AT] GAINESVILLE:

Dispatch received. Preparations will be made to subsist your troops here. Enemy reported moving in the direction of Columbus. Started Forrest's brigade to West Point and Aberdeen and Bell's brigade to Columbus this morning. Will move in the morning with the balance of my command and with the artillery, leaving about 600 here with my wagons.

N. B. Forrest, Major-General.[108]

Forrest to Confederate General James Ronald Chalmers, February 21, 1864:
☞ SEVEN MILES NORTH OF WEST POINT, FEBRUARY 21, 1864—2.30 P.M. BRIGADIER-GENERAL CHALMERS, COMMANDING DIVISION:

General: The enemy are evidently moving up Sakatouchee. They are moving up the railroad and are retreating. I will move on and keep you posted. Send a line of couriers after me to carry dispatches to you. They are now halted in a swamp in front of us, 1 mile south of John A. Walker's.

Respectfully,

N. B. Forrest, Major-General.

P.S.—Colonel Barteau with his brigade is across the Tombigbee moving parallel with the enemy. Move Richardson and General Gholson up the river toward Houston, to prevent enemy crossing Sakatouchee.

N. B. F.[109]

Forrest to Confederate General James Ronald Chalmers, February 21, 1864:
☞ AT JAMES EVANS' PLACE, TWO AND A HALF MILES NORTH OF WEST POINT [MISS.], [FEBRUARY 21, 1864.]

Brig. Gen. J. R. Chalmers: I find that the enemy has taken the Houston road to Winston's farm. I think they are badly scared. I wish you to move everything south of Line Creek and picket the fords. I will follow on until I can ascertain the route they have taken. If they should cross the creek and attempt to move west of Starkville, General [S. D.] Lee and yourself will be in position to follow or cut them off. If they fall back toward Pontotoc I will follow on as long as I think I can do any good. Send the 2,000 and move as rapidly as possible with the light artillery. I ordered Colonel Neely with his force this morning to Tibbee

Station. Recall him at once and Bell's brigade, provided you find the enemy moving west. Direct General Ruggles to keep scouts out in direction of Decatur, Ala.

N. B. Forrest, Major-General.[110]

Forrest to Confederate Colonel Richard Harrison, February 22, 1864:
☛ HEADQUARTERS, EIGHT MILES SOUTH OF EGYPT [MISS.], FEBRUARY 22, 1864.

Col. Richard Harrison: If General Ruggles is at Columbus you will assume command of all the mounted force of General Ruggles and move up to Cotton Gin Port. The enemy is at Okolona and may attempt to cross at that point or above. Should they do so you will harass and prevent them from doing so. Should they cross you will check them all you can. Keep in their front ,burn all bridges behind you, and keep me advised of all their movements. Send a copy of this to General Ruggles.

N. B. Forrest, Major-General.[111]

From Forrest to Confederate General Leonidas Polk, February 26, 1864:
☛ HEADQUARTERS, STARKVILLE, MISS., FEBRUARY 26, 1864.
[TO: LIEUT. GEN. L. POLK:]

General: I have the honor to acknowledge receipt of your letter of 20th instant, and am under many obligations for the ordnance stores and train sent to Gainesville. I am also gratified at being able to say that your wishes in regard to the enemy's forces under [Union] Generals Smith and Grierson are realized—at least to the extent of defeat and utter rout. We met them on Sunday morning last at Ellis Bridge, or Sakatonchee Creek, 3 miles south of West Point, in front of which Colonel Forrest's brigade was posted to prevent the enemy from crossing. After a brisk engagement of an hour and a half the enemy retired toward West Point. It was not my intention to attack them or bring on a general engagement, but to develop their strength, position, and movements. I moved forward with my escort and a portion of Faulkner's Kentucky regiment and found the enemy had begun a systematic retreat, and being unwilling they should leave the country without a fight, ordered the advance of my column. Will forward a detailed official report as soon as reports from brigade commanders are received.

It is sufficient for me to say here that with 2,500 men[,] the enemy, numbering from 6,000 to 7,000 strong, were driven from West Point to within 10 miles of Pontotoc in two days. All his efforts to check our advance failed, and his forces at last fled utterly defeated and demoralized, leaving 6 pieces of artillery, 100 killed, over 100 prisoners, and wounded estimated at 300 or over. The seriously wounded, about 50 in number fell into our hands. They took in their retreat every carriage, buggy, cart, and wagon along the road to remove their killed and wounded officers, and all their slightly wounded, according to report of citizens, were moved in front with their pack train.

Our loss is about 25 killed, 75 wounded, and probably 8 or 10 captured.

Among the killed are my brother, Col. Jeff. E. Forrest, commanding brigade Lieutenant-Colonel Barksdale, commanding George's regiment, and several other officers whose names are not now remembered.

It affords me pleasure to mention the fortitude and gallantry displayed by the troops engaged, especially the new troops from West Tennessee, who, considering their want of drill, discipline, and experience, behaved handsomely, and the moral effect of their victory over the best cavalry in the Federal service will tell in their future operations against the enemy, inspiring them with courage and confidence in their ability to whip them again. Considering the disparity in numbers, discipline, and drill, I consider it one of the most complete victories that have occurred since the war began.

After the enemy succeeded in reaching the hills between Okolona and Pontotoc, the resistance of the enemy was obstinate, compelling me frequently to dismount my advance to drive them from favorable positions defended by the broken condition of the country. About 800 men of the Second Tennessee Cavalry, under Colonel Barteau, and the Seventh Tennessee Cavalry, Colonel Duckworth, received the repeated charges of seven regiments of the enemy in open ground, drove them back time after time, finally driving them from the field, capturing three stand of colors and another piece of their artillery. A great deal of the fighting was almost hand to hand, and the only way I can account for our small loss is the fact that we kept so close to them that the enemy overshot our men. Owing to the broken down and exhausted condition of men and horses, and being almost out of ammunition, I was compelled to stop pursuit.

Major-General Gholson arrived during Monday night, and his command, being comparatively fresh, continued the pursuit, and when last heard from was still driving the enemy, capturing horses and prisoners. The enemy had crossed the Tallahatchie River on the night of the 28d, burning the bridge behind them at New Albany and retreating rapidly toward Memphis, with Gholson still in pursuit.

I am, general, very respectfully, your obedient servant,

N. B. Forrest, Major-General.[112]

Forrest to Confederate General James Ronald Chalmers, March 5, 1864:
☞ HEADQUARTERS, ARTESIA, MISS., MARCH 5, 1864.

General Chalmers, [at] Starkville: You will move your entire command to the vicinity of Tibbee and Mayhew Stations and report to me in person at Columbus to-morrow. Send my escort and headquarters wagons with Morton's battery direct to Columbus.

N. B. Forrest, Major-General.[113]

Forrest to Confederate Lieutenant Colonel Thomas M. Jack, March 8, 1864, concerning the Battles of West Point (February 21, 1864) and Okolona (February 22, 1864):
☞ HEADQUARTERS FORREST'S CAVALRY DEPARTMENT, COLUMBUS, MISS., MARCH 8, 1864. [LIEUTENANT COLONEL THOMAS M. JACK, ASSISTANT ADJUTANT-GENERAL:]

Colonel: I have the honor to submit the following report of the movements and operations of my command against the Federal forces under command of General Smith, in the engagements of the 20th, 21st, and 22d ultimo:

Learning on the 14th ultimo, at Oxford, that the enemy was moving in heavy force in the direction of Pontotoc, and believing his destination to be the Prairies, and from thence a junction with Sherman, I withdrew all my forces from the Tallahatchie and Yazoo Rivers and moved rapidly to Starkville, which place I reached on the evening of the 18th ultimo.

On the 19th, the enemy were reported at Okolona, but his movements or intended course was not developed, and fearing he might cross the Tombigbee, I ordered Bell's brigade to Columbus and also dispatched General Ruggles to use all his effective force to prevent them from doing so. At the same time ordered Brigadier-General Chalmers, commanding division, to send Forrest's brigade to Aberdeen, or in that direction, to meet and ascertain the movements of the enemy; and also with McCulloch's brigade of his division, and Richardson's brigade, under Colonel Neely, to move out to West Point, leaving General Richardson at Starkville in command of all the dismounted men of the command to protect my wagon train, and send out scouts in the direction of Houston in order to give timely notice should the enemy divide his forces and move in that direction.

On the morning of the 20th, Colonel Forrest met the enemy in force and fell back toward West Point, skirmishing with them, but avoiding an engagement. In repelling their attacks he lost 2 men killed and several wounded and captured. I moved over to his assistance with General Chalmers and his remaining brigade, taking with me also Richardson's brigade and two batteries of artillery, joining Colonel Forrest within 3 miles of West Point. Finding the enemy in heavy force, and having been informed that General [S. D.] Lee was moving to my assistance, and desiring to delay a general engagement as long as possible, I determined at once to withdraw my forces south of Sakatonchee Creek, which I did, camping a portion of them near Ellis Bridge and the remainder at Siloam. After crossing the river a courier reported the enemy as having crossed the river 8 miles above Ellis Bridge, destroying mills and taking horses and negroes. With five companies of Faulkner's regiment and my escort I moved rapidly to the point, clearly designated by the smoke of the burning mill, gained the bridge, and succeeded in capturing the squad, which proved to be a lieutenant and 22 privates of the Fourth Regulars, U. S. Cavalry. Fearing the enemy might attempt to cross at the upper bridge during the night, I ordered its destruction and concentrated my force at Ellis Bridge, 3 miles from West Point. This bridge I determined, if possible, to defend and preserve, because it was necessary in the event we could drive back the enemy to use it in advancing on them; and had I allowed the enemy to cross it and then succeeded in driving them back they would have burned it behind them, rendering pursuit impossible without heading the stream.

During the night all was quiet. On Sunday morning, the 21st, the vedettes and pickets were driven in, and the enemy reported advancing from West Point in full force. I had ordered General Chalmers to dismount his division, throwing Forrest's brigade across the creek in front of the bridge, while McCulloch's brigade took possession of the south bank of the stream to support Colonel Forrest and protect him in the event he was compelled to retire and recross the stream. Dispatches were sent to General Richardson to move up all his force to the bridge across Line Creek, 8 miles of Starkville and 4 miles in my rear; also to Colonel Barteau to move across the Tombigbee, to keep on the flank, and, if possible, to gain the enemy's rear. I ordered Colonel Neely to move his (Richardson's) brigade at once, and to guard all the ferries and fords across Tibbee River from the mouth of Line Creek to Tibbee Station, sending Major-General Gholson with the State forces under his command to Palo Alto to watch any movement of the enemy from the direction of Houston. In making these necessary dispositions my effective force in front of the enemy was reduced to Chalmers' division, my escort, and two batteries. The enemy attacked Colonel Forrest at 8 o'clock, and after a fight of two hours were repulsed with considerable loss. The hastily-improvised breast-works of rails and logs thrown up by Colonel Forrest greatly protected his men, and our casualties during this fight were 7 men wounded.

As the enemy withdrew I followed them with my escort and a portion of Faulkner's regiment, mounted; also with a section of Morton's battery, supported by a regiment from McCulloch's brigade on foot. Our advance at first was necessarily slow and cautious. I soon ascertained, after a few well-directed shots from our artillery, that the enemy had begun a rapid and systematic retreat, and dashed on after them, sending back orders to General Chalmers to send forward to me, as rapidly as possible, 2,000 of his best mounted men and Hoole's battery of mountain howitzers. I soon came on their rear guard, charged it with my escort and Faulkner's command, and drove it before me. They made several stands, but Colonel McCulloch, with his brigade, having caught up, we continued to charge and drive them on, killing and wounding 15 or 20 of them and capturing a number of prisoners.

Night came on, and we kept so close to the enemy that my men mistook each other for the enemy and fired a volley at each other, without, however, doing any damage. Fearing a recurrence of such mistakes, and considering the great risk necessarily incurred in following and fighting a superior force after dark, I determined to encamp for the night and resume the chase at daylight next morning. Early next morning, the column moved forward, taking a different road. With my escort I came upon and charged the enemy 4 miles from Okolona, and drove their rear guard into town, when I found them drawn up in line of battle and apparently awaiting our arrival. Colonel Barteau, with Bell's brigade, had also reached Okolona, and was in line of battle awaiting the arrival of the balance of my forces. Leaving my escort in line as skirmishers, with my staff I made a circuit around the town, took command of Bell's brigade and advanced upon them. They received us with a volley and charged with yells, but were handsomely repulsed in the open field and forced to retreat, which they did rapidly and in confusion, using every exertion to check pursuit by ambuscading and forming regiments on either side of the road, who would fire and retreat successively. Before attempting or being able to make a stand of any kind they were crowded so closely that they cut out the horses and abandoned five pieces of artillery (some of the pieces spiked), and gaining the broken and hilly country on the Pontotoc road their resistance became more stubborn. They had every advantage in selecting position, and to drive and dislodge them I was compelled to dismount most of my command, and fought the last 9 miles on foot. About 5 miles from Okolona they formed and awaited us, making a determined stand, McCulloch's and Forrest's brigades both arriving with Hoole's battery. After a short but obstinate resistance the enemy gave way.

In this engagement Colonel Forrest was killed while rallying and leading his men. In a few miles they again formed, and having dismounted a portion of their men and made breast-works of the fences on each side of the road, they were[,] with some difficulty and hard fighting[,] compelled again to retire. In driving them at this point, Lieutenant-Colonel Barksdale, commanding Fifth Mississippi Regiment, fell mortally wounded.

Ten miles from Pontotoc they [the Yanks] made a last and final effort to check pursuit, and from their preparations, numbers, and advantageous position no doubt indulged the hope of success. They had formed in three lines across a large field on the left of the road, but which a turn in the road made it directly in our front. Their lines were at intervals of several hundred paces, and the rear and second lines longer than the first. As the advance of my column moved up they opened on us with artillery. My ammunition was nearly exhausted, and I knew that if we faltered they would in turn become the attacking party, and that disaster might follow. Many of my men were broken down and exhausted with clambering the hills on foot and fighting almost constantly for the last 9 miles. I determined, therefore, relying upon the bravery and courage of the few men I had up, to advance to the attack. As we moved up, the whole force charged down at a gallop, and I am proud to say that my men did not disappoint me. Standing firm, they repulsed the grandest cavalry charge I ever witnessed. The Second and Seventh Tennessee drove back the advance line, and as it wheeled in retreat poured upon them a destructive fire. Each successive line of the enemy shared the same fate and fled the field in dismay and confusion, and losing another piece of artillery, and leaving it strewn with dead and wounded men and horses.

Half of my command were out of ammunition, the men and horses exhausted and worn down with two days' hard riding and fighting, night was at hand, and further pursuit impossible.

Major-General [Samuel J.] Gholson arrived during the night. His command was small, but comparatively fresh. I ordered him to follow on the next morning and press them across the Tallahatchie. Having received no official report from him, I cannot give any details of his pursuit after them.

Considering the disparity in numbers and equipments, I regard the defeat of this force, consisting as it did of the best cavalry in the Federal army, as a victory of which all engaged in it may justly feel proud. It has given, for a time at least, peace and security to a large scope of rich country whose inhabitants anticipated and expected to be overrun, devastated and laid waste, and its moral effect upon the raw, undisciplined and undrilled troops of this command is in value incalculable. It has inspired them with courage and given them confidence in themselves and their commanders. Although many of them were but recently organized, they fought with a courage and daring worthy of veterans.

I herewith transmit you a list of casualties, which, under all the circumstances, is small, and especially so when compared with that of the enemy.

The killed and wounded of the enemy who fell into our hands amounts to over 100. We captured 6 pieces of artillery, 3 stand of colors, and 162 prisoners. By pressing every horse, buggy, carriage, and vehicle along the road they were enabled to take off all their wounded, except those severely or mortally wounded, and it is but reasonable to suppose amid a low estimate to place their loss in killed, wounded, and missing at 800.

My force in the fight did not exceed 2,500 men, while that of the enemy was twenty-seven regiments of cavalry and mounted infantry, estimated at 7,000 strong.

I regret the loss of some gallant officers. The loss of my brother, Col. J. E. Forrest, is deeply felt by his brigade as well as myself, and it is but just to say that for sobriety, ability, prudence, and bravery he had no superior of his age. Lieutenant-Colonel Barksdale was also a brave and gallant man, and his loss fell heavily on the regiment he commanded, as it was left now without a field officer.

I desire to testify my appreciation of the skill and ability of Colonels McCulloch, Russell, and Duckworth, commanding brigades. Colonel McCulloch, although wounded on the evening of the 22d, continued in command. Colonel Russell assumed command of Bell's brigade after the injury to Colonel Barteau, and Colonel Duckworth took command of Forrest's brigade after Colonel Forrest fell on the morning of the 22d ultimo.

I have formally congratulated and returned my thanks to the officers and troops of my command for their gallant and meritorious conduct; for their energy, endurance, and courage, and it would afford me pleasure to mention individual instances of daring and dash which came under my own observation but for fear of doing apparent injustice to others who in other parts of the field perhaps did as well.

My escort deserves especial mention: Commanded by Lieut. Thomas S. Tate on the 21st, and by its commander, Captain Jackson, on the 22d, its battle-flag was foremost in the fray, sustaining its reputation as one of the best fighting cavalry companies in the service. I also desire to acknowledge, as I have often done before, my indebtedness to Maj. J. P. Strange, my assistant adjutant-general; Capt. Charles W. Anderson, my aide-de-camp, and Lieutenant Tate, assistant inspector-general, for prompt and faithful services rendered in the delivery and execution of all my orders on the field.

All of which is respectfully submitted.

N. B. Forrest, Major-General.[114]

Forrest to Confederate Colonel Thomas M. Jack, March 10, 1864:

☛ HEADQUARTERS FORREST'S CAVALRY DEPARTMENT, COLUMBUS [MISS.], MARCH 10, 1864. COL. T. M. JACK, ASSISTANT ADJUTANT-GENERAL:

Colonel: If nothing occurs to prevent, will leave here on Monday next with General Buford's division and four small pieces of artillery. Will get from the First and Forty-third Mississippi Infantry about 100 horses. Will need 150 horses to complete the four batteries, and 150 more for mounting the three Kentucky regiments under Colonel Thompson. I have also about 200 men of Chalmers' and Buford's divisions without horses, most of whom lost their horses in the recent engagements with the enemy.

My scouts report six regiments of Federal cavalry moving from Memphis to Nashville, and that there are no Federals on the Memphis and Charleston Railroad east of Germantown. Scouting parties, however, are sent out daily.

[Yankee General Fielding] Hurst is still reported in West Tennessee, and a portion of Jackson and Brownsville have been burned by his men.

Will order six companies of Colonel Forrest's regiment, under Captain Warren, to Marion County, Ala., to protect the foundries, &c., against tories and deserters. Will also send Colonel McCulloch, commanding Chalmers' division, with the brigade now here with orders to divide his command and breast the country from this toward Memphis and Panola, arresting all stragglers and deserters.

I am, very respectfully, your obedient servant,

N. B. Forrest, Major-General.[115]

Forrest to Confederate Colonel Thomas M. Jack, March 10, 1864:

☛ HEADQUARTERS FORREST'S CAVALRY DEPARTMENT, COLUMBUS [MISS.], MARCH 10, 1864. COL. T. M. JACK, ASSISTANT ADJUTANT- GENERAL:

Colonel: I have the honor respectfully to forward you a copy of letter received from Brig. Gen. James R. Chalmers, and to state that I have relieved him from duty with my command and ordered him to report to the lieutenant-general commanding for assignment. I am satisfied that I have not and shall not receive the co-operation of Brigadier-General Chalmers, and that matters of the smallest moment will continue, as they have heretofore done, to be a source of annoyance to myself and detrimental to the service, and, holding myself responsible to the proper authority for all orders I have or may hereafter issue, I deem it both necessary and beneficial that we should separate.

Hoping that the lieutenant-general commanding may be able to place Brigadier-General Chalmers in a position more congenial to his taste and wishes than the one he now occupies, I am, very respectfully, your obedient servant,

N. B. Forrest, Major-General.[116]

In an attempt to belittle the South and tarnish Forrest's reputation, Union General Ulysses S. Grant tried to suppress the facts about Forrest's magnificent win at the Battle of Okolona.[117] On March 11, 1864, however, Forrest issued the following circular to his men, immortalizing the truth:

☛ HDQRS. FORREST'S CAVALRY DEPARTMENT, COLUMBUS, MARCH 11, 1864. [DICTATED TO FORREST'S ASSISTANT MAJOR JOHN P. STRANGE:]

The major-general commanding desires to return his thanks and acknowledgments to the officers and men of his command for their recent gallant and meritorious conduct in defeating and routing the largest, most carefully selected, and best equipped cavalry and mounted infantry command ever sent into the field by the enemy. And it affords him both pleasure and pride to say that by your ability, unflinching bravery, and endurance, a force three times your own was defeated, routed, demoralized, and driven from the country, his plans frustrated, his ends unaccomplished, and his forces cut to pieces. Thus by your valor and courage you have given safety and security to the homes and firesides of the defenseless and helpless inhabitants of the country, whose grateful acknowledgments are showered upon you and whose prayers daily and nightly ascend to heaven for your future prosperity and success.

The major-general commanding deplores the loss of some of his bravest officers and men. They have fallen in the discharge of their duty as soldiers and patriots, and have yielded up their lives in defense of all that man holds dear. He desires that you cherish their memory, emulate their example, and achieve your independence or perish in the attempt.

In conclusion, the major-general commanding desires to say that all who were engaged may feel justly proud of their participation in a victory so pregnant with disaster to the enemy and so glorious in its results to our cause, and which has delivered a grateful people from that oppression, devastation, and destruction which follows the footsteps of a dastardly and brutal foe.

By your past conduct and heroism he confidently relies upon and predicts your future success in whipping the enemy wherever you meet them.

By command of Major-General Forrest: J. P. Strange, Assistant Adjutant-General.[118]

Forrest to Confederate General Leonidas Polk, March 12, 1864:
☛ HEADQUARTERS FORREST'S CAVALRY COMMAND, COLUMBUS [MISS.], MARCH 12, 1864. LIEUT. GEN. L. POLK, COMMANDING:

General: I have the honor to acknowledge the receipt of yours yesterday; am glad to know that Brigadier-General Armstrong will report to me.

I regretted the necessity of relieving Brigadier-General Chalmers, but his letter addressed to me, a copy of which I have forwarded you, speaks for itself. He has never been satisfied since I came here, and being satisfied that I have not had and will not receive his support and co-operation, deemed it necessary that we should separate. I must have the cordial support of my subordinate officers in order to succeed and make my command effective, and holding myself responsible for all my acts and orders to the proper authority, have forwarded his letter, also his application for a court of inquiry. I hope you may be able to place him where he will be better satisfied than with me.

Brigadier-General Richardson is relieved on account of charges preferred against him by Colonel Green, and is ordered to report to you at Demopolis.

I am, general, very respectfully, your obedient servant,
N. B. Forrest, Major-General.[119]

Forrest to Confederate General Charles Clark, March 15, 1864:
☛ HEADQUARTERS FORREST'S CAVALRY, ABERDEEN, MARCH 15, 1864. HIS EXCELLENCY GOVERNOR CHARLES CLARK, GOVERNOR OF MISSISSIPPI:

Governor: I have the honor to say that General Gholson has returned here, and states that you are willing to turn over the State troops under his command to the Confederate States. I have promised, if possible, to make him a brigade of 1,800 men, and recommend him to be appointed its brigade commander.

I respectfully suggest, therefore, that General Gholson be ordered and authorized to reorganize the State cavalry and fill up and consolidate the commands into full regiments, and then to turn them over.

I desire to give, or that by this arrangement General Gholson shall have, a large Mississippi brigade, for which I desire to fit him up a battery, &c., but consider it of the first importance that the regiments shall be full and well officered and organized, and that it be done as early as practicable. I desire the brigade to defend this portion of the country, and will keep it in this section unless ordered away by the lieutenant-general commanding this department.

I am, very respectfully, your obedient servant,
N. B. Forrest, Major-General.[120]

Forrest to Confederate General Leonidas Polk, March 18, 1864:
☛ HEADQUARTERS, TUPELO [MISS.], MARCH 18, 1864. LIEUTENANT-GENERAL POLK, DEMOPOLIS:

Dispatches received; orders to Colonel Jackson revoked. Will leave this morning for West Tennessee. All important reports from North Alabama and elsewhere will be sent you through General Gholson at this place. Scouts at Austin report five large transports passed up the river with 3,500 troops from 7th to 11th instant. Sherman and staff at Memphis on the 11th. Memphis scout reports expedition fitting out for Red River. Cavalry at Memphis reported as ordered to East Tennessee. Governor Clark as consented to transfer the State cavalry to Confederate service, to be formed into a Mississippi brigade and be kept, if not required elsewhere. I recommend that enough of the unattached companies of this portion of the State be ordered to General Gholson to fill up his three regiments.

N. B. Forrest, Major-General.[121]

Forrest to Confederate Lieutenant Colonel Thomas M. Jack, March 21, 1864:

☞ HEADQUARTERS FORREST'S CAVALRY, JACKSON, TENN., MARCH 21, 1864. COL. THOMAS M. JACK, ASST. ADJT. GEN. DEPT. OF ALA., MISS., AND EAST LA.:

Colonel: I forward, for the information of the lieutenant-general commanding, the inclosed statement [below] of outrages committed by the commands of [Union] Col. Fielding Hurst and others of the Federal Army. I desire, if it meets with the approval of the lieutenant-general commanding, that this report may be sent to some newspaper for publication. Such conduct should be made known to the world.

Very respectfully, colonel, your obedient servant,

N. B. Forrest, Major-General, Commanding.

[INCLOSURE ATTACHED TO PREVIOUS LETTER]

☞ Hdqrs. Cav. Dept. of West Tenn. and North Miss., Jackson, March 21, 1864. Lieut. Col. T. M. Jack, Assistant Adjutant-General:

Colonel: I have the honor to report the arrival of my advance at this place on yesterday morning at 11 o'clock, and deem it proper to give the lieutenant-general commanding a report of the condition of the country through which I have passed, also the state of affairs as they exist, with such suggestions as would naturally arise from observations made and a personal knowledge of facts as they exist. From Tupelo to Purdy the country has been laid waste, and unless some effort is made either by the Mobile and Ohio Railroad Company or the Government[,] the people are bound to suffer for food. They have been[,] by the enemy and by roving bands of deserters and tories[,] stripped of everything; have neither negroes nor stock with which to raise a crop or make a support. What provisions they had have been consumed or taken from them, and the majority of families are bound to suffer. They are now hauling corn in ox wagons and by hand-cars from Okolona and below to Corinth, and as far north as Purdy, also east and west of Corinth, on the

Memphis and Charleston Railroad, but their limited means of transportation will not enable them to subsist their families, and my opinion is that the railroad can be easily and speedily repaired, and that any deficiency in iron from Meridian north can be supplied from the Memphis and Charleston Railroad, and that a brigade of cavalry with a regiment or two of infantry placed at Corinth would afford protection to that section, and would be the means of driving out of the country or placing in our army the deserters and tories infesting that region, whose lawless appropriation of provisions, horses, and other property is starving out the defenseless and unprotected citizens of a large scope of country. Repairing and running the railroad would enable the inhabitants to procure provisions from the prairies and would prove an invaluable acquisition in the transportation of supplies and troops from this section. But little can be done in returning the deserters from our army now in West Tennessee, and collecting and sending out all persons subject to military duty, unless the railroad is rebuilt or repaired, as they will have to be marched through a country already, for want of labor and supplies, insufficient for the subsistence of its own inhabitants. With a conscript post or an established military post at Corinth and the railroad from thence south they could be rapidly forwarded to the army. The wires can also be extended and a telegraph office established. The whole of West Tennessee is overrun by bands and squads of robbers, horse thieves, and deserters, whose depredations and unlawful appropriations of private property are rapidly and effectually depleting the country. The Federal forces at Paducah, Columbus, and Union City are small. There is also a small force at Fort Heiman, on the Tennessee, and Fort Pillow, on the Mississippi River. About 2,000 men of Smith's forces, composed of parts of many regiments, have crossed the Tennessee River at Clifton and Fort Heiman, and returned to Nashville; four regiments of Illinois cavalry have re-enlisted and have gone home on furlough. The cavalry force at Memphis is therefore small.

Numerous reports having reached me of the wanton destruction of property by Col. Fielding Hurst and his regiment of renegade Tennesseans, I ordered Lieut. Col. W. M. Reed to investigate and report upon the same, and herewith transmit you a copy of his report. Have thought it both just and proper to bring these transactions to the notice of the Federal commander at Memphis, and by flag of truce will demand of him the restitution of the money taken from the citizens of Jackson, under a threat from Hurst to burn the town unless the money was forthcoming at an appointed time. Have also demanded that the murderers be delivered up to Confederate authority for punishment, and reply from that officer as to the demand, &c., will be forwarded you as soon as received. Should the Federal commander refuse to accede to the just demands made, I have instructed the officer in charge of the flag to deliver the notice inclosed outlawing Hurst and his command.

I am, general, very respectfully, your obedient servant,

N. B. Forrest, Major-General.[122]

Forrest to Union General Ralph Pomeroy Buckland, March 22, 1864:
☞ HDQRS. DEPT. OF WEST TENN. AND NORTH MISS., IN THE FIELD, MARCH 22, 1864. BRIGADIER-GENERAL BUCKLAND OR COMMANDING OFFICER U. S. FORCES, MEMPHIS, TENN.:

General: I have the honor to transmit the inclosed report, prepared from a thorough investigation of all the facts in the premises :

I respectfully demand that restitution be made by the U.S. authorities in the sum of $5,139.25 to the citizens of Jackson, Tenn., the amount extorted from them by [Yankee] Col. Fielding Hurst, on or about the 12th day of February, 1864, under threats of burning the town. It appears that within the past two months seven cases of deliberate murder have been committed in this department, most of them known and all believed to have been perpetrated by the command of Colonel Hurst. I therefore demand the surrender of Col. Fielding Hurst and the officers and men of his command guilty of these murders, to be dealt with by the C.S. authorities as their offenses require. It has also come to my knowledge that many citizens of this portion of the State are now held in confinement by the U.S. authorities against whom no charges have been preferred, among them the Rev. G. W. D. Harris, of Dyer County, Tenn., now in confinement at Fort Pillow.

I demand that Mr. Harris be granted a fair trial before a competent tribunal, or else unconditionally and promptly released, or otherwise I shall place in close confinement 5 Federal soldiers, now in my hands, as hostages for his protection, and in case he should die in your hands from ill treatment these men shall be duly executed in retaliation.

Lieut. Col. W. M. Reed, bearer of these dispatches and temporarily attached to my staff, is hereby authorized to examine any communications which may be delivered in reply to the above, and also to conclude such arrangements as may arise from the subjects hereinbefore mentioned, or otherwise to deliver such papers as by me he is authorized in possible contingencies to present.

I am, general, very respectfully, your obedient servant,

N. B. Forrest, Major-General, Commanding.[123]

Still angry over the outrages of Union General Fielding Hurst, Forrest fired off a second dispatch on March 22, 1864:

☞ HDQRS. DEPT. OF WEST TENN. AND NORTH MISS., IN THE FIELD, MARCH 22, 1864.

To whom it may concern: Whereas it has come to the knowledge of the major-general commanding that Col. Fielding Hurst, commanding [Sixth] Regiment U.S. [Tennessee Cavalry] Volunteers, has been guilty of wanton extortion upon the citizens of Jackson, Tenn., and other places, guilty of depredations upon private property, guilty of house burning, guilty of murders, both of citizens and soldiers of the Confederate States; and whereas demand has been duly made upon the military authorities of the United States for the surrender of said Col. Fielding Hurst and such officers and men of his command as are guilty of these outrages; and whereas this just demand has been refused by said authorities: I therefore declare the aforesaid Fielding Hurst, and the officers and men of his command, outlaws, and not entitled to be treated as prisoners of war falling into the hands of the forces of the Confederate States.

N. B. Forrest, Major-General, Commanding.

Note.—Lieutenant-Colonel Reed is authorized to deliver this notice in the event an unsatisfactory answer is given to the demands made.[124]

Forrest to Union Colonel Isaac R. Hawkins, March 24, 1864, during an engagement with the Yanks near Union City, Tennessee:

☞ HEADQUARTERS C.S. FORCES, IN THE FIELD, MARCH 24, 1864. OFFICER U.S. FORCES AT UNION CITY, TENN.:

Sir: I have your garrison completely surrounded, and demand an unconditional surrender of your forces. If you comply with the demand, you are promised the treatment due to prisoners of war, according to usages in civilized warfare. If you persist in defense, you must take the consequences.

By order of Maj. Gen. N. B. Forrest.[125]

Forrest to U.S. Colonel Stephen G. Hicks, March 25, 1864, during the Battle of Paducah, Kentucky:

☞ HEADQUARTERS FORREST'S CAVALRY CORPS, COLONEL HICKS, PADUCAH, KY., MARCH 25, 1864. COMMANDING FEDERAL FORCES AT PADUCAH:

Colonel: Having a force amply sufficient to carry your works and reduce the place, and in order to avoid the unnecessary effusion of blood, I demand the surrender of the fort and troops, with all public property. If you surrender, you shall be treated as prisoners of war; but if I have to storm your works, you may expect no quarter.

N. B. Forrest, Major-General, Commanding Confederate Troops.[126]

Forrest to U.S. Colonel Stephen G. Hicks, March 26, 1864, after beating him at the Battle of Paducah:

☞ HEADQUARTERS FORREST'S CAVALRY CORPS NEAR PADUCAH, KY., MARCH 26, 1864. COL. S. G. HICKS, COMMANDING FEDERAL FORCES AT PADUCAH, KY.:

Sir: I understand you hold in your possession in the guard-house at Paducah a number of Confederate soldiers as prisoners of war. I have in my possession about 35 or 40 Federal soldiers who were captured here yesterday, and about 500 who were captured at Union City. I propose to exchange man for man, according to rank, so far as you may hold Confederate soldiers.

Respectfully,

N. B. Forrest, Major-General, Commanding Confederate Forces.[127]

Forrest to General Leonidas Polk, March 27, 1864:

☞ REPORTS OF MAJ. GEN. NATHAN B. FORREST, C.S. ARMY, COMMANDING CAVALRY. DRESDEN, TENN., MARCH 27, 1864. [TO: LIEUTENANT-GENERAL POLK, DEMOPOLIS:]

General: Left Jackson on the 23d. Captured Union City on the 24th, with 450 prisoners, among them the renegade Hawkins and most of his regiment, about 200 horses, and 500 small-arms; also took possession of Hickman, the enemy having passed it. I moved now with Buford's division direct from Jackson to Paducah in fifty hours; attacked it on the evening of the 26th; drove the enemy to their gun-boats and forts; held the town for ten hours, and could have held it longer, but found the small-pox was raging and evacuated the place. Captured many stores and horses, burned up sixty bales of cotton, one steamer and the dry-dock, bringing out 50 prisoners.

My loss at Union City and Paducah, as far as known, is 25 killed and wounded, among them Colonel Thompson, commanding Kentucky brigade, killed; Lieutenant-Colonel Lannom, Faulkner's regiment, mortally wounded, and Colonel Crossland, of the Seventh Kentucky, and Lieutenant-Colonel Morton, of the Second Tennessee, slightly wounded.

Enemy's loss in Paducah 50 killed, wounded, and prisoners; in all, 500.

Have dispatched Gholson, at Tupelo, to meet prisoners at Corinth and take them to you.

I hold possession of all this country except posts on the river. Think if I can remain unmolested here fifteen days I will be able to add 2,000 men to my command.

N. B. Forrest, Major-General.[128]

Forrest to Confederate General Leonidas Polk, April 2, 1864:
☞ JACKSON, TENN., APRIL 2, 1864. LIEUTENANT-GENERAL POLK:

Sir: Six hundred Federal prisoners will arrive at Ripley, Miss., to-day en route for Demopolis.

Colonel Neely engaged Hurst on the 29th of March near Bolivar, capturing his entire wagon train, routing and driving him to Memphis, killing 30 and capturing 35 prisoners, killing 2 captains and capturing 1. I am moving McCulloch's brigade to Gibson County. Must rest my horses ten or fifteen days; many broken down.

If General [S. D.] Lee was here with his command we could gather 5,000 men in ten days.

N. B. Forrest, Major-General.[129]

Forrest to Lieutenant Colonel Thomas M. Jack, April 4, 1864, shortly before the Battle of Fort Pillow:

☞ HEADQUARTERS FORREST'S CAVALRY DEPARTMENT, JACKSON, TENN., APRIL 4, 1864. [TO: LIEUT. COL. THOMAS M. JACK, ASSISTANT ADJUTANT-GENERAL:]

Colonel: I desire respectfully and briefly to state that Lieutenant-Colonel Crews, commanding battalion, met the enemy yesterday morning, and after a sharp little engagement repulsed and drove them back to Raleigh. The enemy's force was two regiments of cavalry of Grierson's command. The fight occurred 15 miles east of Raleigh, on Somerville road. Colonel Crews lost 1 man severely and 1 slightly wounded. The enemy had 6 killed and 15 or 20 wounded and 3 prisoners.

In all engagements so far in West Tennessee my loss in the aggregate is 15 killed and 42 wounded. Among the killed[,] Colonel Thompson, commanding Kentucky brigade, whose death was reported to you by telegraph. Lieutenant-Colonel Lannom, of Faulkner's regiment, reported mortally wounded, is, I am glad to say, rapidly recovering.

The loss of the enemy thus far is as follows: 79 killed, 102 wounded, and 612 captured. I have as far as prudent allowed my troops an opportunity of going home. Am now concentrating and preparing for any move the enemy may make, or for offensive operations, provided they do not move on me. I feel confident of my ability to whip any cavalry they can send against me, and can, if necessary, avoid their infantry. If permitted to remain in West Tennessee, or rather, if it is not the purpose of the lieutenant-general commanding to order me elsewhere until driven out by the enemy, would be glad to have my artillery with me, and will send for it as I could operate effectively with my rifle battery on the rivers. With the small guns I have here it would be folly to attempt the destruction or capture of boats. I am yet in hopes the lieutenant-general commanding will repair and operate the railroad to Corinth, as suggested in a former letter. I, of course, cannot tell what demands are being made on him for troops, but am clearly of opinion that with a brigade of infantry at Corinth as a force upon which I could fall back if too hard pressed, that I can hold West Tennessee against three times my numbers, and could send rapidly out from here all conscripts and deserters for service in infantry. At present it is impracticable, as I am without the transportation necessary to supply them with rations to Okolona through a country already depleted and whose inhabitants are suffering for food. I find corn scarcer than I had thought, but I have plenty of meal, flour, and bacon for troops. If supplied with the right kind of money or cotton can furnish my command with all small-arm ammunition required, and I think with small-arms also

General Chalmers is here, and will be kept in readiness for any move that may be made from Memphis. General Buford's division is above this, and concentrating at Eaton, 10 miles west of Trenton. As I came up here [I] employed a man to get up lead. He writes me that he has from 8,000 to 10,000 pounds at Corinth, which I shall send out as soon as possible, and will continue to get up all that can be had. There is a Federal force of 500 or 600 at Fort Pillow, which I shall attend to in a day or two, as they have horses and supplies which we need. There are about 6,000 troops now at Memphis; all else gone up the river. It is clear that they are concentrating all their available force before Richmond and at Chattanooga. They have attempted to send their cavalry across the country to Pulaski, Tenn. Have driven them back and hope yet to be able to make them take water. I have ordered everything belonging to my command at Columbus moved up to Aberdeen, and Morton's battery up to Tupelo to report to General Gholson, and shall bring it on here unless ordered to the contrary, as the little guns I have are of no use to me. You will please send any orders or dispatches for me through General Gholson, at Tupelo.

I am, colonel, very respectfully, your obedient servant,

N. B. Forrest, Major-General, Commanding.[130]

Forrest to Confederate General Joseph Eggleston Johnston, April 6, 1864:
☞ HEADQUARTERS FORREST'S CAVALRY, JACKSON, TENN., APRIL 6, 1864. GENERAL JOSEPH E. JOHNSTON:

General: I desire to return you my thanks for past favors received while you were in command of this department and to say that so far I have been successful in every engagement with the enemy and have accomplished all that could be reasonably expected of me. I have in my command four small brigades of cavalry of about 1,200 men each, and if permitted to hold this country will increase it in a short time to perhaps 2,000 more. One of my brigades is composed exclusively of Kentuckians, and Col. T. G. Woodward is exceedingly anxious to become attached to it. His command is very small and was raised in Southern and Southwestern Kentucky, and I think if transferred to me could be readily filled up. At any rate, if the transfer be made I will send to your army from the conscripts and deserters in this portion of the State at least two men for every one of Colonel Woodward's command that may be sent to me. As to whether the good of the service requires or permits the change is a matter left entirely to your better judgment. Am exceedingly anxious to further Colonel Woodward's wishes, provided it meets with your approbation. I have at present entire possession of West Tennessee and Kentucky south and west of Tennessee River, except the posts on the river of Memphis, Fort Pillow, Columbus, and Paducah. My men are in fine spirits and my command harmonious, and I hope to accomplish much during the spring and summer. My loss in all engagements and skirmishes with the enemy since I re-entered West Tennessee is 15 killed and 42 wounded; that of the enemy over 800. Have sent to [Confederate] General Polk over 600 prisoners, and their killed was 72 and balance of the 800 wounded. The Sixteenth and Twentieth Army Corps (Federal) have gone up the river from Memphis—reported destination Chattanooga and Pulaski [Tenn.]. I am of the opinion that everything available is being concentrated against General Lee and yourself. Am also of opinion that if all the cavalry of this and your own department could be moved against Nashville that the enemy's communication could be utterly broken up.

I am, general, with great respect, your most obedient servant, N. B. Forrest, Major-General.[131]

Forrest to Confederate Colonel Thomas M. Jack, April 10, 1864:
☞ HEADQUARTERS FORREST'S CAVALRY DEPARTMENT, JACKSON, TENN., APRIL 10, 1861. LIEUT. COL. THOMAS M. JACK, ASSISTANT ADJUTANT-GENERAL:

Colonel: I have the honor to state that Captain Oliver has reported to these headquarters with orders to thoroughly inspect my command, and regret very much that the position and the duties of the troops render it totally impossible for him to do so. In order to watch the enemy in all directions the command is much scattered, and heavy scouting as well as frequent moves are rendered unavoidable by scarcity of forage, preventing concentration at any one point, and no report or inspection can take place until I can draw in the regiments on outpost duty and get returns also from that portion of my command stationed on the Tallahatchie [River] and those with my wagon trains at Aberdeen.

I expect in the course of ten or twelve days to move back into North Mississippi and expect to take out with me at least 2,000 more troops, conscripts amid deserters included; if not moved upon by the enemy in that time will probably get out with even a greater number. Will then have my command together and full reports and thorough will be made. I have four regiments in Southern Kentucky, with orders as they move back to bring with them every man they can get hold of between the ages of eighteen and forty-five. Governor Harris is at Paris with a detachment of men who are performing the same duty. Bell's brigade, of Buford's division, is posted from Bolivar around by Raleigh, with orders to take up and send to Jackson every one subject to military duty and all absentees from the army. Would be glad if the lieutenant-general commanding would give me instructions as to what disposition to make of them; only those will be received in the cavalry who are well mounted. Old commands will be, as far as practicable, filled up; the balance will be forwarded or held as you may direct.

The enrollment of men between the ages of seventeen and eighteen and forty-five and fifty years of age is in my opinion of doubtful policy (at least for the present) in this section, as, according to law, they are held to duty only in the State and could only be removed temporarily from the State. Will carry out, however, as far as practicable, any orders the lieutenant-general may give in regard to this or other measures deemed necessary to secure the enrollment or conscription in West Tennessee or North Mississippi.

I am, colonel, very respectfully, your obedient servant,
N. B. Forrest, Major-General, Commanding.[132]

Forrest to Confederate General Stephen Dill Lee, April 10, 1864:
☛ HEADQUARTERS FORREST'S CAVALRY, JACKSON, TENN., APRIL 10, 1864. MAJOR-GENERAL LEE, COMMANDING

CAVALRY:

General: Your dispatch of the 6th instant is this moment received. I have heard nothing from General Polk since leaving Columbus. I requested General Polk to allow you to move with your command to this place for the purpose of operating against the enemy and conscripting this portion of the State. I would advise that you move immediately from Holly Springs to Brownsville, as that portion of the country is more abundantly supplied with forage, and also because I have a pontoon bridge at Brownsville. I will order that rations be procured for your division at that point. I move to-morrow on Fort Pillow with two brigades, the force at that point being 300 whites and 600 negroes. [Union General] Grierson is reported moving up the State line road from Memphis, and I would suggest that you look well to that quarter. Colonel Neely, commanding Richardson's brigade, is near Raleigh and east of Wolf River. I will return to this point by the 15th.

I am, general, with respect, your obedient servant,

N. B. Forrest, Major-General, Commanding.[133]

On April 12, 1864, Forrest and his men fought at the infamous Battle of Fort Pillow, where, according to Yankee mythology, the General and his men slaughtered surrendering Union soldiers, disproportionately targeting black Union soldiers. I have discussed this slanderous anti-South propaganda at length in my work A Rebel Born *and so need not go over the same territory here. Instead, we will allow Forrest's reports of the engagement to speak for themselves. The first is an April 12, 1864, battlefield dispatch from Forrest to Union Major Lionel F. Booth, commander of Yankee forces at the conflict:*

☛ HEADQUARTERS, CONFEDERATE CAVALRY, NEAR FORT PILLOW, TENN., APRIL 12, 1864. MAJ. L. F. BOOTH, COMMANDING U.S. FORCES AT FORT PILLOW:

Major: The conduct of the officers and men garrisoning Fort Pillow has been such as to entitle them to being treated as prisoners of war. I demand the unconditional surrender of the [entire] garrison, promising that you shall be treated as prisoners of war. My men have [just] received a fresh supply of ammunition, and from their present position can easily assault and capture the fort. Should my demand be refused, I cannot be responsible for the fate of your command.

Very respectfully, your obedient servant,

N. B. Forrest, Major-General, Commanding Confederate Cavalry.[134]

When Booth made an attempt to delay this demand, Forrest quickly followed it with another:

☞ HEADQUARTERS CONFEDERATE CAVALRY, NEAR FORT PILLOW, APRIL 12, 1864. MAJ. L. F. BOOTH, COMMANDING U.S. FORCES AT FORT PILLOW:

I have the honor to acknowledge the receipt of your note, asking one hour to consider my demand for your surrender. Your request cannot be granted. I will allow you twenty minutes from the receipt of this note for consideration; if at the expiration of that time the fort is not surrendered, I shall assault it. I do not demand the surrender of the gun-boat.

Very respectfully, your obedient servant,

N. B. Forrest, Major-General, C.S. Army.[135]

Forrest to U.S. Captain James Marshall, April 12, 1864, after the Battle of Fort Pillow:

☞ HEADQUARTERS FORREST'S CAVALRY. CAPTAIN MARSHALL, PORT PILLOW. APRIL 12, 1864. COMMANDING GUN-BOAT NO. 7, U. S. NAVY:

Sir: My aide-de-camp, Capt. Charles W. Anderson, is fully authorized to negotiate with you for the delivery of the wounded of the [Federal] garrison at this place [upon your own or any other U.S. vessel] on board your vessel.

I am, very respectfully, yours, &c.,

N. B. Forrest, Major-General.[136]

Forrest to Confederate General James Ronald Chalmers, April 13, 1864:

☞ DURHAMVILLE, TENN., APRIL 13, 1864. BRIG. GEN. J. R. CHALMERS:

General: I am directed by Lieutenant-General Polk to move with my command to Alabama, to join General Lee to meet a Federal raid upon that State. You will collect McCulloch's and Bell's brigades together as rapidly as possible, and move to Brownsville and prepare to move to Tupelo with these two brigades, the artillery, wagons, and prisoners. I have ordered Lieutenant-Colonel Forrest, with all of Bell's men at Trenton, to join you at Brownsville. I wish you to come on to Brownsville at once to see me before I go to Jackson. Bring Colonel Bell with you if no damage threatens your command. I will remain at Brownsville until 12 m. [midnight] to-morrow.

Respectfully,

N. B. Forrest, Major-General, Commanding.[137]

Forrest to Confederate General Leonidas Polk, April 15, 1864, concerning the Battle of Fort Pillow:

☞ JACKSON, TENN., APRIL 15, 1864. [TO: LIEUTENANT-GENERAL POLK, DEMOPOLIS:]

General: I attacked Fort Pillow on the morning of the 12th instant with a part of Bell's and McCulloch's brigades, numbering 1,500, under Brig. Gen. James R. Chalmers. After a short fight drove the enemy, 700 strong, into the fort under the cover of their gun-boats. Demanded a surrender, which was declined by Maj. L. F. Booth commanding U. S. forces. I stormed the fort, and after a contest of thirty minutes captured the entire garrison, killing 500 and taking 200 horses and a large amount of quartermaster's stores. The officers in the fort were killed, including Major Booth. I sustained a loss of 20 killed and 60 wounded. Among the wounded is the gallant Lieut. Col. Wiley M. Reed while leading the Fifth Mississippi. Over 100 citizens who had fled to the fort to escape conscription ran into the river and were drowned. The Confederate flag now floats over the fort. N. B. Forrest, Major-General.

N. B. Forrest, Major-General.[138]

Forrest to Confederate Lieutenant Colonel Thomas M. Jack, April 15, 1864:

☞ HEADQUARTERS FORREST'S CAVALRY, JACKSON, TENN., APRIL 15, 1864. [TO: LIEUT. COL. THOMAS M. JACK:]

A dispatch of the 9th instant from the lieutenant-general commanding reached me on the morning of the 13th at Fort Pillow. Orders were issued at once to have the same complied with. Brigadier-General Chalmers, commanding MoCulloch's and Bell's brigades, was ordered to make the necessary preparations for moving to Okolona by way of Abbeville, that being the only route upon which forage could be obtained with facility. Col. J. J. Neely, commanding Richardson's brigade, was ordered to put himself in readiness to report to and follow General Chalmers as early as possible. Brigadier-General Buford, commanding one brigade in Kentucky, is ordered to this point, and will be here by Tuesday next (the 19th), when he will follow on also. They will proceed to Okolona and there report to you. I am in hopes to be able to come on at the same time, but am now suffering from exhaustion, caused by hard riding and bruises received in the late engagement. I will leave Colonel Duckworth's regiment and Lieutenant-Colonel Crews' battalion for the purpose of conscripting the State and holding the guerrillas in check. You will please give such instructions as you may desire to my quartermaster and commissary, whom I ordered to remain at Aberdeen, that being a central point. Please communicate your instructions to me or Brigadier-General Chalmers at Okolona. Have dispatched by telegraph of the capture of Fort Pillow.

Arrived there on the morning of the 12th and attacked the place with a portion of McCulloch's and Bell's brigades, numbering about 1,500 men, and after a sharp contest captured the garrison and all of its stores. A demand was made for the surrender, which was refused. The victory was complete, and the loss of the enemy will never be known from the fact that large numbers ran into the river and were shot and drowned. The force was composed of about 500 negroes and 200 white soldiers (Tennessee Tories). The river was dyed with the blood of the slaughtered for 200 yards [this sentence was an off-the-cuff exaggeration on Forrest's part, one that, unfortunately, was later used against him in the creation of the "Fort Pillow Massacre Myth"].[139] There was in the fort a large number of citizens who had fled there to escape the conscript law. Most of these ran into the river and were drowned.

The approximate loss was upward of 500 killed, but few of the officers escaping.

It is hoped that these facts will demonstrate to the Northern people that [Northern] negro soldiers cannot cope with [white and black] Southerners. We still hold the fort.

My loss was about 20 killed and about 60 wounded. Among the latter I regret to state Lieut. Col. W. M. Reed, commanding Georges regiment. He was shot in three places, and it is feared that his wounds may prove mortal. The country can ill afford to lose the services of so good and brave an officer at this time.

There has been no larger force up the Tennessee River than 1,500 Yankees, who came out to Purdy but were driven back to their boats by one regiment, when they went up to Waterloo and thence across to Athens, Ala. A small squad of about 50 cavalry came across the river, but hearing of our force immediately returned.

I have done but little conscripting from being so constantly employed in operating against the enemy. Large numbers of the Tories have been killed and made away with, and the country is very near free of them. Greenbacks [Confederate money] have gone down, and are being refused. Could I but stay here a month would have everything in fine condition. Parties have come up and expressed their willingness to take Confederate money. Kentucky could be placed in the same condition had I the time.

In conclusion, I desire to bring to the notice of the lieutenant-general commanding the great want of artillery, and it is hoped that the guns recently captured will be fitted up and put in such a condition as will enable the battery to move with the command. I have been unable to supply my artillery with horses, from the fact that the captured stock is very inferior and has to supply the place of the horses killed in action. The enemy's navigation of the rivers has been uninterrupted from the want of this important branch of the service, and it is to be hoped that the lieutenant-general commanding will give the matter his earliest attention.

I am, colonel, with respect, your obedient servant,

N. B. Forrest.[140]

Forrest to Confederate President Jefferson Davis, April 15, 1864:
☞ HEADQUARTERS FORREST'S CAVALRY JACKSON, TENN., APRIL 15, 1864. [TO: HIS EXCELLENCY JEFFERSON DAVIS, PRESIDENT CONFEDERATE STATES OF AMERICA:]

Dear Sir: Having an opportunity of sending a letter direct to Richmond by a friend who leaves here in the morning, and believing that your Excellency would be glad to receive as information a detailed statement of the condition of things in this section, I have taken the liberty of addressing you this communication. North Mississippi, West

Tennessee, and Southern Kentucky, west of the Tennessee River, are free from Federal rule and occupation, except by their garrisons at Memphis and Paducah. There may be a small force at Columbus, but my last advices were that the enemy had or intended evacuating it. They look upon Memphis as being the next point of attack, and are reported as having moved all stores and valuables within their fortifications at Fort Pickering.

I am glad to state that in all the engagements I have had with them since I re-entered West Tennessee we have been successful. The bands of guerrillas, horse-thieves, and robbers which infested this region have been broken up and dispersed, and many men heretofore Union in sentiment are openly expressing themselves for the South. There are yet a large number of men in West Tennessee who have avoided the service, and there is but little prospect for adding to our strength by volunteering. Conscription, however, would, I think, give us from 5,000 to 8,000 men, perhaps more. I have not, from constant marches and active operations in the field, been able to do much in conscripting those to military duty, but design doing so effectively whenever I can with safety send detachments in all directions to scour the country for deserters and conscripts. My command consists of four small brigades, numbering about 5,000 men, and being in a country entirely surrounded (except at the south) by navigable streams, by which the enemy could gain my rear, it has required constant watchfulness to protect myself against possible movements and act offensively at the same time.

I left Columbus, Miss., on March 16 with Buford's division (without wagons) with five days cooked rations and 60 rounds of ammunition to the man, and reached this place on the 23d. After resting my horses and preparing more rations moved rapidly northward against Union City and Paducah; captured Union City on the 24th with over 400 prisoners, 200 horses, and several hundred stand of arms.

While the move of a portion of the command was made against Union City, with the balance I moved rapidly on Paducah, drove the enemy to their boats and fortifications, held the town for ten hours, capturing a large amount of clothing, several hundred horses, a large lot of medical stores for the command, burning a steamer, the dock, and all cotton on the lauding. Could have held the place longer, but on account of the prevalence of small-pox in the place thought it prudent to withdraw.

On Monday last I moved against Fort Pillow, and attacked it on Tuesday morning with Chalmers' division. The advance of our troops after getting within the outer works was cautiously and slowly made. The cannonading from the fort and the gun-boats was very heavy and rapid. Having gained the desired position, surrounding the fort with the troops from the river above to its bluff below, a surrender was demanded, which they asked an hour, but were given twenty minutes, to consider. It was held by about 700 white and negro troops. At the expiration of the twenty minutes the fire was renewed, the assault was made, and the works carried without a halt, the men and officers displaying great gallantry and courage. The enemy attempted to retreat to the river, either for protection of gun-boats or to escape, and the slaughter was heavy. There were many Union men who had taken shelter in the fort also, many of whom in their fright leaped into the river and were drowned. It is safe to say that in troops, negroes, and citizens the killed, wounded, and drowned will range from 450 to 500.

My loss is 20 killed and 60 wounded.

After securing all the stores we could remove and the artillery (six pieces) I withdrew my troops and destroyed all the buildings and the works as far as practicable, burying the dead and removing the wounded. The victory was complete, and the conduct of my troops and the officers commanding them shall meet with due attention and mention in my official report.

I am ordered back to Okolona, Miss., by General Polk with my command to meet, in conjunction with General [S. D.] Lee, an anticipated raid through Alabama from Middle Tennessee. It is my opinion that no such raid will be made from Decatur or any point west of there. General Lee has about 7,000 cavalry, and with our forces united a move could be made into Middle Tennessee and Kentucky which would create a diversion of the enemy's forces and enable us to break up his plans, and such an expedition, managed with prudence and executed with rapidity, can be safely made.

I am gratified in being able to say that the capture of Hawkins at Union City, and Bradford at Fort Pillow, with a recent defeat (by Richardson's brigade, of my command) of Colonel Hurst, has broken up the Tennessee Federal regiments in the country. Their acts of oppression, murder, and plunder made them a terror to the whole land. For murders committed I demanded that Fielding Hurst and such of his men as were guilty of murder should be delivered to me, to be dealt with as their offenses required. The demand has been referred to the proper Federal authorities and investigations ordered. Hurst and his command have, as I learn, been sent, in consequence of this demand, to some other locality.

Mr. William McGee, who carries you this, belongs to a Louisiana battery. He is a native of Tennessee, and his relatives and friends are here. He is anxious to change his command and report to me, and if consistent with the good of the service, and it meets your approbation, I should be glad to have him ordered to me for duty, as I am in great need of competent artillerists. They are required to drill and render efficient as speedily as possible the new men with which our batteries are being filled up.

I am, sir, with great respect, your obedient servant,

N. B. Forrest, Major-General.[141]

Forrest to Confederate General Leonidas Polk, April 16, 1864:
☛ JACKSON, TENN., [APRIL?] 16, 1864. (RECEIVED 21ST.) LIEUTENANT-GENERAL POLK, DEMOPOLIS:

Yours of 11th instant with General Johnston's dispatch just received. Lieutenant-Colonel Kelley, of my old regiment, arrived yesterday from Tuscumbia. He states there are only two regiments at Decatur. No enemy west of Tennessee River from Decatur down. Have also just received dispatch from Colonel [D. M.] Wisdom, dated Purdy, 15th instant, as follows:

> [Colonel Wisdom speaking] "No enemy in this vicinity, and my information induces me to believe that all is quiet in the direction of Eastport. I dispatched you yesterday stating that Brigadier-General Chalmers, commanding McCulloch's and Bell's brigades, were ordered to Okolona by way of Abbeville, and Colonel Neely's brigade was ordered to follow without delay, to report to you on their arrival, 22d instant. No enemy this side of Decatur as far as I can learn. A force came to Tennessee River, opposite Waterloo; burned all the corn in that region and returned to Athens. If forage and rations can be sent to Tupelo, would, on account of position and water, prefer to stop there. Orders will

reach me at Tupelo or General Chalmers at Okolona."

N. B. Forrest, Major-General.[142]

Forrest to Confederate General Thomas M. Jack, April 20, 1864:
☞ HEADQUARTERS FORREST'S CAVALRY COMMAND, JACKSON, TENN., APRIL 20, 1864. COL. T. M. JACK, ASSISTANT ADJUTANT-GENERAL:

Colonel: Governor Harris leaves for department headquarters this morning, and can give the lieutenant-general commanding a statement of affairs as they exist in West Tennessee.

I shall leave here with General Buford as soon as he arrives from Kentucky. A few days delay have unavoidably occurred, as he had detachments out conscripting and recruiting when he received orders to move southward, and it was necessary to gather all up before leaving. I expect to leave here on 22d, day after to-morrow, as I think his Kentucky brigade will reach here to-morrow evening.

General Chalmers with three brigades will be at Okolona before this reaches you. Would be glad if the lieutenant-general commanding would send me orders to Tupelo, and designate the point at which he desires I should hold my command until a move is necessary. My scouts report no enemy west of Decatur, and if a move is made into Alabama I am of opinion it will be from Decatur, or between that and Guntersville.

Have ordered my chief quartermaster and commissary to move to Aberdeen, provided they do not receive orders to the contrary from the lieutenant-general commanding, which he will please give should he deem it proper for them to remain at Columbus. I have ordered Major Rambaut, acting commissary of subsistence, to get up some rations for the command at Okolona, as they can be used there or transported by rail to other points. My scouts have just returned from Florence, and report no enemy between that place and Clifton. The force which came to Waterloo has returned to Athens. There are a few scattering companies of tories on the east side of Tennessee River.

I am, very respectfully, your obedient servant,

N. B. Forrest, Major-General.[143]

Forrest to Confederate General Thomas M. Jack, April 20, 1864:

☞ HEADQUARTERS FORREST'S CAVALRY, JACKSON, TENN., APRIL 20, 1864. LIEUT. COL. THOMAS M. JACK, ASSISTANT ADJUTANT-GENERAL:

Colonel: I wrote you on yesterday morning, per Governor Harris, giving you the movements of my command. After his departure, I received through General Chalmers a dispatch countermanding or revoking the orders to move south; as General Chalmers received the orders before they reached me, he sent back Bell's and Richardson's brigades, and orders were immediately sent then to Colonel Neely, commanding Richardson's brigade, to move down toward Memphis and drive the country back to this place, gathering all conscripts and absentees, and Colonel Bell was ordered to Cherryville to begin close to the Mississippi River, and moving back to this place, to perform the same service. General Buford, then moving south, was ordered to spread out his Kentucky brigade and sweep the country.

Consequently, with the necessary detachments requisite to be sent out in all directions to protect me against any movement of the enemy, my command is much scattered, and it will take time to get them together.

This morning I received a letter from the lieutenant-general commanding, in which he expresses disappointment at not hearing from me oftener; also indicating requirements of my command against the forces of [Union] General [William T.] Sherman.

I have written and forwarded by couriers letters to the lieutenant-general commanding as frequently as I was able to do so; also sent telegraphic dispatches to Tupelo to be forwarded, and am at a loss to know why they have not reached department headquarters. It is true that for more than a week at a time, during my trips to Union City, Paducah, and Fort Pillow, it was impossible to write or dispatch you, being in the saddle myself and commanding my troops in person; results, however, of all my operations as soon as they had transpired have been promptly forwarded.

It will require until the 1st of May to get all my troops together and move out, and my orders to brigade commanders sent out this morning direct that all be gathered up and concentrated at this place on that day, and expect to reach Tupelo with my entire command by the 5th

of May, with all conscripts and deserters we catch. Have also ordered Brigadier-General Chalmers to leave one regiment of McCulloch's brigade on the Tallahatchie [River] and to move back with the balance within the lines of my department and gather up all squads, detached companies, and conscripts found in the country and meet me at Tupelo on the 5th proximo, with his entire wagon and ordnance train.

I have also directed all my wagons and artillery to be moved up to Tupelo; have also ordered my commissary to get up 20,000 rations for my troops and all the forage possible by the 5th, using my teams to haul it to the depots and get the trains, if possible, to bring it up to Tupelo or this side of there, provided it meets with the approval of the lieutenant-general commanding.

I would like to have everything there in order to fully organize the command and shoe up the horses, most of which are in bad condition for want of shoes. I would be glad also, if the lieutenant-general commanding could spare the time, that he would come up on the train and meet me at Tupelo on the 6th or 7th proximo. His presence would facilitate me in disposing of conscripts and organizing commands. As preparatory to the move indicated in his letter, it will require me to be all the time with my command.

I am, colonel, very respectfully, your obedient servant,

N. B. Forrest, Major-General.[144]

Forrest to Confederate Colonel Thomas M. Jack, April 22, 1864:
☞ JACKSON, TENN., APRIL 22, 1864. LIEUT. COL. THOMAS M. JACK:

Colonel: I respectfully acknowledge receipt of orders last night which places McCulloch's brigade at Grenada to co-operate in protecting the country east of Yazoo River, &c., which orders have been promptly given to Brigadier-General Chalmers. I had hoped, however, to collect my entire command at Tupelo (except one regiment), and before it moved again to have it thoroughly inspected, organized, and full and satisfactory reports made as to its numbers, condition, &c.; and if at all consistent with the good of the service I trust the lieutenant-general commanding will order back McCulloch's brigade, except the regiment deemed absolutely necessary to remain on the Tallahatchie [River], to report at Tupelo for the purposes above stated, and place on duty at

Grenada some command whose duties have not been so arduous, and whose animals are in suitable condition for service.

A review of the operations of my command since December last will, I think, justify me in saying that time and opportunity should, if possible, be given me to shoe up and rest my horses, and place my troops in the best possible condition for future service, and to render to the department proper field returns and inspection reports, and to thoroughly organize it at the earliest moment practicable.

I am making arrangements to have all my troops, conscripts, and deserters at Tupelo by the 5th or 6th proximo, and to prepare them for any service required.

There has been no movement of the enemy of any importance since I last wrote you.

[Union General] Grierson came out with about men as far as Mount Pleasant and within 12 miles of Holly Springs, but has returned. He dare not venture across the Wolf or Tallahatchie [Rivers], consequently his scouts are confined to the State Line road and the country between those rivers.

I am, colonel, very respectfully, yours, &c.,
N. B. Forrest, Major-General.[145]

Forrest to Confederate Colonel Thomas M. Jack, April 25, 1864:
☞ HEADQUARTERS FORREST'S CAVALRY, JACKSON, TENN., APRIL 21, 1864. (VIA HOLLY SPRINGS, APRIL 23, 1864; VIA MERIDIAN, APRIL 25, 1864. RECEIVED DEMOPOLIS, APRIL 25, 1864.) COL. THOMAS M. JACK, ASSISTANT ADJUTANT-GENERAL:

Your dispatch of the 19th is just received. McCulloch's brigade from Holly Springs has been ordered to move to Grenada, but owing to long and rapid marches will be compelled to advance slowly. Twelve transports loaded with infantry have passed up the Mississippi River; destination not known. All quiet in this section and on Tennessee River.
N. B. Forrest, Major-General.[146]

Forrest to Confederate Colonel Thomas M. Jack, April 25, 1864:
☞ HEADQUARTERS FORREST'S CAVALRY, JACKSON, APRIL 25, 1864. LIEUT. COL. THOMAS M. JACK, ASSISTANT

ADJUTANT-GENERAL:

Colonel: Everything quiet in this section. One brigade of infantry and fourteen pieces of artillery have been landed at Memphis. They came up the river. My entire command is engaged conscripting and arresting deserters. They are scattered in all directions, but are moving toward this place; will have all concentrated here by the 30th, and will reach Tupelo by the 5th or 6th proximo. I shall move myself via Bolivar and Ripley, and any dispatches for me will meet me on the road.

I would be glad if the [railroad] cars would run as far above Tupelo as possible, as I have about 30,000 pounds of bacon which I shall carry in wagons to Corinth, and send it down for my command on hand-cars until it meets a train.

I am, colonel, very respectfully, yours, &c.,

N. B. Forrest, Major-General.[147]

Forrest to Confederate General Leonidas Polk, April 25, 1864:

☞ HEADQUARTERS FORREST'S CAVALRY, JACKSON, APRIL 25, 1864. LIEUTENANT-GENERAL POLK, COMMANDING DEPARTMENT:

General: A reliable man named Griswell, who used to be a scout of mine in Middle Tennessee, has just arrived. He reports that the enemy are evacuating the Northwestern Railroad, and that they are moving everything to the front by the Nashville and Chattanooga and Tennessee and Alabama Railroads to Chattanooga, and I am satisfied that the enemy's move will be on Dalton. He represents everything as being moved in that direction.

Much having been said in the Northern press in regard to the massacre at Fort Pillow, I shall forward you by next courier copies of all the correspondence in regard to the demand for surrender and a statement of all material facts; an extra copy of same will also be sent you, with a request to forward to the [Confederate] President [Jefferson Davis]. [Union] Captain Young, the provost-marshal at Fort Pillow, now a prisoner, can corroborate all the facts, as he was the bearer of the enemy's flag of truce, and it would be well to have him taken care of on that account.

I am, general, very respectfully, yours, &c.,

N. B. Forrest, Major-General.[148]

What follows is General Forrest's full official field report of the Battle of Fort Pillow. Written on April 26, 1864, it completely contradicts the fictitious Northern version of events:

☞ HEADQUARTERS FORREST'S CAVALRY DEPARTMENT, JACKSON, TENN., APRIL 26, 1864. [TO: PROBABLY LIEUT. COL. THOMAS M. JACK]:

Colonel: I have the honor respectfully to forward you the following report of my engagement with the enemy on the 12th instant at Fort Pillow:

My command consisted of McCulloch's brigade, of Chalmers' division, and Bell's brigade, of Buford's division, both placed for the expedition under the command of Brig. Gen. James R. Chalmers, who, by a forced march, drove in the enemy's pickets, gained possession of the outer works, and by the time I reached the field, at 10 a. m., had forced the enemy to their main fortifications, situated on the bluff or bank of the Mississippi River at the mouth of Cold Creek. The fort is an earth-work, crescent shaped, is 8 feet in height and 4 feet across the top, surrounded by a ditch 6 feet deep and 12 feet in width, walls sloping to the ditch but perpendicular inside. It was garrisoned by 700 troops with six pieces of field artillery. A deep ravine surrounds the fort, and from the fort to the ravine the ground descends rapidly. Assuming command, I ordered General Chalmers to advance his lines and gain position on the slope, where our men would be perfectly protected from the heavy fire of artillery and musketry, as the enemy could not depress their pieces so as to rake the slopes, nor could they fire on them with small-arms except by mounting the breast-works and exposing themselves to the fire of our sharpshooters, who, under cover of stumps and logs, forced them to keep down inside the works. After several hours hard fighting the desired position was gained, not, however, without considerable loss. Our main line was now within an average distance of 100 yards from the fort, and extended from Cold Creek, on the right, to the bluff, or bank, of the Mississippi River on the left.

During the entire morning the gun-boat kept up a continued fire in all directions, but without effect, and being confident of my ability to take the fort by assault, and desiring to prevent further loss of life, I sent, under flag of truce, a demand for the unconditional surrender of the garrison, a copy of which demand is hereto appended, marked No. 1, to which I received a reply, marked No. 2. The gun-boat had ceased firing, but the smoke of three other boats ascending the river was in view, the foremost boat apparently crowded with troops, and believing the request for an hour was to gain time for re-enforcements to arrive, and that the desire to consult the officers of the gun-boat was a pretext by which they desired improperly to communicate with her, I at once sent this reply, copy of which is numbered 3, directing Captain [W. A.] Goodman, assistant adjutant-general of Brigadier-General Chalmers, who bore the flag, to remain until he received a reply or until the expiration of the time proposed.

My dispositions had all been made, and my forces were in a position that would enable me to take the fort with less loss than to have withdrawn under fire, and it seemed to me so perfectly apparent to the garrison that such was the case, that I deemed their [capture] without further bloodshed a certainty. After some little delay, seeing a message delivered to Captain Goodman, I rode up myself to where the notes were received and delivered. The answer was handed me, written in pencil on a slip of paper, without envelope, and was, as well as I remember, in these words: "Negotiations will not attain the desired object." As the officers who were in charge of the Federal flag of truce had expressed a doubt as to my presence, and had pronounced the demand a trick, I handed them back the note saying: "I am General Forrest; go back and say to Major Booth that I demand an answer in plain, unmistakable English. Will he fight or surrender?" Returning to my original position, before the expiration of twenty minutes I received a reply, copy of which is marked No. 4.

While these negotiations were pending the steamers from below were rapidly approaching the fort. The foremost was the *Olive Branch*, whose position and movements indicated her intention to land. A few shots fired into her caused her to leave the shore and make for the opposite. One other boat passed up on the far side of the river, the third one turned back.

The time having expired, I directed Brigadier-General Chalmers to prepare for the assault. Bell's brigade occupied the right, with his extreme right resting on Coal Creek. McCulloch's brigade occupied the left, extending from the center to the river. Three companies of his left regiment were placed in an old rifle-pit on the left and almost in the rear of the fort, which had evidently been thrown up for the protection of sharpshooters or riflemen in supporting the water batteries below. On the right a portion of Barteau's regiment, of Bell's brigade, was also under the bluff and in rear of the fort. I dispatched staff officers to Colonels Bell and McCulloch, commanding brigades, to say to them that I should watch with interest the conduct of the troops; that Missourians, Mississippians, and Tennesseans surrounded the works, and I desired to see who would first scale the fort. Fearing the gun-boats and transports might attempt a landing, I directed my aide-de-camp, Capt. Charles W. Anderson, to assume command of the three companies on the left and rear of the fort and hold the position against anything that might come by land or water, but to take no part in the assault on the fort. Everything being ready, the bugle sounded the charge, which was made with a yell, and the works carried without a perceptible halt in any part of the line. As our troops mounted and poured into the fortification the enemy retreated toward the river, arms in hand and firing back, and their colors flying, no doubt expecting the gun-boat to shell us away from the bluff and protect them until they could be taken off or re-enforced. As they descended the bank an enfilading and deadly fire was poured into them by the troops under Captain Anderson, on the left, and Barteau's detachment on the right. Until this fire was opened upon them, at a distance varying from 30 to 100 yards, they were evidently ignorant of any force having gained their rear. The regiments which had stormed and carried the fort also poured a destructive fire into the rear of the retreating and now panic-stricken and almost decimated garrison. Fortunately for those of the enemy who survived this short but desperate struggle, some of our men cut the halyards, and the United States flag, floating from a tall mast in the center of the fort, came down. The forces stationed in the rear of the fort could see the flag, but were too far under the bluff to see the fort, and when the flag descended they ceased firing. But for this, so near were they to the enemy that few, if any, would have survived unhurt another volley. As it was, many rushed into the river and were drowned, and the actual loss of life will perhaps never be known, as there were quite a number of refugee citizens in the fort, many of whom were drowned and several killed in the retreat from the fort. In less than twenty minutes from the time the bugles sounded the charge, firing had ceased, and the work was done. One of the Parrott guns was turned on the gun-boat. She steamed off without replying. She had, as I afterward understood, expended all her ammunition, and was therefore powerless in affording the Federal garrison the aid and protection they doubtless expected of her when they retreated toward the river. Details were made, consisting of the captured Federals and negroes, in charge of their own officers, to collect together and bury the dead, which work continued until dark.

I also directed Captain Anderson to procure a skiff and take with him Captain Young, a captured Federal officer, and deliver to Captain Marshall, of the gun-boat, the message, copy of which is appended and numbered 5. All the boats and skiffs having been taken off by citizens escaping from the fort during the engagement, the message could not be delivered, although every effort was made to induce Captain Marshall to send his boat ashore by raising a white flag, with which Captain Young walked up and down the river in vain signaling her to come in or send out a boat. She finally moved off and disappeared around the bend above the fort. General Chalmers withdrew his forces from the fort before dark and encamped a few miles east of it.

On the morning of the 13th, I again dispatched Captain Anderson to Fort Pillow for the purpose of placing, if possible, the Federal wounded on board their transports, and report to me on his return the condition of affairs at the river. I respectfully refer you to his report, numbered 6.

My loss in the engagement was 20 killed and 60 wounded. That of the enemy unknown. Two hundred and twenty-eight were buried on the evening of the battle, and quite a number were buried the next day by details from the gun-boat fleet.

We captured 6 pieces of artillery, viz., two 10-pounder Parrott guns, two 12-pounder howitzers, and two brass 6-pounder guns, and about 350 stand of small-arms. The balance of the small-arms had been thrown in the river. All the small-arms were picked up where the enemy fell or threw them down. A few were in the fort, the balance scattered from the top of the hill to the water's edge.

We captured 164 Federals, 75 negro troops, and about 40 negro women and children, and after removing everything of value as far as able to do so, the warehouses, tents, &c., were destroyed by fire.

Among our severely wounded is Lieut. Col. Wiley M. Reed,

assigned temporarily to the command of the Fifth Mississippi Regiment, who fell severely wounded while leading his regiment. When carried from the field he was supposed to be mortally wounded, but hopes are entertained of his ultimate recovery. He is a brave and gallant officer, a courteous gentleman, and a consistent Christian minister.

I cannot compliment too highly the conduct of Colonels Bell and McCulloch and the officers and men of their brigades, which composed the forces of Brigadier-General Chalmers. They fought with courage and intrepidity, and, without bayonets, assaulted and carried one of the strongest fortifications in the country.

On the 15th, at Brownsville, I received orders which rendered it necessary to send General Chalmers, in command of his own division and Bell's brigade, southward; hence I have no official report from him, but will, as soon as it can be obtained, forward a complete list of our killed and wounded, which has been ordered made out and forwarded at the earliest possible moment.

In closing my report I desire to acknowledge the prompt and energetic action of Brigadier-General Chalmers, commanding the forces around Fort Pillow. His faithful execution of all movements necessary to the successful accomplishment of the object of the expedition entitles him to special mention. He has reason to be proud of the conduct of the officers and men of his command for their gallantry and courage in assaulting and carrying the enemy's work without the assistance of artillery or bayonets.

To my staff, as heretofore, my acknowledgments are due for their prompt and faithful delivery of all orders.

I am, colonel, very respectfully, your obedient servant,

N. B. Forrest, Major-General, Commanding.[149]

Forrest to Confederate General Leonidas Polk, April 28, 1864:

☞ HEADQUARTERS FORREST'S CAVALRY, JACKSON, APRIL 28, 1864. LIEUTENANT-GENERAL POLK, MERIDIAN [MISS.]:

Dispatch of 25th received. Will be at Tupelo on 4th May. My command will be there on the 6th. Desire it thoroughly inspected. Dispatch General Gholson to detain officer from Richmond until I arrive. Hope to meet you there also before organizing my command. All quiet.

N. B. Forrest, Major-General.[150]

Forrest to Confederate General Leonidas Polk, April 29, 1864:
☞ JACKSON, TENN., APRIL 29, 1864:

Lieutenant-General Polk: Enemy reported pressing horses and shops to prepare for a move against me from Memphis. Have the regiment on Tallahatchie [River] left by General Chalmers, and will send Colonel Duckworth, of Seventh Tennessee Cavalry, to watch their movements; also will keep you advised.

N. B. Forrest, Major-General.[151]

Forrest to Confederate General Stephen Dill Lee, May 12, 1864:
☞ TUPELO, MISS., MAY 12, 1864.

Maj. Gen. S. D. Lee: The enemy have all returned to Memphis, cavalry and infantry passing below La Grange.

N. B. Forrest, Major-General.[152]

Forrest to Confederate General Stephen Dill Lee, May 13, 1864:
☞ TUPELO, MISS., MAY 13, 1864.

Maj. Gen. S. D. Lee: Scouts report one load troops passed Austin on 7th, upward bound. [Union General] Hurst's men at Commerce burning and stealing.

N. B. Forrest, Major-General.[153]

Forrest to Confederate General Stephen Dill Lee, May 13, 1864:
☞ TUPELO, MISS., MAY 13, 1864. MAJ. GEN. S. D. LEE:
Following just received:

> [Samuel Carter speaking] "Near Memphis, May 13, 1864. (Via Holly Springs.) Federals all returned to Memphis and vicinity; four regiments at White's Station. Good many Red River troops landing at Memphis. Lines closed permanently after the 15th. Two furloughed regiments, Second Iowa and Third Michigan, have returned to Memphis considerably recruited. Still impressing horses in Memphis. Saml. Carter, Henderson Scouts."

N. B. Forrest, Major-General.[154]

Forrest to Confederate General James Ronald Chalmers, May 14, 1864:
☞ TUPELO [MISS.], MAY 14, 1864. GENERAL CHALMERS, [at]

VERONA:

Have three days' cooked rations for Fifth Mississippi and Duckworth's regiment. Order sent by courier to move immediately.

N. B. Forrest, Major-General.[155]

Forrest to Confederate General James Ronald Chalmers, May 14, 1864:

☞ TUPELO [MISS.], MAY 14, 1864.

General Chalmers: If you have not the ammunition for the two regiments, send to this point for it.

N. B. Forrest, Major-General.[156]

Forrest to Confederate General Stephen Dill Lee, May 15, 1864:

☞ TUPELO, MISS., MAY 15, 1864.   GENERAL S. D. LEE, DEMOPOLIS, ALA.:

Have three regiments at Panola and Grenada (Buford's division) move south to Corinth to-morrow. Forage tax in kind is getting scarce on the road. I propose, with your permission, to leave McCulloch's brigade here and send General Chalmers with Gholson's and Neely's brigades, near Aberdeen, to have their horses shod up and to be drilled, and where they can get corn.

N. B. Forrest, Major-General.[157]

Forrest to Confederate General Stephen Dill Lee, May 15, 1864:

☞ TUPELO, MISS., MAY 15, 1864. GENERAL S. D. LEE:

There are about 1,000 men in my command who left the army at its reorganization in spring of 1862. Orders are here to return these men to their command. This will break up Bell's and Neely's brigades and lead to desertion. The immediate execution of orders will be productive of harm, and I ask a suspension of their surrender for sixty days. On being furnished with rolls of their names I can hereafter safely effect their return without injury to my command and detriment to the public service. As it is important, be good enough to telegraph at once to War Office and ask that the order may be suspended for the present.

N. B. Forrest, Major-General.[158]

Forrest to Confederate General Stephen Dill Lee, May 15, 1864:

☞ HEADQUARTERS FORREST'S CAVALRY, TUPELO, MISS.,

MAY 15, 1864. GENERAL S. D. LEE, DEMOPOLIS, ALA:

General: I telegraphed you this evening, suggesting the removal of a portion of my command to Aberdeen, or that vicinity, for the purpose of drilling, shoeing, and to procure a supply of forage. I also telegraphed you to-day in regard to members of my command who are deserters or absentees from other commands. Some officers are here from infantry to identify and get their men. I have given them free access to the muster-rolls in order to get a list of men claimed, but I am firmly of the opinion that until such times as all time regiments who have absentees here can be represented and have officers present to identify their men, that any attemnpt on the part of the few officers now here to recover their men will result in the loss of 800 or 900 men; for, as soon as you commence arresting, the balance, anticipating a similar fate, will take to the woods with arms, equipments, and horses. If all were known and could be taken at once, it might do; but I recommend, under existing circumstances, that the delivery of any portion of these troops be suspended for at least sixty days, or until my command is at some point where it can be surrounded with infantry and the men taken, and arms, equipments, and horses retained. General Buford's division and Morton's and Rice's batteries go to Corinth to-morrow. I shall go up there myself on Wednesday evening or Thursday morning with General Hodge, and remain until the last of the week, leaving my office and headquarters here. I have three regiments at Grenada and Panola, amounting to 1,100 men, which I presume will be force sufficient. McGuirk's, or rather General Gholson's brigade, is green and imperfectly armed, and I think it best to leave Colonel McCulloch's brigade at this place, and let General Chalmers take Neely's and Gholson's commands to some place near Aberdeen and shoe up their stock. The difficulty of getting tax corn delivered on the road for the [railroad] cars is that the planters cannot well spare their teams to haul it, all their stock being required to cultivate their crops.

I am, general, very respectfully, your obedient servant,
N. B. Forrest, Major-General.[159]

Forrest issued the following circular to his troops, May 16, 1864:
☞ $500 REWARD [about $7,500 in today's currency]. TUPELO, MISS., MAY 16, 1864:

The crime of horse stealing has become one of the most frequent, if it is not one of the most common, crimes in all and around the army. Not a day passes without many complaints being made from both officers and soldiers and citizens. It must be stopped, and the major-general commanding is determined if severe punishment inflicted on those convicted of it will stop it that it shall be done. No mercy will be shown in those cases. The above reward will be paid by me for the detection, delivery, and conviction of any officer or private of this command guilty of horse stealing.

N. B. Forrest, Major-General.[160]

Forrest to Confederate General Stephen Dill Lee, May 16, 1864:
☞ HEADQUARTERS FORREST'S CAVALRY, TUPELO, MISS., MAY 16, 1864. MAJ. GEN. S. D. LEE, DEMOPOLIS, ALA.:

General: So much has been said by the Northern press in regard to the engagement at Fort Pillow that, at the suggestion of Colonel Brent and others, I have sent Judge Scruggs down for the purpose of conversing with, and procuring the statements of, Captain Young and other Federal officers in regard to the matter. They are survivors of the so-called massacre, and Captain Young, who received and delivered the correspondence relative to the demand for surrender, was also with my aide-de-camp, Captain Anderson, with flag of truce on the day succeeding the capture in delivering the wounded on board the U. S. vessels. I respectfully suggest, therefore, that you furnish Judge Scruggs with such papers as will enable him to make the examination desired, as it may prove important; and inasmuch as the investigating committee appointed by the Federal President have reported, a communication to Confederate authority may be made on the subject, and it is due to my command to place at the command of the War Department all the facts in the premises.

I am, general, very respectfully &c., your obedient servant,
N. B. Forrest, Major-General.[161]

Forrest to Confederate General Stephen Dill Lee, May 17, 1864:
☞ TUPELO [MISS.], MAY 17, 1864.

Maj. Gen. S. D. Lee: Dispatch received. Will await further orders. Will be at Corinth to-morrow. Write you fully this evening.

N. B. Forrest, Major-General.[162]

Forrest to Confederate Major William Elliott, May 17, 1864:
☞ HEADQUARTERS FORREST'S CAVALRY, TUPELO [MISS.], MAY 17, 1864. MAJ. WILLIAM ELLIOTT, ASSISTANT ADJUTANT-GENERAL:

Major: Since writing to the major-general commanding this morning, I have had an interview with several persons from Memphis and from that neighborhood, and all agree in the opinion that preparations are being made by the enemy for a move or raid into Mississippi. Unless there are indications of a move on Yazoo City and from thence on Central road by the enemy, I would suggest to the major-general commanding that the two regiments at Grenada, under command of Colonel Duckworth, be ordered up to Oxford, for the purpose of meeting any move from Memphis in that direction. Have ordered Captain Henderson, commanding scouts, to telegraph you promptly all information of importance.

I am, very respectfully, your obedient servant,

N. B. Forrest, Major-General.[163]

Forrest to Confederate General Stephen Dill Lee, May 17, 1864:
☞ HEADQUARTERS FORREST'S CAVALRY, TUPELO [MISS.], MAY 17, 1861. [GENERAL S. D. LEE:]

General: Your dispatch ordering a suspension of orders as to the move across the Tennessee was received and answered this morning. There is no doubt in my mind but that a move by the enemy will be made from Memphis, and it may be from Vicksburg also at the same time; at any rate with such a force at Memphis it would be manifestly impolitic to send off the forces ordered and leave the prairie country almost unprotected. If they are strong enough to move on me with my whole force together, they would assuredly do so the moment they learned of my crossing the Tennessee. The effective total of my command is 9,220; total number of guns, 5,416—3,804.

Take the 3,500 best armed and equipped for the expedition ordered and 1,400 at Grenada and Panola, and it would leave General Chalmers here with balance of his division and Gholson's brigade with less than700 guns. It is due to the families of absent soldiers, many of whom are now suffering for bread, that the railroad and the breadstuffs and provisions in the valley should be abundantly protected, and for our army it is a necessity, for in this department it is only abundant and available in country or region referred to. Again, I think 3,500 men too small a force to send into Middle Tennessee, and 700 muskets wholly insufficient for the defense of the railroad and forage below here. General Gholson has arrived and requisitions will be made out for his arms and equipments. As soon as armed I shall, unless otherwise ordered or circumstances change, send him with his brigade over to Grenada and Panola and return the regiments now there to the division to which they belong, believing it better, as far as practicable, to keep the commands of each division together. I find I shall need thirty or forty more horses to fit up my caissons, and would be glad if you would remind Colonel Kennard as to forwarding as promptly and as rapidly as possible everything which has been required for; nothing has reached here yet but some ammunition. I shall go up to Corinth to-morrow. Had written [Confederate General Philip D.] Roddey to prepare a crossing and to meet me at Bear Creek with all the wagons he had or could get to assist in carrying up corn. Have sent him a special courier advising him of the suspension of the order. If you get the guns at Selma or Montgomery please forward them with the utmost dispatch.

I am, general, very respectfully, your obedient servant,

N. B. Forrest, Major-General.[164]

Forrest to Confederate General Stephen Dill Lee, May 18, 1864:
☛ TUPELO [MISS.], MAY 18, 1864.

Maj. Gen. S. D. Lee: Gholson's command has nothing. Dispatch received countermanding move.

N. B. Forrest, Major-General.[165]

Forrest to Confederate General Stephen Dill Lee, May 21, 1864:
☛ HEADQUARTERS FORREST'S CAVALRY, TUPELO [MISS.], MAY 21, 1864. MAJ. GEN. S. D. LEE, COMMANDING DEPARTMENT:

General: According to your verbal instructions, I have been collecting all unattached companies for the purpose of completing organizations, and find, according to the letter of Captain Armstrong, that in one case my order has clashed with yours. Wishing to avoid anything of the kind, I have thought it best to send Major Harris, who commands a battalion in General Gholson's brigade, down to see you and confer with you as to filling up his command to a regiment. Orders have been given prohibiting the raising of new cavalry commands, and, if desirable to fill up the two battalions of General Gholson's brigade, I presume it will have to be done with detached companies already organized. General Gholson's brigade is composed of three regiments and two battalions, but has only men enough to make about three full regiments. General Bragg's order was to receive them as they were, and General Gholson to command them, and I send Major Harris down to confer with you in regard to filling them up or consolidating them, respectfully asking that you will give such orders as may be necessary in the premises. I would also be glad to have a list of all companies in this section acting under your orders, not attached to any regular command or detached from other commands for conscript or other duty, that my orders to gather up companies may not interfere with your own. Major Harris is anxious to fill up his battalion to a regiment, and has several companies on their way to him, and if it can be done with unattached Mississippi companies I think it ought to be done.

I am, general, very respectfully, your obedient servant,
N. B. Forrest, Major-General.[166]

Forrest to Confederate General Stephen Dill Lee, May 22, 1864:
☞ TUPELO, MAY 22, 1864.

Maj. Gen. S. D. Lee: General Chalmers will start in the morning with his division and Gholson's brigade, about 4,000 strong. I have no baggage train, have not transportation for other troops. Send cooking utensils from Selma to Montevallo for Gholson, and twenty wagons if possible. Two batteries will be sent with Chalmers.

N. B. Forrest, Major-General.[167]

Forrest to Confederate General Stephen Dill Lee, May 22, 1864:
☞ TUPELO [MISS.], MAY 22, 1864. [TO: MAJ. GEN. S. D. LEE:]
Following received today:

[Captain William Hezekiah Forrest, the General's younger brother, speaking] "Holly Springs, May 22, 1864.

"Brigadier-General Chalmers: Fought the enemy thirteen miles west this evening eighty strong, killing 12, wounding and capturing 5, without losing a man or horse. W. H. Forrest, Captain, Commanding Squadron."

N. B. Forrest, Major-General.[168]

Forrest to Confederate Major William Elliott, May 23, 1864:
☞ HEADQUARTERS FORREST'S CAVALRY, TUPELO, MISS., MAY 23, 1864. MAJ. WILLIAM ELLIOTT, ASSISTANT ADJUTANT-GENERAL, MERIDIAN, MISS.:

Major: I have the honor to herewith inclose a tabular report [below] of the number of troops carried away by Brig. Gen. J. R. Chalmers this morning.

I am, sir, very respectfully, your obedient servant,
N. B. Forrest, Major-General.

[INCLOSURE ATTACHED TO PREVIOUS LETTER]
☞ Field return of Brigadier-General Chalmers' division.
Aggregate present for duty:
Brigadier-General Gholson's brigade: 1,265.
First Brigade, Col. J. J. Neely commanding: 1,389.
Second Brigade, Col. R. McCulloch commanding: 1,029.
One battery: 78.
Total: 4,361.

Duff's regiment, Eighteenth Mississippi Regiment, and Duckworth's regiment, two 10-pounder Parrott guns, and two 12-pounder field howitzers, numbering about 1,200 men, are at Oxford and Panola on detached service.

Headquarters First Division, Tupelo, May 23, 1864.
Respectfully forwarded.
No return from this brigade this morning.
The following report of deserters from the brigade since yesterday has been received:
From Twelfth Tennessee: 7.

From Fourteenth Tennessee: 50.

From Fifteenth Tennessee: 58.

Higg's company: 11.

Total: 126.

Aggregate present:

On yesterday: 1,629.

Deducted: 126.

Total: 1,503.

Jas. R. Chalmers, Brigadier-General.

Respectfully submitted.

  [by] N. B. Forrrest, Major-General.[169]

Forrest to Confederate General Stephen Dill Lee, May 24, 1864:

☞ HEADQUARTERS FORREST'S CAVALRY, TUPELO [MISS.], MAY 24,1864. [GENERAL S. D. LEE:]

  General: Before General Chalmers left here his surgeon came to me (or rather was sent by General Chalmers), and represented to me that the general was suffering from fistula and unable to ride, and unless he could rest and have time to be operated upon would in all probability be unable to do anything during the summer. General Chalmers also spoke of the matter but did not like to apply for leave of absence while his command was needed in the field. He was compelled to leave here in his ambulance. I have made you acquainted with these facts and believe were you to write to General Chalmers that you would place General Pillow or Armstrong or some other officer in his stead until he could be operated upon, he would be glad to accept a leave until he could be restored, and able to take his command.

  I am, general, very respectfully, your obedient servant,

  N. B. Forrest, Major-General.[170]

Forrest to Confederate Major William Elliott, May 26, 1864:

☞ HEADQUARTERS FORREST'S CAVALRY, TUPELO [MISS.], MAY 26, 1864. MAJ. WILLIAM ELLIOTT, ASSISTANT ADJUTANT-GENERAL:

  Major: I have ordered scouts to Memphis on all sides, with a view to ascertain certainly what troops are there, and desire to know of the major-general commanding whether an expedition against the place would meet his approbation. I could have a supply of forage and rations sent to Panola and Abbeville by rail and could leave both points one morning and attack it the next; if the force is too heavy I can move above to Randolph with my command and batteries, and it would take 10,000 men to drive me off. A few hours' work would enable me to fight successfully all the so-called gun-boats they have, or I could move onto the Mississippi River at Commerce and obstruct the navigation of the river, having my flank well protected by Rucker's brigade in the direction of Memphis. It may be the means of preventing re-enforcements to the Trans-Mississippi Department, and I think it more than likely we can capture transports and supplies. Such a move may create diversions which will be of advantage. Anticipating a move into Middle Tennessee, I am satisfied the enemy have a force at Athens and Huntsville. I write for the purpose of knowing the wish of the major-general commanding or his views. If it should be thought best to go above Memphis on the river, I should leave Colonel Rucker, with 1,400 men, as at present, at Abbeville and Panola; if to Commerce, throw his force up to Coldwater and threaten Memphis; if to Memphis, would take everything with me, leaving my wagons, &c., at Abbeville and Panola. If it should become necessary to move into Middle Tennessee, it would be better to move from here than from Corinth, as it would be much nearer and the enemy would have but little opportunity to know of it until we reached Tuscumubia.

I am, very respectfully,

N. B. Forrest, Major-General.[171]

Forrest to Confederate General Stephen Dill Lee, May 29, 1864:
☛ TUPELO [MISS.], MAY 29, 1864.

Maj. Gen. S. D. Lee: The time has arrived, and if I can be spared and allowed 2,00 picked men from Buford's division and a battery of artillery[,] will attempt to cut enemy's communication in Middle Tennessee.

N. B. Forrest, Major-General.[172]

Forrest to Confederate General Stephen Dill Lee, May 29, 1864:
☛ TUPELO [MISS.], MAY 29, 1864.

Maj. Gen. S. D. LEE: Following just received:

[C. T. Barton speaking] "Headquarters Johnson's Brigade, Tuscumbia, Ala., May 28, 1864.

"General Forrest: Colonel Johnson directs me to say that the enemy's Seventeenth Army Corps, 10,000 or 12,000 infantry, cavalry, and artillery, are pressing General [Philip D.] Roddey heavily, and have gotten him as far back as Jonesborough, this side of Courtland, Ala. They have 4,000 or 5,000 cavalry. Have forwarded dispatches to you from General Roddey asking for assistance this morning.

"C. T. Barton, Acting Assistant Adjutant-General."

Respectfully submitted.   N. B. Forrest, Major-General. (Forwarded to General [S. D.] Lee at Selma.)[173]

Forrest to Confederate General Stephen Dill Lee, May 29, 1864:
☞ TUPELO [MISS.], [MAY 29,] 1864.

Maj. Gen. S. D. Lee: General [Philip D.] Roddey dispatches me from near Decatur that the Seventeenth Army Corps has moved to Decatur. Four thousand cavalry and 4,000 infantry came out on 20ᵗʰ, skirmished two hours and a half and returned. The river fordable for large horses. Railroads all guarded by negro troops. He has not moved his troops yet to Talladega; will retain them to develop movements of enemy.

N. B. Forrest, Major-General. (Forwarded to General [S. D.] Lee at Selma.)[174]

Forrest to Confederate General Stephen Dill Lee, May 31, 1864:
☞ TUPELO, MAY 31, 1864.

Maj. Gen. S. D. Lee, McDowell's, Ala., (Selma): Following just received:

[General Philip D. Roddey speaking] "Moulton, Ala., May 29, 1864. On 27ᵗʰ large force infantry, cavalry, and artillery crossed Flint River at Redbank, near Somerville, with very large train of wagons. On 28ᵗʰ another large train of wagons guarded by two regiments cavalry, several of infantry, was traveling in direction of Somerville from Decatur. On 27ᵗʰ six regiments cavalry, four of infantry, four pieces of artillery, advanced from Decatur toward Courtland; impeded their progress as much as possible as far as Courtland. Following morning cavalry was retired in direction of

Moulton and infantry toward Decatur. Last night moved my command here and attacked at daylight, fight lasting three hours; force engaged estimated at 3,000. I withdrew three miles south for position; enemy not pursuing, and is now going in direction of Somerville. Roddey."

General Roddey thinks they are moving to the interior of the State and estimates their force at 8,000 or 9,000, half of which is mounted, and which guard about 400 wagons. Will leave here in the morning with command at daylight, via Fulton and Russellville.

N. B. Forrest, Major-General.[175]

Forrest to Confederate Major William Elliott, May 31, 1864:
☞ HEADQUARTERS FORREST'S CAVALRY, TUPELO, MISS., MAY 31, 1864. MAJ. WILLIAM ELLIOTT, ASSISTANT ADJUTANT-GENERAL:

Major: I have the honor of acknowledging the receipt of yonr favor of the 28th instant. The plan of operations, as suggested by the major-general commanding, is entirely satisfactory to me. I shall leave herein the morning, per Russeliville, Ala., with about 2,200 men, six pieces of artillery, and with ten days rations. I shall leave Colonel Russell in command at this point with his own and Newsom's regiment and the dismounted men of the other six regiments, and with two pieces of artillery. Four companies of Russell's regiment and Kizer's scouts will be kept at Corinth. The force at these two points will number about 1,400 men. Colonel [Edmund Winchester] Rucker is at Oxford with three regiments and a squadron of 150 men under Capt. W. H. Forrest, in all numbering 1,500 men. These officers have been ordered to report to the major-general commanding and to receive such instructions from him as may be necessary.

I am, major, very respectfully, your obedient servant,

N. B. Forrest, Major-General.[176]

Forrest to Confederate General Stephen Dill Lee, June 10, 1864:
☞ BALDWYN, JUNE 10, 1864—10 A.M. MAJOR-GENERAL LEE, [at] OKOLONA:

The enemy are advancing directly to this place. Johnson's brigade is here. Buford's division and Rucker's brigade with two

batteries are moving up and will be here by 12 o'clock. Our pickets
have already commenced firing.

N. B. Forrest, Major-General.[177]

*Forrest to Confederate General James Ronald Chalmers, June 14, 1864 (note:
General Leonidas Polk is purposefully killed—by cannon fire—by Union General
William T. Sherman this day at Pine Mountain, near Marietta, Georgia.
Forrest's correspondence with Polk thus ends, and the "fightin' preacher's" vacant
post is filled by Confederate Major General William W. Loring):*

☞ GUNTOWN, MISS., JUNE 14,1864. BRIGADIER-GENERAL
CHALMERS, COLUMBUS:

Move across Tombigbee River. Remain near Columbus and fit
up your command as early as practicable. If you need any wagons, or,
if any of yours are out of repair, I can supply you. Notify me at Tupelo
of your location.

N. B. Forrest, Major-General.[178]

Forrest to Confederate General James Ronald Chalmers, June 14, 1864:

☞ GUNTOWN [MISS.], JUNE 14, 1864. BRIGADIER-GENERAL
CHALMERS, COLUMBUS:

Barton will be near enough. Shoe up your horses at Columbus
and Aberdeen. Meet me at Columbus on Friday next.

N. B. Forrest, Major-General.[179]

Forrest to Union General Cadwallader Colden Washburn, June 14, 1864:

☞ HEADQUARTERS FORREST'S CAVALRY, IN THE FIELD, JUNE
14, 1864. [MAJ. GEN. C. C. WASHBURN:]

General: I have the honor herewith to inclose copy of letter
received from Brigadier-General Buford, commanding U.S. forces at
Helena, Ark., addressed to [Confederate] Col. E. W. Rucker [Edmund
Winchester Rucker], commanding Sixth Brigade of this command; also
a letter from myself to General Buford, which I respectfully request you
to read and forward to him.

There is a matter also to which I desire to call your attention,
which until now I have not thought proper to make the subject of a
communication. Recent events render it necessary, in fact demand it.

It has been reported to me that all the negro troops stationed in

Memphis took an oath on their knees, in the presence of [Union] Major-General Hurlbut and other officers of your army, to avenge Fort Pillow, and that they would show my troops no quarter. Again, I have it from indisputable authority that the troops under [Union] Brigadier-General [Samuel D.] Sturgis, on their recent march from Memphis, publicly and in various places proclaimed that no quarter would be shown my men. As his troops were moved into action on the 11th [10th] the officers commanding exhorted their men to remeumber Fort Pillow, and a large majority of the prisoners we have captured from that command have voluntarily stated that they expected us to murder them; otherwise they would have surrendered in a body rather than taken to the bush after being run down and exhausted. The recent battle of Tishomingo Creek [Brice's Cross Roads] was far more bloody than it would otherwise have been but for the fact that your men evidently expected to be slaughtered when captured, and both sides acted as though neither felt safe in surrendering, even when further resistance was useless. The prisoners captured by us say they felt condemned by the announcement, &c., of their own commanders, and expected no quarter.

In all my operations since the war began I have conducted the war on civilized principles, and desire still to do, but it is due to my command that they should know the position they occupy and the policy you intend to pursue. I therefore respectfully ask whether my men now in your hands are treated as other Confederate prisoners; also, the course intended to be pursued in regard to those who may hereafter fall into your hands.

I have in my possession quite a number of wounded officers and men of General Sturgis' command, all of whom have been treated as well as we were able to treat them, and are mostly in charge of a surgeon left at Ripley by General Sturgis to look after the wounded. Some of them are too severely wounded to be removed at present. I am willing to exchange them for any men of my command you may have, and as soon as they are able to be removed will give them safe escort through my lines in charge of the surgeon left with them. I made such an arrangement with Major-General Hurlbut when he was in command at Memphis, and am willing to renew it, provided it is desired, as it would be better than to subject them to the long and fatiguing trip necessary to a regular exchange at City Point, Va.

I am, very respectfully, your most obedient servant,

N. B. Forrest, Major-General.[180]

Forrest to Confederate General Stephen Dill Lee, June 15, 1864:

☞ TUPELO [MISS.], JUNE 15, 1864. [TO: GENERAL S. D. LEE:]

General: This is the latest I have, and I forward for your information. I think every preparation should be made to meet the enemy in case they should move out.

Yours, respectfully,

N. B. Forrest, Major-General.[181]

Forrest to Confederate General Stephen Dill Lee, June 22, 1864:

☞ TUPELO [MISS.], JUNE 22, 1864. MAJ. GEN. S. D. LEE:

I am satisfied the enemy are preparing to move against me in large force from Memphis.

N. B. Forrest, Major-General.[182]

Forrest to Union General Cadwallader Colden Washburn, June 23, 1864:

☞ HEADQUARTERS FORREST'S CAVALRY, IN THE FIELD, JUNE 23, 1864. MAJ. GEN. C. C. WASHBURN, COMMANDING U. S. FORCES, MEMPHIS, TENN.:

General: Your communication of the 19th instant is received, in which you say "you are left in doubt as to the course the Confederate Government intends to pursue hereafter in regard to colored troops."

Allow me to say that this is a subject upon which I did not and do not propose to enlighten you. It is a matter to be settled by our Governments through their proper officers, and I respectfully refer you to them for a solution of your doubts. You ask me to state whether "I contemplate either their slaughter or their return to slavery." I answer that I slaughter no man except in open warfare, and that my prisoners, both white and black, are turned over to my Government to be dealt with as it may direct. My Government is in possession of all the facts as regards my official conduct and the operations of my command since I entered the service, and if you desire a proper discussion and decision, I refer you again to the President of the Confederate States.

I would not have you understand, however, that in a matter of so much importance I am indisposed to place at your command and disposal any facts desired, when applied for in a manner becoming an officer holding your rank and position, for it is certainly desirable to every one occupying a public position to be placed right before the world, and there has been no time since the capture of Fort Pillow that I would not have furnished all the facts connected with its capture had they been applied for properly; but now the matter rests with the two Governments. I have, however, for your information, inclosed you copies of the official correspondence between the commanding officers at Fort Pillow and myself; also copies of a statement of Captain Young, the senior officer of that garrison, together with (sufficient) extracts from a report of the affair by my aide-de-camp, Capt. Charles W. Anderson, which I approve and indorse as correct.

As to the death of Major Bradford, I knew nothing of it until eight or ten days after it is said to have occurred. On the 13th (the day after the capture of Fort Pillow) I went to Jackson, and the report that I had of the affair was this: Major Bradford was with other officers sent to the headquarters of Colonel McCulloch, and all the prisoners were in charge of one of McCulloch's regiments. Bradford requested the privilege of attending the burial of his brother, which was granted, he giving his parole to return; instead of returning he changed his clothing and started for Memphis. Some of my men were hunting deserters, and came on Bradford just as he had landed on the south bank of Hatchie, and arrested him. When arrested he claimed to be a Confederate soldier belonging to Bragg's army; that he had been home on furlough, and was then on his way to join his command. As he could show no papers he was believed to be a deserter and was taken to Covington, and not until he was recognized and spoken to by citizens did the guards know that he was Bradford. He was sent by Colonel Duckworth, or taken by him, to Brownsville. All of Chalmers' command went south from Brownsville via La Grange, and as all the other prisoners had been gone some time, and there was no chance for them to catch up and place Bradford with them, he was ordered by Colonel Duckworth or General Chalmers to be sent to me at Jackson. I knew nothing of the matter until eight or ten days afterward. I heard that his body was found near Brownsville. I understand that he attempted to escape, and was shot. If he was improperly killed nothing would afford me more pleasure than to punish the perpetrators to the full extent of the law, and to show you how I regard such transactions I can refer you to my demand upon Major-General Hurlbut (no doubt upon file in your office) for the delivery to Confederate authorities of one Col. Fielding Hurst and others of his regiment, who deliberately took out and killed 7 Confederate soldiers, one of whom they left to die after cutting off his tongue, punching out his eyes, splitting his mouth on each side to his ears, and cutting off his privates.

I have mentioned and given you these facts in order that you may have no further excuse or apology for referring to these matters in connection with myself, and to evince to you my determination to do all in my power to avoid the responsibility of causing the adoption of the policy which you seem determined to press.

In your letter you acknowledge the fact that the negro troops did take an oath on bended knee to show no quarter to my men; and you say further, "you have no doubt they went to the battle-field expecting to be slaughtered," and admit also the probability of their having proclaimed on their line of march that no quarter would be shown us. Such being the case, why do you ask for the disavowal on the part of the commanding general of this department or the Government in regard to the loss of life at Tishomingo Creek? That your troops expected to be slaughtered, appears to me, after the oath they took, to be a very reasonable and natural expectation. Yet you, who sent them out, knowing and now admitting that they had sworn to such a policy, are complaining of atrocities, and demanding acknowledgments and disavowals on the part of the very men you went forth sworn to slay whenever in your power. I will in all candor and truth say to you that I had only heard these things, but did not believe them to be true; at any rate, to the extent of your admission; indeed, I did not attach to them the importance they deserved, nor did I know of the threatened vengeance, as proclaimed along their lines of march, until the contest was over. Had I and my men known it as you admit it, the battle of Tishomingo Creek would have been noted as the bloodiest battle of the war. That you sanctioned this policy is plain, for you say now "that if the negro is treated as a prisoner of war you will receive with pleasure the announcement, and will explain the fact to your colored troops at once, and desire (not order) that they recall the oath; but if they are either to be slaughtered or returned to slavery, let the oath stand."

Your rank forbids a doubt as to the fact that you and every officer and man of your department is identified with this policy and responsible for it, and I shall not permit you, notwithstanding, by your studied language in both your communications, you seek to limit the operations of your unholy scheme and visit its terrible consequences alone upon that ignorant, deluded, but unfortunate people, the negro, whose destruction you are planning in order to accomplish ours. The negroes have our sympathy, and so far as consistent with safety will spare them at the expense of those who are alone responsible for the inauguration of a worse than savage warfare.

Now, in conclusion, I demand a plain, unqualified answer to two questions, and then I have done with further correspondence with you on this subject. This matter must be settled. In battle and on the battle-field, do you intend to slaughter my men who fall into your hands? If you do not intend to do so, will they be treated as prisoners of war? I have over 2,000 of Sturgis' command prisoners, and will hold every officer and private as hostage until I receive your declarations and am satisfied that you carry out in good faith the answers you make, and until I am assured that no Confederate soldier has been foully dealt with from the day of the battle at Tishomingo Creek to this time. It is not yet too late for you to retrace your steps and arrest the storm.

Relying as I do upon that Divine Power which in wisdom disposes of all things; relying also upon the support and approval of my Government and countrymen, and the unflinching bravery and endurance of my troops, and with a consciousness that I have done nothing to produce, but all in my power consistent with honor and the personal safety of myself and command to prevent it, I leave with you the responsibility of bringing about, to use your own language, "a state of affairs too fearful for contemplation."

I am, general, very respectfully, yours, &c.,

N. B. Forrest, Major-General.[183]

Forrest to Confederate General Stephen Dill Lee, June 24, 1864:
☛ HEADQUARTERS FORREST'S CAVALRY, TUPELO, JUNE 24, 1864. MAJ. GEN. S. D. LEE, COMMANDING DEPARTMENT, MERIDIAN:

General: I have the honor herewith to inclose you copy of letter addressed to Major-General [C. C.] Washburn; also his letter addressed to you or the commanding officer Confederate forces near Tupelo. I have not in anywise compromised you, and leave the answer to General Washburn to yourself, provided you deem it necessary or advisable to communicate with him further. I deemed it due myself and command to say what I have said to him, but did not think it proper to make any communication over your signature.

I also have the honor to inclose you statements of Captain Young, who was captured at Fort Pillow, and you can make such use of them as you may deem necessary. As my official reports are in the hands of the Department at Richmond I did not, nor do I, consider that I have any defense to make, or attempt any refutations of the charges made by General Washburn. The character and tenor of his letter is also so outrageously insulting that but for its importance to my men—not myself—I should not have replied to it at all.

I shall forward you tomorrow a statement of the capture of Fort Pillow, by giving you a copy of communication asked for unofficially by Colonel Brent, assistant adjutant-general, and made by my aide-de-camp, Capt. C. W. Anderson.

I have taken pains, also, in my official report made to Lieutenant-General Polk, to place all the facts in the possession of the Government in order that they might meet any demands made by Federal authority.

Should you, however, think proper to place in the hands of General Washburn the papers sent you upon this subject, you are, of course, at liberty to use them. As for myself, entirely conscious of right, I have no explanations, apologies, or disavowals to make to General Washburn nor to any one else but my Government, through my superior officers.

I am, general, very respectfully, your most obedient servant, N. B. Forrest, Major-General.[184]

Despite the obvious truth that there was no Confederate "massacre" at Fort Pillow, the General received many unkind, biased, and threatening letters from Yankee officers afterward. As mentioned above by Forrest in one of his reports, some of the more caustic missives came from Union General Cadwallader Colden Washburn (later to become one of the organizers of the food production company now known as General Mills).[185] *Forrest's replies to Washburn follow. In them he forcefully describes, and clears up, many of the mysteries surrounding the conflict at the Tennessee garrison. The first is from Forrest to Washburn, June 25, 1864:*

☞ HEADQUARTERS FORREST'S CAVALRY, TUPELO, JUNE 25 [23], 1864. MAJ. GEN. C. C. WASHBURN, COMMANDING U. S. FORCES, MEMPHIS:

General: I have the honor to acknowledge the receipt (per flag of truce) of your letter of 17th instant, addressed to Maj. Gen. S. D. Lee, or officer commanding Confederate forces near Tupelo. I have forwarded it to General Lee with a copy of this letter.

I regard your letter as discourteous to the commanding officer of this department, and grossly insulting to myself. You seek by implied threats to intimidate him, and assume the privilege of denouncing me as a murderer and as guilty of the wholesale slaughter of the garrison at Fort Pillow, and found your assertions upon the *ex parte* testimony of your friends, the enemies of myself and country.

I shall not enter into the discussion, therefore, of any of the questions involved nor undertake any refutation of the charges made by you against myself; nevertheless, as a matter of personal privilege alone, I unhesitatingly say that they are unfounded and unwarranted by the facts. But whether these charges are true or false, they, with the question you ask as to whether negro troops when captured will be recognized and treated as prisoners of war, subject to exchange, &c., are matters which the Government of the United States and Confederate States are to decide and adjust, not their subordinate officers.

I regard captured negroes as I do other captured property and not as captured soldiers, but as to how regarded by my Government and the disposition which has been and will hereafter be made of them, I respectfully refer you through the proper channel to the authorities at Richmond. It is not the policy nor the interest of the South to destroy the negro—on the contrary, to preserve and protect him—and all who have surrendered to us have received kind and humane treatment.

Since the war began I have captured many thousand Federal prisoners, and they, including the survivors of the Fort Pillow massacre (black and white), are living witnesses of the fact that with my knowledge or consent, or by my order, not one of them has ever been insulted or in any way maltreated.

You speak of your forbearance in not giving to your negro troops instructions and orders as to the course they should pursue in regard to Confederate soldiers that might fall into their (your) hands, which clearly conveys to my mind two very distinct impressions. The first is that in not giving them instructions and orders you have left the matter entirely to the discretion of the negroes as to how they should dispose of prisoners; second, an implied threat to give such orders as will lead to "consequences too fearful for contemplation." In confirmation of the correctness of the first impression (which your language now fully develops), I refer you most respectfully to my letter from the battle-field of Tishomingo Creek and forwarded you by flag of truce on the 14th instant. As to the second impression, you seem disposed to take into your own hands the settlements which belong to, and can only be settled by, your Government, but if you are prepared to take upon yourself the responsibility of inaugurating a system of warfare contrary to civilized usages, the onus as well as the consequences will be chargeable to yourself.

Deprecating, as I should do, such a state of affairs, determined as I am not to be instrumental in bringing it about, feeling and knowing as I do that I have the approval of my Government, my people, and my own conscience, as to the past, and with the firm belief that I will be sustained by them in my future policy, it is left with you to determine what that policy shall be—whether in accordance with the laws of civilized nations or in violation of them.

I am, general, yours, very respectfully,
N. B. Forrest, Major-General.[186]

Forrest to Confederate Major William Elliott, June 25, 1864:
☛ HEADQUARTERS FORREST'S CAVALRY, TUPELO [MISS.], JUNE 25,1864. [MAJ. WILLIAM ELLIOTT:]

Major: From the information I have, am clearly of the opinion that the force now moving from Memphis meditate the destruction of the Mobile and Ohio Railroad as far down as possible and then turn across to the Central railroad, destroy it and return to Memphis. I therefore advise the removal of all surplus stores from Grenada and other points across in the direction of Meridian. I do not believe they design joining Sherman. Most of their force consists of 100-days' men—at any rate, a large number of that character have arrived and are arriving at Memphis. My scouts report that 184 wagons and 20 ambulances passed Forest Hill, twenty-four miles east of Memphis, and that 12,000 troops had passed up but I think that an overestimate of the number which has thus far left Memphis for up the road. I have no doubt but that they have and will probably move with 18,000 to 20,000 men, a portion of which will be used to garrison the points already fortified on the Memphis and Charleston Railroad, with a base secured as far east as practicable. They will then attempt the programme previously referred to. I respectfully suggest, therefore, that the major-general commanding order up, as far this way as forage will permit, all the available troops of his department. Besides three companies of scouts, I have 200 men at Ripley, and intend sending 200 more under Colonel Forrest, to go as near La Grange as possible and ascertain what is going on and keep me fully posted. Would move a greater force there but for the difficulty of supplying it with forage, not having a sufficiency of mules. Have ordered all of General Roddey's force to Corinth, except 300 men to be left in the valley to meet any raids from Decatur; also ordered him to send his wagon train and all his unserviceable and broken-down stock to this place, to be provided for and pastured.

I am, major, very respectfully, &c.,

N. B. Forrest, Major-General.[187]

Forrest to Confederate General James Ronald Chalmers, June 25, 1864:
☛ TUPELO, MISS., JUNE 25,1864.

Brigadier-General Chalmers, [at] Aberdeen: I wish you to have your command as near Okolona as nature of forage will permit, and prepare your command with five days rations and 100 rounds small-arm ammunition to the man, and hold yourself in readiness to move at a moments notice.

N. B. Forrest, Major-General.[188]

Forrest to Confederate General Stephen Dill Lee, June 25, 1864:
☛ TUPELO [MISS.], JUNE 25, 1864. MAJOR-GENERAL LEE:

Have just received dispatches that there are 3,000 enemy at La Grange. Have ordered Chalmers up to this place. Would it not be well for you to order Mabry up also?

N. B. Forrest, Major-General.[189]

Forrest to Confederate General James Ronald Chalmers, June 26, 1864:
☞ TUPELO, MISS., JUNE 26,1864.

Brigadier-General Chalmers, [at] Okolona: Not necessary to make a forced march. Bring all men except those needed to get up forage.

N. B. Forrest, Major-General.[190]

Forrest to Confederate General Gideon Johnson Pillow, June 26, 1864, concerning a dispute with over the men in Forrest's command:
☞ HEADQUARTERS FORREST'S CAVALRY, TUPELO [MISS.], JUNE 26,1864.

Respectfully returned, accompanied by a report from Col. T. H. Bell. The troops now under Colonel Bell I do not claim as my troops, but are Confederate troops, and subject to the orders of the major-general commanding department. I do claim, however, to have perfected and completed their organization and to have been the means of gathering them up and placing them effectively and promptly in the service, by consolidating and placing together the various parts of which the brigade was to be composed. Russell's, Wilson's, Greer's, and a portion of Newsom's regiments were consolidated into two regiments. I have since organized a third regiment, composed of a part of Newsom's regiment, the Tennessee companies of Forrest's (Alabama) regiment, and other unattached companies. The troops and their officers are desirous of remaining in my command. I am much attached to them and desire them to remain with me, and am of the opinion that it would not be for the good of the service to take them from the command against their wish. At the same time they, with all other troops in my command, are subject to orders from department headquarters.

N. B. Forrest, Major-General.[191]

Forrest to Confederate General Stephen Dill Lee, June 27, 1864:
☞ TUPELO [MISS.], JUNE 27, 1864. MAJOR-GENERAL LEE:

The enemy's cavalry is at Saulsbury, their main force reaching La Grange. [Railroad] Car ran to La Grange yesterday evening. The

[rail] road has been badly broken from Saulsbury to Corinth. If they come out at all they will move from Saulsbury.

    N. B. Forrest, Major-General.[192]

Forrest to Confederate General Stephen Dill Lee, June 28, 1864:
☞ TUPELO [MISS.], JUNE 28, 1864. LIEUTENANT-GENERAL LEE:

    Cannot write. Roddey and Mabry take into the field more than 6,000 men.

    N. B. Forrest, Major-General.[193]

Forrest to Confederate General Stephen Dill Lee, June 28, 1864:
☞ TUPELO [MISS.], JUNE 28, 1864. LIEUT. GEN. S. D. LEE:

    Allow me to congratulate you on your promotion. I am suffering with boils. If the enemy should move out I desire you to take command of the forces. Our force is insufficient to meet this command. Can't you procure some assistance?

    N. B. Forrest, Major-General.[194]

Forrest to Confederate General Stephen Dill Lee, June 28, 1864:
☞ TUPELO [MISS.], JUNE 28, 1864. LIEUTENANT-GENERAL LEE:

    Have ordered Mabry as near Okolona as he can get water and forage, his headquarters at or near Okolona. Chalmers division is at Verona. Will go myself to Corinth to-day to prepare Roddey's command. Have ordered his unserviceable horses and wagon train to this place. Several of my scouts have been captured near La Grange, amongst them 2 officers, all of whom were brutally murdered after capture.

    N. B. Forrest, Major-General.[195]

At the Battle of Brice's Cross Roads (also known as the Battle of Tishomingo Creek) on June 10, 1864, Forrest led his men in one of the most decisive and brilliant Confederate victories of the entire War. A few weeks later, on June 28, 1864, the General gave these moving words to his men:
☞ HEADQUARTERS FORREST'S CAVALRY, TUPELO, MISS., JUNE 28, 1864.

Soldiers: After a long and laborious campaign, the major-general commanding deems it an appropriate occasion to address you a few words of recapitulation, acknowledgment, and congratulation. About the 15th of February last the campaign which so gloriously terminated at Tishomingo Creek was inaugurated. Major-General Sherman with a large and well-appointed army undertook to penetrate the central counties of Alabama and Mississippi. His object was avowedly to capture Selma and Mobile, and to desolate that productive region of country, from which the granaries of a large section of the Confederacy were supplied. Generals Smith and Grierson had their duties assigned them, and were to act a conspicuous part in the work of spoliation and piracy. With a large co-operating cavalry force, thoroughly armed and equipped, they were to descend through Northern Mississippi, carrying fire and sword with them. On they came, like a blighting sirocco [storm]. At West Point you met them. There you threw yourselves across the rich prairies, a living bulwark, to stay the desolating tide. Compared with the enemy you were but few in numbers, but every man became a hero, for all seemed impressed with the importance of the momentous struggle. You proved yourselves equal to the expectations of the country. You met the proud and exultant enemy. The result is known to the world; you drove him howling back in ignominy and shame; broken and demoralized. Sherman's campaign was thus brought to an abrupt conclusion, and Mississippi and Alabama saved. The victory was a glorious one, and with heartfelt pride the general commanding acknowledges your unexampled gallantry. This great work was accomplished by Colonel Bell's brigade, commanded by Colonel Barteau, Colonel McCulloch's, and Colonel Forrest's brigades. But great as was this victory, it is not without its alloy. The laurel is closely entwined with the cypress, and the luster of a brilliant triumph is darkened by the blood with which it was purchased. It was here that Colonel [James A.] Barksdale gave up his life[,] a willing sacrifice upon the altar of his country. He fell in front of the battle, gallantly discharging his duty. He sleeps, but his name is imperishable. Here, too, fell the noble brother of the general commanding, Col. Jeffrey E. Forrest. He was a brave and chivalrous spirit, ever foremost in the fight. He fell in the flower of his youth and usefulness, but his dying gaze was proudly turned upon the victorious field, which his own valor had aided in winning. Peace to the ashes of these gallant young heroes.

After a short repose you were called to a new theater of action. By long and rapid marches, which you endured without murmur or complaint, you found yourselves upon the waters of the Ohio, sweeping the enemy before you wherever you met him, capturing hundreds of prisoners, valuable and needed stores in the quartermaster's and ordnance departments, while securing for yourselves a character for endurance, valor, and efficiency which might well excite the envy of the most famous legions in military history. At Fort Pillow you exhibited the same conspicuous gallantry. In the face of a murderous fire from two gun-boats and six pieces of artillery on the fort, you stormed the works and either killed or captured the entire garrison, a motley herd of negroes, traitors, and Yankees. This noble work was accomplished by parts of Chalmers' and Buford's divisions, composed of Bell's and McCulloch's brigades, commanded by Brigadier-General Chalmers; and for his gallantry on this and other occasions General Chalmers deserves the enduring gratitude of his countrymen. For the exhibitions of high soldierly bearing on these fields you have earned from your country and its government the most grateful and well-deserved plaudits. Congress has voted you complimentary resolutions of thanks and tendered you a nation's homage.

But the crowning glory of your great deeds has yet to be named. Tishomingo Creek is the brightest leaf in your chaplets of laurels. General Grierson, not satisfied with his test of your prowess, united with General Sturgis, at the head of one of the best appointed forces ever equipped by the Yankee nation, complete in infantry, cavalry, artillery, and supply trains. They came forth with threats of vengeance toward you and your commander for the bloody victory of Fort Pillow, made a massacre only by dastardly Yankee reporters. Again you responded bravely to your general's call. You met the enemy and defeated him. Victory was never more glorious, disaster never more crushing and signal. From a proud and defiant foe, en route to the heart of your country, with declarations both by negro and white troops of "no quarters to Forrest or his men," he became an enemy beaten, defeated, routed, destroyed. You drove the boasted minions of despotism in confused flight from the battle-field. Seventeen guns, 250 wagons, 3,000 stand of arms, 2,000 prisoners, and killed and wounded 2,000 more, are the proud trophies which adorn your triumphant banners. The remainder is still wandering in the bushes and bottoms, forever lost to the enemy. There were not over 3,000 of you who achieved this victory over 10,000 of the enemy. Had you never before raised an arm in your country's cause this terrible overthrow of her brutal foe would entitle you to her deepest gratitude. Again, your general expresses his pride and admiration of your gallantry and wonderful achievements. You stand before the world an unconquerable band of heroes. Whether dismounted, and fighting shoulder to shoulder like infantry veterans, or hurling your irresistible squadrons on the flying foe, you evinced the same courageous bravery.

Soldiers! Amid your rejoicing do not forget the gallant dead upon these fields of glory. Many a noble comrade has fallen[,] a costly sacrifice to his country's independence. The most you can do is to cherish their memory and strive to make the future as glorious as you and they have made the past.

To Brigadier-General Buford, commanding division, my obligations are especially due. His gallantry and activity on the field were ever conspicuous, and for the energy displayed in pursuing the enemy he deserves much of his Government. He has abundant cause to be proud of his brigade commanders, Colonels Lyon and Bell, who displayed great gallantry during the day. Col. Edward Winchester Rucker was prompt in the discharge of every duty. His brigade displayed conspicuous steadiness during the fight. Colonel Johnson, commanding brigade from General Roddey's command, merits notice for his coolness and bravery on this occasion, and for the valuable services rendered by his troops. Nor can the general commanding forget to mention the efficient aid rendered by the artillery, commanded by Capt. John W. Morton. He moved rapidly over the roughest ground and was always in action at the right time, and his well-directed fire dealt destruction in the masses of the enemy. The general commanding also takes pleasure in noticing the intelligent alacrity with which Maj. C. W. Anderson, Capt. W. H. Brand, Lieutenants Otey, Donelson, Titus, and Galloway, of my staff, conveyed orders to all parts of the field. They were ever near my person, and were prompt in the discharge of every duty.

Soldiers! You have done much, but there is still work for you to do. By prompt obedience to orders and patient endurance you will be enabled to repeat these great achievements. The enemy is again preparing to break through the living wall erected by your noble bosoms and big hearts. In the name and recollection of ruined home, desolated fields and the bleaching bones of your martyred comrades, you are appealed to again. The smoke of your burning homesteads, the screams of your insulted women, and the cries of starving children will again nerve your strong arms with strength. Your fathers of '76 had much to fight for, but how little and unimportant was their cause compared with yours. They fought not against annihilation, but simply to be independent of a foreign yet a constitutional and free Government. You are struggling against the most odious of all tyranny, for existence itself, for your property, your homes, your wives, and children, against your own enslavement, against emancipation, confiscation, and subjugation, with all their attendant horrors.

In conclusion, your commanding general congratulates you on the brilliant prospects which everywhere pervade our cause. The independence of the Confederate States is a fixed, accomplished, immutable fact. The ray of peace is glimmering like bright sunshine around the dark clouds. Be true to yourselves and your country a little while longer and you will soon be enabled to return to your desolated homes, there to collect together once more your scattered household goods.

By order of Maj. Gen. N. B. Forrest.[196]

Forrest to Confederate General James Ronald Chalmers, June 29, 1864:
☛ TUPELO [MISS.], JUNE 29,1864.

Brigadier-General Chalmers, [at] Verona: Need not cook rations until further orders. Keep the quantity on hand as ordered ready to be cooked.

N. B. Forrest, Major-General.[197]

Forrest to Confederate General James Ronald Chalmers, June 29, 1864:
☛ TUPELO [MISS.], JUNE 29,1864.

Brigadier-General Chalmers, [at] Verona: Organize your dismounted men into companies under competent officers; furnish them with wagon and cooking utensils and send them to Tupelo.

N. B. Forrest, Major-General.[198]

Forrest to Confederate Major William Elliott, June 30, 1864:
☞ TUPELO [MISS.], JUNE 30,1864. MAJ. WILLIAM ELLIOTT, ASSISTANT ADJUTANT-GENERAL, MERIDIAN, MISS.:

Major: I have the honor to acknowledge the reception of dispatch for [Union] Major-General [C. C.] Washburn. Will forward it to-day by flag of truce to La Grange. I am gratified to know that my reply met the approval of the lieutenant-general commanding.

I am, very respectfully, yours, &c.,

N. B. Forrest, Major-General.[199]

Forrest to Confederate General James Ronald Chalmers, June 30, 1864:
☞ TUPELO [MISS.], JUNE 30,1864.

Brigadier-General Chalmers, [at] Verona: You will send up all your dismounted [men] this evening with Enfield or Australian rifles, with forty rounds of ammunition to the man. Send one six-mule wagon, with cooking utensils, under proper officer.

N. B. Forrest, Major-General.[200]

Forrest to Confederate General James Ronald Chalmers, June 30, 1864:
☞ TUPELO [MISS.], JUNE 30,1864.

Brigadier-General Chalmers, [at] Verona: Have Seventh Tennessee Regiment and Forrest's regiment ready to move at an hour's notice, with sixty rounds of ammunition. Have six days' rations of hard bread and bacon ready for them provided they are ordered to move.

N. B. Forrest, Major-General.[201]

Forrest to Union General Andrew Jackson Smith, June 30, 1864:
☞ HEADQUARTERS FORREST'S CAVALRY, IN THE FIELD, JUNE 30, 1864. MAJ. GEN. A. J. SMITH, COMMANDING U.S. FORCES:

General: I have received information of the killing (after capture) of several of my scouts, also the brutal murder of several citizens by troops of your command. Two of my scouts were captured and killed by the Ninth Illinois Cavalry, and one by the Seventh Kansas, whose major I learn has vowed to kill every man they find in Confederate uniform. I do not intend acting hastily, but am causing an official report of these transactions to be made out. In the mean time I shall hold, under the order of Lieutenant-General [S. D.] Lee, commanding, all the officers captured at Tishomingo Creek as hostages, and shall certainly execute them man for man, or in any other proportion to stop it. I cannot of course believe that you approve such conduct on the part of your men, and believe that you will do all in your power to prevent it. At the same time it forces upon us alternatives recognized as legitimate, but which are, to say the least, unpleasant and unsatisfactory, although it is the recognized remedy, yet the innocent suffer and the guilty go unpunished. If, however, I am at all deceived as regards yourself, and these acts have been committed by authority of yourself or any other general officer, I respectfully ask that you will so state it.

I am, general, respectfully, yours,

N. B. Forrest, Major-General.[202]

Forrest to Confederate Major P. Ellis, July 1, 1864, giving his official report on the Battle of Brice's Cross Roads:

☞ REPORT OF MAJ. GEN. NATHAN B. FORREST, C.S. ARMY. HEADQUARTERS FORREST'S CAVALRY, TUPELO [MISS.], JULY 1, 1864. [TO: MAJ. P. ELLIS, ASSISTANT ADJUTANT-GENERAL, MERIDIAN, MISS.:]

Major: I have the honor to submit the following report of the operations of my command in the battle of Tishomingo Creek, fought near Guntown, Miss., June 10, 1864:

I received orders from Maj. Gen. S. D. Lee, commanding department, to move into Middle Tennessee with 2,000 men from my own command and 1,000 from the division of Brigadier-General [Philip D.] Roddey, commanding cavalry of North Alabama, and two batteries of artillery, for the purpose of destroying the railroad from Nashville and breaking up the lines of communications connecting that point with Sherman's army in Northern Georgia. In pursuance of that order I left Tupelo on the 1st day of June with Buford's division and Morton's and Rice's batteries. Prior to leaving Tupelo I dispatched my aide-de-camp, Capt. Charles W. Anderson, and Capt. John G. Mann, of the engineer department, to make all necessary arrangements for crossing the Tennessee River, which they did through Brigadier-General Roddey.

On the morning of the 3d a dispatch reached me at Russellville from Major-General [S. D.] Lee, stating that the enemy were moving in force from Memphis in the direction of Tupelo, and ordering my immediate return. The order was promptly obeyed, and the column reached Tupelo on the 5th, at which time the enemy were reported at Salem, fifty miles from this place, west.

On the 7th my scouts reported the enemy moving in the direction of Ruckersville, and to meet him I moved with Buford's division to Baldwyn, and on the morning of the 8th from thence to Booneville. Major-General Lee had ordered Colonel Rucker, commanding Sixth Brigade of my command, to move to my assistance, and in pursuance of the order he had joined me at Booneville on the evening of the 9th. Major-General Lee had also dispatched Brigadier-General Roddey to leave a small force in the valley near Decatur, and re-enforce me with the balance of his command. I received a dispatch from General Roddey stating that Col. W. A. Johnson, commanding brigade, was moving and ordered to report to me at Tupelo; also informing me that the balance of his command was then between Decatur and Rome on the flank of a force of the enemy moving from Decatur to Sherman's army. Johnson's brigade reached Baldwyn on the 9th, and was ordered to join me at Booneville. The enemy had endeavored to cross the Hatchie River in the direction of Rienzi, but owing to high water had only succeeded in throwing forward about 500 cavalry, which entered Rienzi on the morning of the 7th and attempted the destruction of the railroad, but left hastily after burning the depot and destroying a few yards of the railroad track. Supposing the main body would move in that direction, General Buford was ordered on the 9th to send Bell's brigade to Rienzi, holding Lyon's brigade, with two batteries of artillery, to await further developments.

On the night of the 9th I received dispatches reporting the enemy, in full force, encamped twelve miles east of Ripley on the Guntown road, having abandoned the upper route as impracticable. Orders were issued to move at 4 o'clock on the following morning (10th instant). General Buford was also directed to order the immediate return of Bell's brigade from Rienzi to Booneville. The wagon train of my entire command, in charge of Maj. C. S. Severson, chief quartermaster, was ordered to the rear and southward from Booneville, east of the railroad to Verona. I moved as rapidly as the jaded condition of my horses would justify, intending, if possible, to reach Brice's Cross-Roads in advance of the enemy. On arrival at Old Carrollville, in advance of the command, I received intelligence that the enemy's cavalry were within four miles of the cross-roads. I immediately sent forward Lieutenant Black, temporarily attached to my staff, with a few men from the Seventh Tennessee Cavalry, who soon reported that he had met the advance of the enemy one mile and a half north of the cross-roads, and was then skirmishing with them. I ordered Colonel Lyon, whose brigade was in front, to move forward and develop the enemy, and wrote back to General Buford to move up with the artillery and Bell's brigade as rapidly as the condition of the horses and roads would permit, and ordered him also to send one regiment of Bell's brigade from Old Carrollville across to the Ripley and Guntown road, with orders to gain the rear of the enemy or attack and annoy his rear or flank. Moving forward Colonel Lyon threw out one company as skirmishers, and soon after dismounted his brigade and attacked the enemy's line of cavalry, driving them back to near the cross-roads, at which place his infantry was arriving and being formed. Desiring to avoid a general engagement until the balance of my troops and the artillery came up, Colonel Lyon was not pushed forward, but in order to hold his position secure he made hasty fortifications of rails, logs, and such other facilities as presented themselves. I ordered up Colonel Rucker's brigade dismounting two regiments and forming them on the left of Colonel Lyon, holding his third regiment, under Colonel Duff, mounted, as a reserve, and throwing it out well on the extreme left to prevent any flank movement on the part of the enemy. Colonel Johnson was also moved into position. We had a severe skirmish with the enemy, which was kept up until 1 o'clock, at which time General Buford arrived with the artillery, followed by Bell's brigade. The enemy had for some time been shelling our position. On the arrival of the batteries I directed General Buford to move them in position and open fire, in order to develop the position of enemy's batteries and his lines. The enemy responded with two guns only. The firing from our batteries was discontinued, while Lyon and Johnson were ordered to move their lines forward. It was now 1 o'clock, and as all my forces were up I prepared to attack him at once. Taking with me my escort and Bell's brigade I moved rapidly around to the Guntown and Ripley road, and advancing on that road, dismounting the brigade, and forming Russell's and Wilson's regiments on the right, extending to Colonel Rucker's left, and placing Newsom's regiment on the left of the road, Duff's regiment, of Rucker's brigade, and my escort were placed on the left of Newsom's, and formed the extreme left of my line of battle. Before leaving General Buford I ordered him the moment the attack began on the left to move the center and right rapidly forward. Owing to the density of the undergrowth Colonel Bell was compelled to advance within thirty yards of the enemy before assaulting him. In a few seconds the engagement became general, and on the left raged with great fury. The enemy having three lines of battle, the left was being heavily pressed, I sent a staff officer to General Buford to move Lyon's and Johnson's brigades forward and press the enemy on the right. Newsom's regiment was suffering severely and had given way. Colonel Duff and my escort, dismounted, were ordered to charge the enemy's position in front of Newsom's regiment, and succeeded in driving the enemy to his second line, enabling the regiment to rally, reform, and move forward to a less exposed position. Fearing my order to General Buford had miscarried, I moved forward rapidly along the lines, encouraging my men, until I reached General Buford on the Blackland road, and finding but two pieces of artillery in position and engaged, I directed my aide-de-camp, Captain Anderson, to bring up all the artillery, and ordered General Buford to place it in action at once, which was promptly done. The battle was fierce and the enemy obstinate; but after two hours hard fighting the enemy gave way, being forced back on his third and last line. Colonel Barteau, in command of the regiment sent from Old Carrollville, had gained the rear of the enemy, and by his presence and attack in that quarter had withdrawn the cavalry from the enemy's flank and created confusion and dismay to the enemy's wagon train and the guard attending it. The cavalry was sent back for its protection, and the enemy now in front made a last attempt to hold the cross-roads; but the steady advance of my men and the concentrated, well-directed and rapid fire from my batteries upon that point threw them back, and the retreat or rout began. He endeavored, after abandoning the cross-roads, one piece of artillery, several caissons, and a quantity of ammunition, to protect his rear and check pursuit, taking advantage of every favorable position along his line of march, but he was speedily driven from them. Pressing forward he was forced to abandon many of his wagons and ambulances. Before reaching Tishomingo Creek the road was so blockaded with abandoned vehicles of every description that it was difficult to move the artillery forward. Ordering up my horses, they were mounted and the pursuit was then continued and the enemy were driven until dark. He attempted the destruction of his wagons, loaded with ammunition and bacon, but so closely was he pursued that many of them were saved without injury, although the road was lighted for some distance. It being dark, and my men and horses requiring rest, I threw out an advance to follow slowly and cautiously after the enemy, and ordered the command to halt, feed, and rest.

At 1 A.M. on the 11th the pursuit was resumed. About 3 o'clock we came again upon the enemy's rear guard of cavalry; but moving forward he gave way and did not attempt to check our advance. In the bottom on the south prong of the Hatchie [River] they had abandoned the balance of their wagon train, all their wounded, and 14 pieces of artillery. We came upon them again about four miles east of Ripley, where they had prepared to dispute our advance, but made only a feeble and ineffectual resistance, the Seventh Tennessee and my escort driving him from his position. He made another stand two miles east of Ripley, but it was followed by another characteristic retreat. On reaching the town of Ripley, about 8 A.M., the enemy was found in line of battle and seemingly prepared for determined resistance, occupying all favorable positions for that purpose. I had but few troops present. My escort was sent to the left and engaged the enemy, and Colonel Wilson's regiment was thrown forward, dismounted, as skirmishers, expecting they would be driven until the balance of my forces came up. The advance of Colonel Wilson and the escort was spirited and determined, and at the first appearance of additional force he again retreated, leaving 21 killed and 70 wounded, among whom was Colonel McKeaig; also leaving another piece of artillery, 2 caissons, and 2 ambulances; and from this place to the end of our pursuit the enemy offered no organized resistance, but retreated in the most complete disorder, throwing away guns, clothing, and everything calculated to impede his flight. Faulkner's (Kentucky) regiment, commanded by Major Tate, and the Seventh Tennessee, Colonel Duckworth, made repeated charges, mounted, and captured many prisoners. I ordered General Buford to continue the pursuit, and taking with me my escort and Colonel Bell, with his brigade, endeavored by taking another road to cut them off at Salem, but reached there an hour after their rear had passed. General Buford had pursued them rapidly and their infantry saved themselves by scattering on all by-roads leading toward the Memphis and Charleston Railroad, retreating through the woods in squads and avoiding capture in that way. Regarding all further pursuit of the enemy's cavalry useless, I ordered General Buford to move in the direction of Mount Pleasant and La Grange, and to scour the country on his return and to gather up prisoners, arms, &c., that could be found. All the troops were ordered back, and details made to gather up prisoners and spoils. Before reaching the battle-field on the return march several hundred prisoners were taken from their hiding places in the woods. My entire command moved to Guntown, and thence to this place.

My available force in the engagement was 3,500. From the reports of the prisoners captured, corroborated by official documents captured on the field, the enemy had in the engagement 10,252.

The loss of the enemy in killed and wounded is not less than 2,000, 250 wagons and ambulances, 18 pieces of artillery, 5,000 stand of small-arms, 500,000 rounds of ammunition, and all his baggage and supplies. I regret to say that during our pursuit the abandoned wagons, &c., of the enemy were pillaged and plundered by citizens and stragglers of the command.

I herewith forward reports from the chief quartermaster and commissary, showing the amount of property belonging to their respective departments received; and but for fire and robbery the entire outfit could have been saved.

The enemy broke, bent, and secreted a large number of their small-arms, but as far as they could be found they have been packed up and sent back for repairs.

A report of the division provost-marshal, showing the prisoners captured and sent south, is also herewith forwarded. Quite a number were captured too far west to be returned to this route, and were sent south via Holly Springs and Grenada. The whole number captured and in our hands is not less than 2,000.

Our loss in the engagement in killed and wounded is, as will be seen by report of chief surgeon, 493.

Colonel Rucker, commanding brigade, reported directly to me, and I take pleasure in speaking of his uniform good conduct. His attack was made with vigor, rapidity, and precision. Capt. John W. Morton, chief of artillery, moved with great promptness, and did admirable execution with his guns. My medical staff, under the direction of Chief Surg. J. B. Cowan, were assiduous in attention to the wounded on the field and in their removal to comfortable hospitals. My chief quartermaster, Maj. C. S. Severson, and Maj. G. V. Rambaut, commissary of subsistence, were highly serviceable and useful in gathering up and taking care of captured property belonging to their respective departments.

Thus did my troops in the hour of need rally to the defense of their country. They deserve well of her gratitude. Notwithstanding the great disparity in numbers they repulsed the foe and achieved a victory as imperishable as it is brilliant.

My obligations are hereby returned to Brigadier-General Buford, commanding division. He was prompt in obeying orders and exhibited great energy both in assaulting and pursuing the enemy. The high praises he bestows upon his brigade commanders, Colonels Bell and Lyon, are truthful and just. They exhibited coolness, skill, courage, and ability. Colonel Johnson, commanding brigade from General [Philip D.] Roddey's command, exhibited throughout the engagement the qualities of a gallant officer.

This victory may be justly considered one of the most complete of the war, and for it I feel indebted to the valor of my troops and the skill of my subordinate officers, and I mention again that to Colonels Bell, Lyon, and Rucker, commanding brigades, I feel mainly indebted for this crowning success over vastly superior numbers.

It would be unjust to close my report without referring to the gallant and meritorious conduct of my escort company, commanded by Capt. J. C. Jackson. Owing to drill, discipline, and material its services were to me on this occasion, as on many other fields, invaluable, and I consider it to-day the best body of men in my command—dashing, daring, and unflinching in the execution of orders given, and as scouts, for reliability and effectiveness, they are without any equal.

In conclusion, my acknowledgments are also due to Maj. Charles W. Anderson, acting assistant adjutant-general, and to Lieutenants Donelson and Galloway, my aides-de-camp. Fully alive to the emergencies of the occasion and the odds against us, they were prompt and faithful in the execution of all orders and untiring in the discharge of every duty devolving upon them from the commencement of the battle until pursuit was ended.

Respectfully submitted.

N. B. Forrest, Major- General.[203]

Forrest to Confederate Major William Elliott, July 3, 1864:
☞ HEADQUARTERS FORREST'S CAVALRY, TUPELO, JULY 3, 1864. [MAJOR ELLIOTT:]

Major: I have now between 500 and 600 dismounted men organized and in camp. They appear very well satisfied, and placing them in camp has caused increased attention to horses on the part of those who are mounted, and the policy will prove highly beneficial. There are yet quite a number that a close inspection will place in the field as infantry, and I respectfully suggest that the lieutenant-general commanding order all the cavalry of his department closely inspected and the unserviceable horses sent to pasture to be recruited, and then order that no dismounted man be allowed to return to his cavalry command until his horse will pass inspection. By this means he will be able to get a good brigade of infantry, or its equivalent, and recruit horses that a few days' service at this time will render worthless. A number of General Roddey's men have run away rather than come to the dismounted camp, but once in the camp and assured of the design to recruit their stock and render it serviceable they appear very well satisfied. If it meets the general's approbation I would be glad if all the dismounted troops should be sent up here for organization, as I am clearly of the opinion that a good brigade, if not more, could be formed. It would also give us credit with the enemy of having an infantry force, and all placed together in one command would make them effective and useful. I shall have my command closely inspected and send to the rear all horses unable to stand the fatigues of service. To do otherwise would result in loss of the services of both man and horse all be productive of straggling and scattering men all along the line of march. There are many men connected with provost guards and in the State reserves between the ages of eighteen and forty-five, also a large number of men acting with these guards as officers who are not officers, and I am of opinion that a rigid inspection of all such troops and of commands on post duty at various points, together with attachés, employés, and detailed men, claimed as purchasing agents, &c., who can be spared, will result in adding at least 2,000 men to the dismounted force.

I hope the lieutenant-general commanding will not think me presumptuous in offering these suggestions. Knowing and appreciating the necessity of having every available man in order to meet the superior force of the enemy now threatening us, is my apology for referring to the matter and making the suggestions.

I am, major, very respectfully, yours, &c.,

N. B. Forrest, Major-General.[204]

Forrest to Confederate Major William Elliott, July 4, 1864:

☛ HEADQUARTERS FORREST'S CAVALRY, TUPELO, MISS., JULY 4, 1864. MAJ. WILLIAM ELLIOTT, ASSISTANT ADJUTANT-GENERAL:

Major: I desire respectfully to call the attention of the lieutenant-general commanding to Neely's brigade, now with General Pillow. If I am correctly informed it is reduced to less than 600 men. I do not believe Colonel Neely an efficient brigade commander, and think for the good of the service a change should be made. A portion of the brigade as originally organized is here with Colonel Rucker, and I believe if the three regiments under Colonel Neely were sent back to this command that in the course of twenty-five or thirty days I could bring them up to double their present number. The scare consequent upon the action of the Government in taking out and sending back absentees from in infantry, together with the removal of the command to Alabama has, no doubt caused many to absent themselves, and the lax discipline and management of the officers, who are, no doubt, in the same dissatisfied condition, has served to deplete the command. If the state of affairs will permit their return, I will take the Seventh Tennessee and my old regiment and place with Neely's command, and give the command of the brigade thus formed to Rucker, ad return the Eighteenth Mississippi and First Mississippi Partisans to Colonel McCulloch's brigade, which would give General Chalmers his division with competent brigade commanders, and will, I believe, result in the restoration of nearly all the absentees.

I am, major, very respectfully, yours,

N. B. Forrest, Major-General.[205]

Forrest to Confederate General James Ronald Chalmers, July 9, 1864:
☞ TUPELO [MISS.], JULY 9,1864.

Brigadier-General Chalmers, [at] Verona: Send one brigade to the dismounted camp at once, and throw out scouts in the direction of Pontotoc and Chesterville. Enemy six miles south of New Albany on the roads from New Albany to Pontotoc and to Chesterville. Move your other brigade to Pontotoc at once and get there ahead of the enemy, keeping me fully advised of everything at Okolona. Send your ordnance and all other wagons to Garvin's Mills, on the Okolona road, to-night.

N. B. Forrest, Major-General.[206]

Forrest to Confederate General Stephen Dill Lee, July 17, 1864:
☞ HEADQUARTERS FORREST'S CAVALRY, OKOLONA [MISS.], JULY 17, 1864. [GENERAL S. D. LEE:]

General: : My wound is much more painful than I supposed it would be. I would like to have permission to go to Columbus in the event circumstances will admit of my doing so. At the same time will remain here and continue nominally in command if it is desired. In the event the enemy does not threaten any immediate movement against us, I respectfully suggest that Roddey's command remain or be encamped at Tupelo, Mabry's at or near Camargo, and Buford's and Chalmers' divisions and Neely's brigade be sent in the neighborhood of Pikeville, on Chuckatouchee Creek, to be fitted up, rested, and reorganized. With this disposition of the command, at least 100 captured negroes now getting up forage can be placed at work on the railroad, and in a short time have it open and running to Corinth. Mabry's brigade can be supplied with forage in the neighborhood of Camargo, and there is plenty of forage (tax in kind) on the Chuckatouchee for the other commands, and the men can also get vegetables, which they very much need. I could establish my office and headquarters at this place, remaining nominally in command, and have to a great extent the direction of affairs in reorganizing and fitting the troops for active service in the field and gathering up the absentees. With the horses being recruited in pastures below, and those of dead and permanently disabled officers and men, I think the battalion of dismounted men can be remounted and sent to their respective regiments. I am also of the opinion that it would be a good plan to send one officer from every company to get absentees and to bring horses to those who have them at home, but have not been granted the privilege of going after them, limiting the absence of the officers to fifteen days.

The manifest indisposition of the management of the Mobile and Ohio [rail] road to do anything unless aided by the army, renders it very certain that if the road is desired we shall have to furnish the labor necessary to repair it, otherwise if the troops are not drawn back to the forage our teams will necessarily be run down in hauling it to the commands, and the negroes also be required to handle it along the railroad and place it on cars to be sent forward as far as the road can carry it. As soon as the road is repaired, General Roddey, with his command, can occupy Corinth again, if it is desirable to do so. His command is small and I think it would be for the good of the service to form one good brigade of his command, as he has present for duty barely men enough to make one good brigade. He can then have direct supervision over them and control the action of his present brigade commanders. His absentees will be gathered up and fewer of them scattered through the country. I believe it would cause General Roddey and his officers to be more zealous in getting up the absent and more vigilant in keeping them in camp when returned. Please let me hear from you as soon as the movements of the enemy will permit. I would like to have 1,000 of the new Enfield rifles for my command. We lost a number in the recent engagement and after dividing out and issuing the 1,000 stand asked for, will turn over to the ordnance officer all excess in unserviceable and inferior guns.

I am, general, very respectfully, your obedient servant,

N. B. Forrest, Major-General.[207]

Forrest to Confederate General James Ronald Chalmers, July 18, 1864:
☞ OKOLONA [MISS.], JULY 18,1864.

Brigadier-General Chalmers, [at] Verona: Move division, Buford's division and the battalion of artillery, with all wagons, ambulances, &c., belonging thereto, to the neighborhood of Pikeville or Gladney's Mills. Neely's brigade is ordered there also. Send out and scour the woods and houses in neighborhood of battle-field to gather up all arms and equipments. Will send Roddey and Mabry orders by courier.

N. B. Forrest, Major-General.[208]

Forrest to Confederate General James Ronald Chalmers, July 29, 1864:
☞ OKOLONA [MISS.], JULY 29,1864.

Brigadier-General Chalmers [at] Columbus: Send a good company, with a prudent officer, to La Fayette County, Ala., near La Fayette Court-House, and arrest Captain Gouldin and his company, and dismount and bring them to your headquarters with as little delay as possible.

N. B. Forrest, Major-General.[209]

Forrest to Confederate Major P. Ellis, August 1, 1864, issuing his official report on the Battle of Tupelo or Harrisburg (fought July 14-15, 1864):
☞ HEADQUARTERS FORREST'S CAVALRY, OKOLONA [MISS.], AUGUST 1, 1864. [TO: MAJ. P. ELLIS, ASSISTANT ADJUTANT-GENERAL, SELMA, ALA.]

Major: I have the honor to make the following report of the action of my troops in the engagements commencing at Pontotoc on the 13th and ending near Harrisburg, Miss., on the 15th of July:

My scouts reported the enemy in strong force at La Grange, Tenn., on the Memphis and Charleston Railroad, and kept me constantly advised of his movements.

On the 5th he was reported advancing upon Ripley.

On the 6th I was advised that he was moving toward Tupelo by Ellistown. I immediately ordered General Buford to send Colonel Bell's brigade to Ellistown to guard the approach of the enemy in that direction.

On the morning of the 9th I ordered General Buford to move from Tupelo and to join Colonel Bell at Ellistown. At the same time I ordered Colonel Mabry, commanding a brigade of Mississippians, to move from Saltillo and report to General Buford at Ellistown. The enemy after reaching Ellis Mills turned abruptly down the road toward New Albany and Pontotoc. I ordered General Buford to pursue him, to hang upon his flanks, and to develop his strength, but to avoid a general engagement by gradually falling back toward Okolona if the enemy pressed him.

On the evening of the 10th I ordered General Chalmers to send one of his brigades to Pontotoc, and if possible to reach there before the enemy arrived, and to move with his other brigade to the infantry camps at the crossing of the Tupelo and Pontotoc with the Chesterville and Okolona roads.

On the night of the 10th I gave General Chalmers full instructions, and ordered General Buford to report to him. The enemy was reported slowly and cautiously advancing. I ordered General Chalmers to hold him in check until I was prepared to give him battle at or near Okolona, where the necessary arrangements were being vigorously made. The enemy was easily held in check, but reached Pontotoc on the evening of the 11th, but made no further effort to advance during the day. General Chalmers advised me of the disposition he had made of the troops, which was most satisfactory. As all the approaches south were strongly guarded I made no change except to order Colonel Barteau's regiment to the rear of the enemy.

On the 12th the enemy made an early advance on the Pontotoc and Okolona road, but was promptly met by General Lyon's brigade and easily driven back. He also attempted an advance on the road leading from Pontotoc to Houston, but here he was met by a part of Colonel McCulloch's brigade and forced to make a hasty retreat. Simultaneous with his other movement he threw out a force on the Pontotoc and Tupelo road but after advancing five miles was met by a part of Rucker's brigade, under the command of Colonel Duff, and driven back. Everything being in readiness to receive the enemy, I ordered General Chalmers to send Rucker's brigade to his rear, and to offer no further resistance if he desired to advance toward Okolona. The delay of the enemy at Pontotoc produced the impression that he designed to fall back toward Memphis, and after a short consultation it was determined to accept battle wherever he offered it and to attack him if he attempted a retreat. Lieutenant-General [S. D.] Lee therefore ordered me to move everything to the front. I immediately dispatched one of my staff officers to General Chalmers, ordering him to resume his former position if he had retired, and to hold it at all hazards until I arrived with the artillery and infantry re-enforcements. I reached the front about 9 o'clock, and found the troops in the position they had occupied during the day.

On the morning of the 13th the enemy was reported retiring from Pontotoc in the direction of Tupelo. Lieutenant-General Lee ordered me, with Mabry's brigade, my escort, and Forrest's old regiment, to attack and press upon the rear of the enemy. At the same time Lieutenant-General Lee moved forward, with Chalmers' and Buford's two divisions on the right, with the view of attacking the enemy's flanks at every vulnerable point. Accordingly, I advanced upon the enemy and found his rear one mile from Pontotoc, on the Okolona road. I threw forward my escort and Forrest's old regiment, and after a short skirmish he was rapidly driven into town and out on the Tupelo road, along which the main column was retreating. I made a vigorous assault upon the enemy's rear for ten miles. He took advantage of every favorable position, and my artillery was kept almost in constant action. Ten miles from Pontotoc he made a formidable stand, as if to contest my farther advance. After a short engagement he was driven from his position and made a rapid retreat across an extended field, while my artillery poured upon him a concentrated fire. I had now driven the enemy ten miles, and as his flanks had not yet been attacked I was fearful that he was driven too rapidly. I therefore halted my command and awaited the attack upon his flanks. After resting about one hour our guns opened upon him about three miles ahead. I resumed the march and hurriedly pressed forward, and on reaching the ground I found General Chalmers had dashed into the road, surprised the enemy, and took possession of his wagon train. The enemy, however, threw back a large force upon General Chalmers and forced him to retire but not until he had killed and wounded many men and horses, which forced the enemy to burn and abandon several wagons, caissons, and ambulances. About this time heavy firing was heard still farther up the road in the direction of Tupelo, which admonished me that General Buford was also attacking the enemy's flank. As night approached the enemy became more obstinate in his resistance, but I attacked his rear with renewed energy until 9 o'clock, when I reached a point two miles from Harrisburg, where I was joined by my entire command, which halted for the night. Being anxious to learn the exact position of the enemy, I moved Mabry's brigade forward and opened upon the enemy with four pieces of artillery. At a late hour in the night, accompanied by one of my staff officers, I approached Harrisburg and discovered the enemy strongly posted and prepared to give battle the next day. Colonel Mabry's brigade having been on duty for twenty-four hours, I ordered General

Buford to send the Kentucky brigade to its relief.

On the morning of the 14th Lieutenant-General Lee ordered the attack to be made, and the troops were disposed for that purpose. The enemy had selected a strong position on a ridge fronting an open field, gradually sloping toward our approach. During the night he had constructed fortifications, and his position being naturally strong it was now almost impregnable. The entire command was dismounted. General [Philip D.] Roddey's troops were placed on the extreme right, Colonel Mabry's brigade on the left, and the Kentucky brigade, commanded by Colonel Crossland, in the center. Bell's brigade was formed in the rear of Colonel Mabry's brigade as a support, but was subsequently moved forward and formed between Mabry's and Crossland's brigades. General Chalmers division of cavalry and General Lyon, who had been placed in command of about 700 infantry, were formed in the rear to be held as a reserve to support the entire front line. Lieutenant-General Lee gave the order to advance, and directed me to swing the right around upon the enemy's left. I immediately repaired to General Roddey's right with all possible speed, which was nearly a mile distant, and after giving him the necessary orders in person I dashed across the field in a gallop for the purpose of selecting a position in which to place his troops, but on reaching the front I found the Kentucky brigade had been rashly precipitated forward, and were retiring under the murderous fire concentrated upon them. I seized their colors, and after a short appeal ordered them to form a new line, when they held their position. The terrific fire poured upon the gallant Kentucky brigade showed that the enemy were supported by overwhelming numbers in an impregnable position, and wishing to save my troops from the unprofitable slaughter I knew would follow any attempt to charge his works, I did not push forward General Roddey's command when it arrived, knowing it would receive the same concentrated fire which had repulsed the Kentucky brigade. I ordered forward four pieces of artillery and formed a new line on the Tupelo and Verona road. Mean time the troops on my left were hotly engaged. Mabry's, Bell's, and Rucker's brigades were steadily advancing. They drove a heavy line of skirmishers back to their fortifications, from which point the enemy opened a furious cannonade and terrific fire of small-arms. Mabry's brigade advanced to within sixty yards of the enemy's fortifications, but the weather was so oppressive that hundreds of men fell fainting with exhaustion, and so deadly was the concentrated fire of small-arms and artillery upon the advancing column that it was compelled to fall back. The troops thus engaged, having exhausted their ammunition, were relieved by McCulloch's brigade, which moved forward and covered their retreat. The enemy still remained behind his works and made no effort to pursue. About 1 o'clock Lieutenant-General Lee ordered me to fall back to the residence of Mrs. Sample, and to form a new line fronting a large open field. The position selected was a strong one. There being no timber in front, it commanded every approach for several hundred yards. I ordered immediate construction of temporary fortifications, and in a short time the men along my entire line were protected behind strong works erected out of the rails, logs, and cotton-bales which the premises of Mrs. Sample so abundantly furnished. The approach of the enemy was anxiously awaited, but he still remained behind his fortifications. About night he commenced burning the houses in Harrisburg. General Chalmers advanced with one piece of artillery, and McCulloch's brigade, which was still in front, and did good execution by throwing shells among the enemy, who could be plainly seen by the light of the burning houses. At the approach of darkness I ordered Rucker's brigade to report to me mounted. With it I moved to the right and cautiously approached the enemy's left, with a view of ascertaining his position and strength in that direction. By meandering through the woods I approached very near his camps before he discovered my presence. I ordered my men to open fire upon him, when the first line fell back to the main body and opened upon me one of the heaviest fires I have heard during the war. The enemy's whole force seemed to be concentrated at this point. There was unceasing roar of small-arms, and his whole line was lighted up by a continuous stream of fire. Not a man was, however, killed, as the enemy overshot us, but he is reported as having suffered much from the fire of my men, and still more from their own men, who fired into each other in the darkness of the night. On returning to camp I ordered General Buford to move to the right with his division, to occupy the road between the enemy and Verona, and to oppose any advance in that direction.

On the morning of the 15th, finding the enemy could not be driven from his fortifications, General Buford was ordered to move up the Verona road and attack his left flank. General Buford pushed forward his troops and drove the enemy back about one mile, where he was protected by his main line. But few men were killed or wounded in this engagement, but I found the road strewn with men fainting under the oppressive heat, hard labor, and want of water. General Chalmers, who had been ordered to the left in the morning, reported the enemy retreating on the Ellistown road. I immediately proceeded to Harrisburg with General Roddey's command and attacked the enemy's rear guard, which, after a short engagement with Colonel Warren's regiment, retired. I ordered General Buford to press forward in the direction of Tupelo and engage the enemy there, if he still occupied the place. On reaching Harrisburg Lieutenant-General Lee ordered me to take command of the troops and to pursue the enemy. I ordered Mabry's brigade on the Chesterville road, and General Chalmers and Buford to pursue the enemy retreating on the Harrisburg and Ellistown road, and to make a vigorous assault upon his rear as soon as it could be overtaken, while I moved with Lieutenant-General Lee to Tupelo for the purpose of consulting and receiving orders. Having learned General Lee's desires I started from Tupelo to join my command. Three miles from Tupelo I heard heavy artillery firing, and as I farther advanced I could also hear the firing of small-arms. On arriving at Old Town Creek I found General Chalmers and General Buford hotly engaged. The enemy had selected a strong position on the crest of a hill, but was driven to the creek bottom by Bell's and Crossland's brigades, where he was heavily re-enforced, which enabled him not only to hold his position, but to press back these two brigades. I ordered General Chalmers to move up with McCulloch's brigade, and Rice's battery to be placed in position, which for a time held the enemy in check. While riding across the field and endeavoring to press forward my left[,] I received a painful wound, which incapacitated me from further service. I sent one of my staff officers back to Tupelo to advise General Lee of my wound. I ordered General Chalmers to assume command and the withdrawal of the troops.

The next morning the enemy renewed his retreat and was for two days [pursued] by General Chalmers with Rucker's and Roddey's brigades. The enemy was thus driven back to the point from which he started and many a home saved from spoliation, and the country preserved from the desolation and ruin which everywhere marks the invader's tracks. But this achievement cost the best blood of the South.

My forces during these engagements did not exceed 5,000; the enemy was 18,000 or 20,000. He fought behind fortifications and in positions of his own selection. Notwithstanding the advantages of the enemy, my troops moved forward with a gallantry which has never been excelled on any field.

The long list of killed and wounded is a sad but truthful tribute to their valor. Three of my brigade commanders (Rucker, McCulloch, and Crossland) were severely wounded. Colonels were either killed or wounded. Two hundred and ten were killed and 1,116 wounded. The enemy's loss was equal to my own.

The battle of Harrisburg will furnish the historian a bloody record, but it will also stamp with immortality the gallant dead and the living heroes it has made. Prominent among the former the names of Col. Isham Harrison and Lieut. Col. Thomas M. Nelson of the Sixth Mississippi; Lieut. Col. John B. Cage, commanding Fourteenth Confederate; Lieutenant-Colonel Sherrill, of the Seventh Kentucky, and Maj. Robert C. McCay, of the Thirty-eighth Mississippi, will shine in fadeless splendor. They were lion-hearted officers and courteous officers. It was a sad blow that struck down these gallant spirits. In unselfish devotion to the cause and high courage they leave no superiors behind among men. Their noble natures and ardent patriotism, it is hoped, will find in the soldier's grave that peace for which their country has thus far struggled in vain, and for the achievement of which they have sacrificed their lives. Future generations will never weary in hanging garlands upon their graves.

My staff on this occasion acted with their accustomed gallantry and promptitude in obeying orders, for which they have my thanks.

All of which is respectfully submitted.

N. B. Forrest, Major-General.[210]

Forrest to Confederate General Dabney Herndon Maury, August 5, 1864:
☞ HEADQUARTERS FORREST'S CAVALRY, MAJ. GEN. D. H. MAURY, COMMANDING DEPARTMENT OF MOBILE, ALA.:

General: I have the honor to acknowledge the receipt of your letter of the 2d instant, and in reply allow me to say that I can well understand and realize the responsibility of your position and the difficulties under which you labor in the command of a large department with forces inadequate for its defense when assailed, as it now appears to be, from all quarters. I regret very much that recent engagements in North Mississippi (Tishomingo and Harrisburg) have reduced my command so much in numbers, but especially am I deficient in field officers and brigade commanders. Colonel Lyon having left the department, McCulloch and Rucker wounded, leaves me, aside from Colonel Bell, without an experienced brigade commander and in Bell's brigade the greater number of field officers are wounded or killed. Nevertheless, all that can be done shall be done in North Mississippi to drive the enemy back. At the same time I have not the force to risk a general engagement, and will resort to all other means in my reach to harass, annoy, and force the enemy back. I have ordered the impressment of negroes for the purpose of fortifying positions, blockading roads and fords upon the rivers, and shall strike him in flank and rear, and oppose him in front to the extent of my ability, and fight him at all favorable positions along his line of march. I am of opinion that his move will be in this direction; that the feints against Central railroad are made to draw my forces west and give him the start toward the prairies. I have ordered Mabry to Grenada, a brigade to Pontotoc, and General Chalmers, with one of the best brigades I have, has gone to Abbeville, with instructions to blockade fords, fortify positions, and repair the works on Tallahatchie and Yalobusha Rivers. With Buford's division I shall await further developments and move as future indications require. I have sent a battery of four guns with General Chalmers, another with the brigade to Pontotoc, and have two batteries here yet. My artillery in all numbers sixteen pieces, and my effective force as formerly reported, with Mabry's added. You may rest assured, general of my hearty co-operation in all things and at all times. I can take the saddle with one foot in the stirrup, and if I succeed in forcing the column back will be ready to move to your assistance at short notice, mounted or by rail. Will arrange with Governor Clark for a proper disposition of the State forces and all reserves he may be able to bring to my assistance. Will write you or telegraph as often as deemed necessary. Captain Carter, of Wheeler's scouts, reports the enemy from Decatur as having returned. The main points are from Vicksburg and Memphis.

I am, general, very respectfully, your obedient servant,

N. B. Forrest, Major-General.[211]

Forrest to Confederate General James Ronald Chalmers, August 7, 1864:
☞ PONTOTOC, MISS., AUGUST 7,1864. BRIG. GEN. JAMES R.
CHALMERS, [AT] OXFORD [MISS.]:

I find that it is necessary for me to return to Okolona this morning, as I see from the papers of 5th from Mobile that the enemy's gun-boats and ships had passed our forts at Mobile, and three of our boats were captured or sunk. General Buford will reach here this evening with Bell's brigade. I will order the Kentucky brigade up on Tuesday next. Order Mabry, with his brigade, to move as far up the road as he can procure corn. If you find that the enemy attempts to cross the Hatchie River, burn the bridge and destroy the road to Oxford and Grenada as you fall back. Destroy the bridge over the Tallahatchie [River] at once, and all the trestles as far toward Oxford as possible. I will be in Okolona in the morning. Put yourself in communication with General Buford at this place at once. Major Warren reports the railroad broken between Water Valley and Oxford. Impress wagons and haul the corn up if the road is not repaired. I don't wish to throw any more force on your front. You will assume command of Mabry's brigade and fall back in front of the enemy, contesting all the ground, while I will operate on his flank and rear. Keep your men well in hand and be certain to destroy the road north of the Tallahatchie, if possible to do so. I send Colonels Duckworth and Kelley, with their regiments, to Lick Spring to blockade that road to-morrow morning, and to watch the river below there. Send the Beck boys to report to Duckworth and Kelley as guides.

I am, yours, &c.,
N. B. Forrest, Major-General.[212]

Forrest to Confederate General James Ronald Chalmers, August 7, 1864:
☞ OKOLONA, MISS., AUGUST 7,1864. BRIG. GEN. JAMES R.
CHALMERS, [AT] OXFORD [MISS.]:

Have Mabry move up as near Abbeville as possible. Dispute the enemy's crossing the Tallahatchie [River], but if forced to fall back destroy the railroad as effectually as possible between Abbeville and Grenada. Have your forces up as near the enemy as possible. Will send you further orders on Wednesday morning. Press teams and negroes, if necessary, to haul up forage for your troops.

N. B. Forrest, Major-General.[213]

Forrest to Confederate President Jefferson Davis, August 7, 1864:

☞ HEADQUARTERS FORREST'S CAVALRY, OKOLONA, MISS. AUGUST 7, 1864. HIS EXCELLENCY JEFFERSON DAVIS PRESIDENT, C.S.A.:

Sir: I have the honor to state that I am just in receipt of letter from Adjutant and Inspector General's Office, under date of 19th ultimo, accompanied by a memorandum of instructions as to the irregularities and illegalities occurring in the organization of the various regiments of my command, which instructions require the election of held officers for several of the regiments as organized by me at Oxford, Miss., in February last. It is due to myself to state that, in organizing the West Tennessee regiments referred to, it was my understanding that elections for field officers could not be held, and that being made up as they were from the odds and ends of some twelve or fifteen reputed commands and of unattached companies and squads raised inside the enemy's lines, the field officers were to be appointed by the War Department; hence, in nominating the field officers for these commands, I was governed by the claims of the parties instrumental in raising the troops, also by their ability and merits as officers. Your Excellency is aware of the condition of affairs as I found them in West Tennessee and North Mississippi, and the circumstances of my entering this department, and the limited means placed at my command for the accomplishment of my mission here. With great labor, and under many difficulties and disadvantages, I succeeded in bringing order out of confusion, and organized and placed in the service a majority of the troops now constituting my command. The enemy in heavy force is in my front, and any attempt, by elections, to fill the field positions of the West Tennessee regiments I am satisfied will disorganize my command and be injurious to the service. They are all contented and everything is moving along harmoniously, and election will surely result in the loss of best field officers I have, who by strict discipline have kept the men together and are not popular with the men. Many of them have distinguished themselves by gallantry in the recent engagements of Tishomingo Creek and Harrisburg, and quite a number are now absent, wounded. I have no desire to see the rights of any one disregarded. I believe the appointing of field officers upon proper recommendations the legal method of supplying field officers of regiments composed of parts of so many different unattached commands, and now that it has been done and has proved satisfactory to all parties, I do hope the appointments will be made as per roster forwarded to the Department. I should not trouble Your Excellency with this matter, but for the fact that the good of the service and the efficiency of my command and justice to the officers, who have served so faithfully, require that I should lay this matter before you. I shall as soon as practicable forward a detailed statement of facts and recommendations relative to all parties referred to by the Department in its instructions, and do hope that no changes will be made in the new commands raised under your authority. At this particular time it would be disastrous to change the field officers of the West Tennessee regiments, and it is my firm conviction that to do so at any time will be highly injurious. I distinctly disavow any assumption of any power or authority to make these appointments, but selected the very best men in the commands for the positions, and in doing so believed I was acting properly and legally and that the officers nominated and placed in command would be appointed to the positions to which they were assigned. Having done all as I conceived for the best, and having organized a fine command, which since its organization has performed more and better duty than perhaps any other new cavalry command ever did in the same length of time, I do hope that nothing will now be done to destroy its effectiveness or weaken my influence and control over them. I regarded them as detached commands, raised under various authorities, at different times, and by different parties, and that field officers could only be made by appointment from the War Department.

I have the honor to be very respectfully your obedient servant, N. B. Forrest, Major-General.[214]

Forrest to Confederate General James Ronald Chalmers, August 8, 1864:
☞ OKOLONA, MISS., AUGUST 8, 1864. BRIG. GEN. JAMES R. CHALMERS, [AT] OXFORD [MISS.]:

Have ordered Mabry, if his horses are broken down, to move his command from Grenada by rail, and report to you. I move everything to-morrow to Pontotoc. Let me hear from you there by courier. Will not move force from Pontotoc until I ascertain what direction enemy takes from Abbeville. I do not think enemy will go down Central road.

N. B. Forrest, Major-General.[215]

Forrest to Confederate General James Ronald Chalmers, August 8, 1864:
☞ OKOLONA, MISS., AUGUST 8,1864. BRIG. GEN. CHALMERS:

What facilities for crossing the river at Panola? How many boats are there?

N. B. Forrest, Major-General.[216]

Forrest to Confederate General James Ronald Chalmers, August 8, 1864:
☞ OKOLONA, MISS., AUGUST 8,1864. BRIGADIER-GENERAL CHALMERS, [at] ABBEVILLE:

Do not fall back to Oxford if you can possibly help it. Contest every inch of ground from Abbeville southward.

N. B. Forrest, Major-General.[217]

Forrest to Confederate General James Ronald Chalmers, August 8, 1864:
☞ OKOLONA, MISS., AUGUST 8,1864. BRIGADIER-GENERAL CHALMERS, [at] ABBEVILLE:

Contest every inch of ground. Do not give back unless forced to do so.

N. B. Forrest, Major-General.[218]

Forrest to Confederate General James Ronald Chalmers, August 8, 1864:
☞ OKOLONA, MISS., AUGUST 8,1864. BRIGADIER-GENERAL CHALMERS, [at] OXFORD:

Will send you a section of rifled artillery to-morrow.

N. B. Forrest, Major-General.[219]

Forrest to Confederate Colonel George Deas, August 15, 1864:
☞ HDQRS. WEST TENNESSEE AND NORTH MISSISSIPPI, OXFORD, MISS., AUGUST 15, 1864. COLONEL DEAS, CHIEF OF STAFF:

Colonel: I herewith inclose copy of orders from these headquarters relieving Lieut. Col. N. Wickliffe from duty with this command. Colonel W[ickliffe] was temporarily assigned to the command of this regiment by Lieutenant-General Polk, who at the same time forwarded a letter recommending him to be promoted to colonel of cavalry, and that he be given the command of the above regiment, at that time without a field officer present for duty. The papers were returned to me with the indorsement that the appointment could not be made, and that Colonel George, although wounded and a prisoner, was still the colonel of the regiment, and that other field positions must remain as per roster forwarded, or vacancies filled by promotion. Aside from this the regiment is much dissatisfied, have mutinied on one occasion, and it has done no good under his command. Colonel W[ickliffe] has repeatedly asked to be relieved, and I think the good of the service as well as the indorsement of the Secretary of War demands that he should be. I trust that Colonel W[ickliffe] may be assigned to a position more agreeable to himself and beneficial to the service than the one he held here.

I am, colonel, very respectfully, your obedient servant,

N. B. Forrest, Major-General.[220]

Forrest to Confederate General James Ronald Chalmers, August 19, 1864:

☛ PANOLA, MISS., AUGUST 19,1864. BRIGADIER-GENERAL CHALMERS, [at] OXFORD:

The streams are so high that I shall send one section of artillery to Grenada, and will put ten horses to the piece, and take one section with me. Will camp about Como to-night. Will send ambulances to Grenada also.

N. B. Forrest, Major-General.[221]

Forrest to Confederate General James Ronald Chalmers, August 19, 1864:

☛ PANOLA, MISS., AUGUST 19,1864. BRIGADIER-GENERAL CHALMERS, [at] OXFORD:

Will move as originally intended, taking one section of artillery, and sending the other to Grenada.

N. B. Forrest, Major-General.[222]

Forrest to Confederate General James Ronald Chalmers, August 20, 1864:

☛ SENATOBIA, MISS., AUGUST 20,1864. BRIGADIER-GENERAL

CHALMERS, [at] OXFORD:

Have fixed a pontoon and am crossing Hickahale. Expect to have to go to Quinn's Mills to cross Coldwater. Hold the enemy hard and press them up so as to engage their whole attention.

N. B. Forrest, Major-General.[223]

Forrest to Confederate General Dabney Herndon Maury, August 21, 1864:
☞ HERNANDO [MISS.], AUGUST 21, 1864.

I attacked Memphis 4 o'clock this morning, driving enemy to his fortifications. We killed and captured 400, capturing their entire camp, with about 300 horses and mules. [Union General Cadwallader C.] Washburn and staff escaped by darkness of morning, leaving his clothes behind. My loss 20 killed and wounded.

N. B. Forrest, Major-General.[224]

Forrest to Union General Cadwallader Colden Washburn, August 21, 1864:
☞ HDQRS. DEPT. OF WEST TENNESSEE AND NORTH MISS., AUGUST 21, 1864. MAJ. GEN. C. C. WASHBURN, COMMANDING U.S. FORCES, MEMPHIS:

General: I have a number of U.S. prisoners in my possession which I propose to exchange for an equal number of C.S. prisoners of equal rank. If you have not an equal number I will parole the remainder I have, with the understanding that if you should capture any of my men you will parole for exchange.

I make the proposition for the sake of humanity to the prisoners. If you have no prisoners belonging to my command I will exchange for any others you may have, but my proposition is for my own first.

I am, general, very respectfully, your obedient servant,

N. B. Forrest, Major-General.[225]

Forrest to Confederate General James Ronald Chalmers, August 22, 1864:
☞ PANOLA, MISS., AUGUST 22,1864. BRIGADIER-GENERAL CHALMERS, [at] SPRINGDALE:

If enemy is falling back, pursue them hard.

N. B. Forrest, Major-General.[226]

Forrest to Confederate General James Ronald Chalmers, August 22, 1864:

☞ PANOLA, MISS., AUGUST 22,1864. BRIGADIER-GENERAL CHALMERS:

Send Buford, with Kentucky brigade, on Sarepta road to capture enemy's foraging parties. Send Wade to the left for same purpose. Keep them close to their camp. Order Captain Henderson to scout well to their right to ascertain if there is any movement this way. I go to Grenada in the morning with prisoners. I wish the troops here to have two or three days' rest if possible.

N. B. Forrest, Major-General.[227]

Forrest to Confederate General James Ronald Chalmers, August 23, 1864:
☞ GRENADA [MISS.], AUGUST 23,1864. GENERAL CHALMERS:

Press the enemy. Ascertain the direction they go. If towar Panola, notify Colonel Bell at that place; also notify me. When the enemy find I have left Memphis he will return this way. Press him across the river, if possible.

N. B. Forrest, Major-General.[228]

Forrest to Confederate General James Ronald Chalmers, August 24, 1864:
☞ GRENADA [MISS.], AUGUST 24,1864. GENERAL CHALMERS, [AT] OXFORD [MISS.]:

You will fall back south of Yockeney and ascertain their movements. I will order up all the trains to you and order Bell and Neely to join you at Springdale as soon as they can come from Panola.

N. B. Forrest, Major-General.[229]

Forrest to Confederate General James Ronald Chalmers, August 25, 1864:
☞ GRENADA [MISS.], AUGUST 25,1864. GENERAL CHALMERS, [AT] WATER VALLEY:

If you are satisfied that the enemy have gone across the Tallahatchie, you can remain where you are unless they move from Abbeville.

N. B. Forrest, Major-General.[230]

Forrest to Confederate General James Ronald Chalmers, August 25, 1864:
☞ GRENADA [MISS.], AUGUST 25,1864. GENERAL CHALMERS, [AT] SPRINGDALE:

If you find the enemy are crossing the river, leaving a small force on this side, you will drive them across, and, if possible, destroy the bridge. If able to do so, follow them on their flanks and drive them still farther.

N. B. Forrest, Major-General.[231]

Forrest to Confederate General James Ronald Chalmers, August 26, 1864:
☛ GRENADA [MISS.], AUGUST 26,1864. GENERAL CHALMERS, [AT] WATER VALLEY:

You had better move one division in the neighborhood of Oakland, where forage can be procured. Let the other remain at Oxford and picket in direction of Holly Springs.

N. B. Forrest, Major-General.[232]

Forrest to Confederate General James Ronald Chalmers, August 26, 1864:
☛ GRENADA [MISS.], AUGUST 26,1864. GENERAL CHALMERS, [AT] WATER VALLEY:

Send Buford's division to Oxford with Rice's battery. Send the other three batteries to this place. Take your division in neighborhood of Oakland. Captain Forrest and Captain Saunders are at Panola; give them orders. Send all unattached companies here. Send and arrest Mitchell and his men. He has no authority from me to raise companies.

N. B. Forrest, Major-General.[233]

Forrest to Confederate Lieutenant Colonel George Deas, August 27, 1864:
☛ HEADQUARTERS FORREST'S CAVALRY, GRENADA, MISS., AUGUST 27, 1864. LIEUT. COL. GEORGE DEAS, CHIEF OF STAFF:

Colonel: I have this day received General Orders, No. 103, from headquarters Department of Alabama, Mississippi, and East Louisiana, assigning certain districts of the State of Mississippi to Brig. Gen. Wirt Adams and myself. General Adams' district is thus bounded in the order, "The Mississippi Central Railroad will hereafter form the eastern boundary line of said district." My district is described as "all that portion of the State of Mississippi lying north of the Southern Railroad, east of the Mississippi Central Railroad, and north and northeast of Brig. Gen. Wirt Adams' district." Having received no previous order districting the State, I do not clearly understand whether any portion of my district extends west of the Mississippi Central Railroad or not. The Southern Railroad extends from Vicksburg to Meridian. The Mississippi Central Railroad commences at Canton and runs north to the State line of Mississippi and Tennessee. Where is the northern boundary of General Wirt Adams' district? Does his district extend north of that portion of the Southern Railroad extending from Jackson, Miss., to Vicksburg; if so, how far north? I would recommend that the northern boundary of his district be described by county lines, which will make it definite.

I have the honor to be, yours, respectfully,

N. B. Forrest, Major-General.[234]

Forrest to Confederate General James Ronald Chalmers, August 27, 1864:
☞ GRENADA, AUGUST 27, 1864. BRIGADIER-GENERAL CHALMERS, [AT] WATER VALLEY:

Let Mabry's command come to Grenada. Keep your division where you can get forage best, so that you be convenient to Central railroad. I will be up on train in morning on my way to Oxford. Meet me at Water Valley.

N. B. Forrest, Major-General.[235]

Forrest to Confederate General Dabney Herndon Maury, August 30, 1864:
☞ GRENADA, AUGUST 30, 1864:

Enemy left Holy Springs at 2 A.M. yesterday, marching rapidly in direction of Memphis and La Grange. They say they are ordered to re-enforce Sherman.

N. B. Forrest, Major-General.[236]

Forrest to Confederate General Samuel Cooper, August 30, 1864:
☞ HEADQUARTERS FORREST'S CAVALRY; GRENADA [MISS.], AUGUST 30,1864. GENERAL S. COOPER, ADJUTANT AND INSPECTOR GENERAL, RICHMOND, VA.:

General: Accompanying [below] you will find General Orders, No. 73, from these headquarters, organizing and designating the different brigades and divisions composing my command. I most respectfully ask and recommend that the organizations as shown and the assignment to duty of the different officers maybe made permanent. The permanent assignment of Colonels Rucker, McCulloch, and Bell to the command of brigades is made upon the efficiency and gallantry of those officers, all of whom have served faithfully in the respective positions they are assigned to, and I take pleasure in saying that upon all occasions I have found them fully competent to perform the duties devolving upon them as brigade commanders. Hoping, general, that the organization as made by me may meet your approval, and the facts herein set forth concerning the officers mention above may have your consideration for permanent assignment ad promotions,

I have the honor to be, very respectfully, your obedient servant, N. B. Forrest, Major-General.[237]

GENERAL ORDERS, NO. 73, HEADQUARTERS FORREST'S CAVALRY, GRENADA [MISS.], AUGUST 30,1864.

I. The troops of this command will be organized and designated as follows: Rucker's brigade, Col. Edmund W. Rucker: Seventh Tennessee Cavalry, Col. William L. Duckworth; Neely's regiment Tennessee cavalry, James J. Neely; Twelfth Tennessee Cavalry, Col. Robert V. Richardson; Stewart's regiment Tennessee cavalry, Col. Francis M. Stewart; Twenty-sixth Tennessee Battalion Cavalry (General Forrest's old regiment), Lieut. Col. David C. Kelley.

McCulloch's brigade, Col. Robert McCulloch: Seventh Mississippi Cavalry (formerly First Mississippi Partisans), Lieut. Col. Samuel M. Hyams, jr.; Second Missouri Cavalry, Lieut. Col. Robert A. McCulloch; Fifth Mississippi Cavalry, Maj. W. G. Henderson; Willis' Battalion Texas Cavalry, Lieut. Col. Leonidas Willis; Eighth Mississippi Cavalry, Col. William L. Duff; Eighteenth Mississippi Cavalry Battalion, Lieut. Col. Alexander H. Chalmers.

Lyon's brigade, Brig. Gen. Hylan B. Lyon: Third Kentucky Cavalry, Col. Gustavus A. C. Holt; Eighth Kentucky Cavalry, Lieut. Col. A. R. Shacklett; Seventh Kentucky Cavalry, Col. Edward Crossland; Twelfth Kentucky Cavalry, Co. W. W. Faulkner.

Bell's brigade, Col. Tyree H. Bell: Barteau's regiment (Second Tennessee), Col. C. R. Barteau; Nineteenth Tennessee Cavalry, Col. John F. Newsom; Twentieth Tennessee Cavalry, Col. Robert M. Russell; Twenty-first Tennessee Cavalry, Col. Andrew N. Wilson.

II. Col. E. W. Rucker is assigned permanently to the command of the brigade designated as "Rucker's brigade."

III. Col. Robert McCulloch is assigned permanently to the command of the brigade designated as "McCulloch's brigade."

IV. Brig. Gen. H. B. Lyon is assigned permanently to the command of the brigade designated as "Lyon's brigade."

V. Col. T. H. Bell is assigned permanently to the command of the brigade designated as "Bell's brigade."

VI. Brig. Gen. J. R. Chalmers is assigned to the command of the division composed of the two brigades designated as Rucker's and McCulloch's brigades, and will be known as "Chalmers division."

VII. Brig. Gen. A. Buford is assigned to the command of the division composed of the two brigades designated as Lyon's and Bell's brigades, and will be known as "Buford's division."

By command of Major-General Forrest: J. P. Strange, Assistant Adjutant-General.[238]

Forrest to Confederate General James Ronald Chalmers, August 30, 1864:
☞ GRENADA [MISS.], AUGUST 30, 1864. BRIGADIER-GENERAL CHALMERS, [AT] WATER VALLEY:

Move to-morrow morning with your entire division and wagon train to this place, leaving Captains Forrest's and Saunders' companies at Panola with directions to guard and report to General Buford any movements of the enemy.

N. B. Forrest, Major-General.[239]

Forrest to Confederate General James Ronald Chalmers, September 2, 1864:
☞ GRENADA [MISS.], SEPTEMBER 2, 1864. BRIGADIER-GENERAL CHALMERS, [AT] WEST POINT.

Ship 2,000 of your best men and horses, and five of your best wagons and teams, and five ambulances to Mobile; the rest of your command and trains to move slowly to Meridian and await orders.

N. B. Forrest, Major-General.[240]

Forrest to Confederate General Dabney Herndon Maury, September 2, 1864:
☞ GRENADA [MISS.], SEPTEMBER 2, 1864:

Reported enemy's cavalry from Memphis will move in direction of Nashville. Trains going east, loaded with forage. Troops at Memphis under McPherson ordered up river.

N. B. Forrest, Major-General.[241]

Forrest to Union General Cadwallader Colden Washburn, September 3, 1864:
☞ HEADQUARTERS FORREST'S CAVALRY. (RECEIVED HDQRS. DIST. OF WEST TENN., SEPTEMBER 3, 1864.) MAJ. GEN. C. C. WASHBURN, COMMANDING U.S. FORCES, MEMPHIS, TENN.:

Sir: I have the honor to acknowledge receipt of your letter of 17th instant, per flag of truce in charge of Lieutenant Kinzie.

On the 14th I sent you, per flag of truce in charge of Lieutenant-Colonel Pitman, a proposition to exchange Colonel McKeaig and other wounded officers and men of your army for men of my command. The flag with your reply has not yet returned, therefore I am unable to determine the disposition to be made of them. I take advantage of the opportunity afforded by the return of Lieutenant-Colonel Hepburn, the bearer of the second flag, to say that unless exchanged for, I of course will have to retain them for regular exchange through the usual channel.

I am, general, very respectfully, your obedient servant,

N. B. Forrest, Major-General.[242]

Forrest to Confederate President Jefferson Davis, September 5, 1864:
☞ MERIDIAN [MISS.], SEPTEMBER 5, 1864.

The President: If permitted to do so with 4,000 picked men and six pieces of artillery of my present command, I believe I can proceed to Middle and West Tennessee, destroy enemy's communication or cripple it, and add 2,000 men to my command.

N. B. Forrest, Major-General.[243]

Forrest to Confederate General James Ronald Chalmers, September 6, 1864:
☞ MERIDIAN [MISS.], SEPTEMBER 6, 1864. BRIGADIER GENERAL CHALMERS:

Move your troops from West Point to Aberdeen. Cheer up and be prepared for a move in the direction of Memphis.

N. B. Forrest, Major-General.[244]

Forrest to Confederate General James Ronald Chalmers, September 6, 1864:
☞ MERIDIAN [MISS.], SEPTEMBER 6, 1864. BRIGADIER GENERAL CHALMERS:

Send the balance of McCulloch's brigade, his cooking utensils, four ordnance and eight other wagons and teams, to Mobile.

N. B. Forrest, Major-General.[245]

Forrest to Confederate General James Ronald Chalmers, September 6, 1864:
☞ MERIDIAN [MISS.], SEPTEMBER 6, 1864. BRIGADIER GENERAL CHALMERS:

Let the balance of McCulloch's men remain until I return from Mobile, but send wagons as previously ordered. Let Neely stay where he is if he can shoe his horses.

N. B. Forrest, Major-General.[246]

Forrest to Confederate General Richard Taylor (son of U.S. President Zachary Taylor and President Jefferson Davis' former brother-in-law), September 18, 1864:
☞ HEADQUARTERS FORREST'S CAVALRY, CHEROKEE, SEPTEMBER 18, 1864. LIEUT. GEN. R. TAYLOR, COMMANDING DEPT. OF ALA., MISS., AND EAST LA., [AT] MOBILE:

General I have the honor to announce my arrival here by rail this evening. Buford's division has also reached here and Rucker's brigade will be here to-morrow. I have not seen Major-General Wheeler yet, but I understand that his command will not number more than 2,000 men; the men have deserted and straggled off to such an extent, and a portion of them cut off or lost, and the above is represented as his effective strength. General Roddey claims to have 2,000 men, but they are much scattered, and it is uncertain what number can be relied on from that quarter. The enemy are reported in heavy force in Middle Tennessee. Nevertheless, I shall go on and do the best I can. I learn from a person who left Memphis a few days since that another move against North Mississippi is in preparation. General Smith has returned to Memphis. Their lines are closed, and under the circumstances I have telegraphed General Chalmers as per copy inclosed. I respectfully suggest that unless much needed at Mobile, McCulloch's brigade be sent to Tupelo or Verona. There is a regiment of State troops at Corinth, but

I do not consider them sufficient for the protection of this road; hence the suggestion in regard to McCulloch's brigade.

I am, general, very respectfully, your obedient servant,

N. B. Forrest, Major-General.[247]

[INCLOSURE ATTACHED TO PREVIOUS LETTER]
☛ HEADQUARTERS CHEROKEE, SEPTEMBER 18, 1864. BRIG. GEN. JAMES R. CHALMERS, OR COMMANDING OFFICER, [AT] GRENADA:

You will send at once a sufficient force to break the railroad from La Grange to as near Memphis as practicable, burning all the bridges and trestles and destroying the road as thoroughly as possible.

N. B. Forrest, Major-General.[248]

Forrest to Confederate General Richard Taylor, September 20, 1864:
☛ HEADQUARTERS FORREST'S CAVALRY, CHEROKEE, SEPTEMBER 20, 1864. LIEUT. GEN. R. TAYLOR, COMMANDING, &C.:

General: I have the honor to state that I met Major-General Wheeler to-day at Tuscumbia. His command is in a demoralized condition. He claims to have about 2,000 men with him; his adjutant-general says, however, that he will not be able to raise and carry back with him exceeding 1,000, and in all probability not over 500. One of his brigades left him and he does not know whether they are captured or have returned, or are still in Middle Tennessee. He sent General Martin back in arrest, and his whole command is demoralized to such an extent that he expresses himself as disheartened, and that, having lost influence with the troops, and being unable to secure the aid and co-operation of his officers, he believes it to the interest of the service that he should be relieved from command. General Roddey is sick, but has ordered three regiments—I suppose about 900 men—to report to me. You will see, therefore, that I can expect but little assistance, but will nevertheless go ahead; am all ready and will move in the morning and have my command across the river to-morrow night. General Wheeler has turned over to me what he has of my old brigade, numbering sixty men. When I left it with him last November it then numbered over 2,300 for duty. I hope to be instrumental in gathering them up. I am satisfied that many will flock to me and I shall greatly need the arms telegraphed for to-night.

I am, general, yours, &c.,

N. B. Forrest, Major-General.[249]

Forrest to Confederate General Richard Taylor, September 24, 1864:

☛ ATHENS, ALA., SEPTEMBER 24, 1864. LIEUT. GEN. R. TAYLOR, [AT] SELMA, ALA.:

My forces captured this place this morning with 1,300 officers and men, 50 wagons and ambulances, 500 horses, 2 trains of cars loaded with quartermaster's and commissary stores, with a large quantity of small-arms, and 2 pieces of artillery. My troops in fine spirits. My loss, 5 killed and 25 wounded.

N. B. Forrest, Major-General.[250]

Forrest to Union Colonel Wallace Campbell of the One Hundred and Tenth U.S. Colored Infantry, September 24, 1867:

☛ HEADQUARTERS FORREST'S CAVALRY, IN THE FIELD, SEPTEMBER 24, 1864. OFFICER COMMANDING U. S. FORCES, ATHENS, ALABAMA:

I demand an immediate and unconditional surrender of the entire force and all government stores and property at this post. I have a sufficient force to storm and take your works, and if I am forced to do so the responsibility of the consequences must rest with you. Should you, however, accept the terms, all white soldiers shall be treated as prisoners of war and the negroes returned to their masters. A reply is requested immediately. Respectfully,

N. B. Forrest, Major-General, C.S. Army.[251]

When Union Colonel Wallace Campbell, the officer in charge, rejected Forrest's demand, Forrest sent him the following the same day:

☛ ATHENS [ALABAMA], SEPTEMBER 24, 1864:

Colonel, I desire an interview with you outside of the fort, at any place you may designate, provided it meets with your views. My only object is to stop the effusion of blood that must follow the storming of the place.

N. B. Forrest, Major-General.[252]

After Forrest tricked Colonel Campbell into thinking he had over 10,000 soldiers (he actually had far less), Campbell surrendered, only to learn that he had been duped by the wily Confederate chieftain. Campbell was then forced to sign the following "terms of capitulation" drawn up by Forrest:

☞ AGREEMENT ENTERED INTO AT ATHENS, ALA., ON THE 24TH DAY OF SEPTEMBER, 1864, BY MAJ. GEN. N. B. FORREST, OF THE C.S. ARMY, AND COL. WALLACE CAMPBELL, ONE HUNDRED AND TENTH REGIMENT U.S. COLORED INFANTRY.

We, on the part of our respective Governments, stipulate and agree that the following articles shall be faithfully executed and maintained: On the part of the U.S. Government, by Col. Wallace Campbell, that the fort and United States and public Government property at this point be, and the same hereby are, surrendered to Maj. Gen. N. B. Forrest, of the C.S. Army. On the part of the C.S. Government, by Maj. Gen. N. B. Forrest, that all commissioned officers surrendered or surrendering as above, be, and hereby are, permitted to go to Meridian or some other point in Mississippi, and the said officers shall, so soon as Major-General Forrest can communicate with Major-General Washburn, U.S. Volunteers, be sent to Major-General Washburn or other commanding officer at Memphis, Tenn., to be retained on their paroles of honor not to act in opposition to the forces of the Confederate States until they are duly exchanged by Generals Washburn and Forrest, which exchange shall occur as speedily as possible. The exchange is to be conducted by an exchange of officers for officers of same rank, and man for man.

Again, said commissioned officers shall and hereby are permitted to retain and keep all their personal property, including horses, saddles, side-arms, and clothing. All this permanently.

Again, the enlisted men (soldiers) of Col. Wallace Campbell's command shall be kindly and humanely treated and turned over to the C.S. Government as prisoners of war, to be disposed of as the War Department of the Confederate States shall direct.

N. B. Forrest, Major-General, Commanding, C.S. Army.

Wallace Campbell, Colonel 110th U.S. Colored Infantry, Commanding.[253]

Forrest to Confederate General Richard Taylor, September 25, 1864:

☞ HEADQUARTERS FORREST'S CAVALRY, NINE MILES NORTH OF ATHENS [ALA.], SEPTEMBER 25, 1864. LIEUT. GEN. R. TAYLOR, COMDG. DEPT. OF ALABAMA, MISSISSIPPI, AND EAST LOUISIANA:

General: I would respectfully suggest that you send a command to Corinth for the purpose of protecting the railroad and other prisoners which I expect to send you. Will leave in the morning for Elkton and Pulaski.

Respectfully,

N. B. Forrest, Major-General.[254]

Forrest to Union Captain H. J. Walker, September 26, 1864:

☞ HEADQUARTERS FORREST'S CAVALRY, IN THE FIELD, SEPTEMBER 26, 1864. CAPTAIN WALKER, COMMANDING [U.S.] GARRISON, ROCKLAND STATION:

I have the garrison commanded by you invested with a force amply sufficient to storm and capture it. In order to prevent the effusion of blood I demand an immediate surrender. All the forts and block-houses from this place to Decatur have surrendered, and I can grant you the same terms upon which they surrendered.

If you force me to storm your works and take them I cannot be responsible for the result.

You can have an interview with me personally, should you desire it, and examine the terms upon which the other forts and block-houses surrendered.

Respectfully,

N. B. Forrest, Major-General, C. S. Army.[255]

Forrest to Confederate General Richard Taylor, September 27, 1864:

☞ SOUTH OF PULASKI, TENN., SEPTEMBER 27,1864. LIEUT. GEN. R. TAYLOR, SELMA, ALA.:

I succeeded yesterday in capturing 4 trestles, 3 block-houses, and the fort at Elk River, with about 50 prisoners, without the loss of a man, and have entirely destroyed the railroad from Decatur to Pulaski and 5 large railroad bridges, which will require sixty days to replace.

N. B. Forrest, Major-General.[256]

Forrest to Confederate General Richard Taylor, September 27, 1864:

☞ HALF MILE SOUTH OF PULASKI, TENN., SEPTEMBER 27, 1864. LIEUT. GEN. R. TAYLOR, SELMA, ALA.:

I have driven enemy, after fighting here all day, into his fortifications at this place, and find [Union] General Rousseau with heavy force well fortified. I will move to Nashville and Chattanooga Railroad. My loss to-day about 100 wounded; enemy's much heavier, having contested ground for several miles. Enemy concentrating heavily against me.

N. B. Forrest.[257]

Forrest to Union Brigadier General Robert Seaman Granger, September 30, 1864:

☞ HEADQUARTERS FORREST'S CAVALRY, IN THE FIELD, NEAR HUNTSVILLE, ALA., SEPTEMBER 30, 1864. BRIGADIER-GENERAL GRANGER, COMMANDING U.S. FORCES, HUNTSVILLE, ALA.:

General: Your communication addressed to [my officer] Brigadier-General Buford, concerning the positions to be assumed by the two belligerent parties, has this moment been referred to me. I respectfully decline acceding to them. I expect to attack you to-morrow morning from every rock, house, tree, and shrub in the vicinity, and feeling confident of my ability to succeed in my anticipated attempt, now bid you prepare yourself for the fray. I, however, cheerfully accept the proposition you made to Brigadier-General Buford, namely, to allow two hours of daylight to-morrow morning for the purpose of allowing non-combatants to remove beyond the lines. At the expiration of the third hour of the coming day I shall commence offensive operations, unless another communication is received from you before that time.

I am, general, with great respect,

N. B. Forrest, Major-General, Provisional Army, C.S., Commanding.[258]

From Forrest to General Richard Taylor, October 8, 1864:

☞ HEADQUARTERS FORREST'S CAVALRY, CHEROKEE, OCTOBER 8, 1864. LIEUT. GEN. R. TAYLOR, GENERAL:

I have been constantly in the field since 1861, and have spent half the entire time in the saddle. I have never asked for a furlough for over ten days in which to rest and recruit, and except when wounded and unable to leave my bed have had no respite from duty. My strength is failing and it is absolutely necessary that I should have some rest. I left a large estate [Green Grove, at Sunflower Landing] in Mississippi and have never given my private affairs a day's attention at any one time since the war began. Will make the trip to West Tennessee, and hope as soon thereafter as you can do so[,] you will relieve me from duty for twenty or thirty days to rest and recruit. I have received letters from Colonel McCulloch at Mobile. He and his command are much dissatisfied, and I respectfully ask that my two divisions be placed as they originally were under the command of Brigadier-Generals Chalmers and Buford, and that Mabry's brigade be substituted for McCulloch's, which change would in my opinion be satisfactory to all parties. I have captured since I came into this department over 30 pieces of artillery, fitting up my command with four batteries (in all sixteen guns). They are now scattered, and I desire if possible to get all my command together, and with General Chalmers as senior officer feel that it would be safe to leave the command for a short time, which in my present state of health is absolutely necessary and which you will confer a favor on me by granting as early as consistent with the good of the service.

I am, general, very respectfully, your obedient servant,

N. B. Forrest, Major-General.[259]

Forrest's to Confederate Major P. Ellis, October 17, 1864, concerning his recent "Operations in Northern Alabama and Middle Tennessee":

☞ REPORT OF MAJ. GEN. NATHAN B. FORREST, C.S. ARMY. HEADQUARTERS FORREST'S CAVALRY CORINTH, OCTOBER 17, 1864. [TO: MAJ. P. ELLIS, ASSISTANT ADJUTANT-GENERAL, SELMA, ALA.]

Major: I have the honor to submit the following report of the action of my command during the recent operations in Northern Alabama and Middle Tennessee:

Pursuant to orders from Lieut. Gen. R. Taylor I moved with my commmd from Verona, Miss., on the 16th of September and arrived at Cherokee on the 18th. Cherokee is the eastern terminus of the Memphis and Charleston Railroad, and at this place I had concentrated everything necessary for the complete outfit of my command preparatory to the contemplated move. My men being provided with ten days rations, and everything in readiness, the command left Cherokee at daylight on the morning of the 21st. The artillery, ordnance and wagon trains were placed under the charge of Maj. C. W. Anderson, of my staff, with instructions to be ferried across the Tennessee River at Newport, where boats had already been sent for that purpose. With my troops I moved down the river to Ross' Ford, or Colbert's Shoals, and forded with but little difficulty. The artillery and wagon trains were safely and rapidly ferried over and joined the main body of the command five miles west of Florence. The command encamped at Florence, having crossed the river and traveled about twenty-five miles during the day.

On the morning of the 22d I moved in the direction of Athens, Ala. At Shoal Creek, six miles east of Florence, I was joined by General Roddey's troops, under the command of Col. William A. Johnson, who had been previously ordered to cross the river at Bainbridge and to join me at this place. My entire force now consisted of General Buford's division, composed of Colonel Bell's and General Lyon's brigades, and Colonel Kelley's brigade with General [Philip D.] Roddey's troops, commanded by Colonel Johnson, who reported directly to me. These commands constituted an available force of 4,500 men. About 400 of these were dismounted, which I moved with my command on foot, with the expectation of being able to mount them on horses captured from the enemy. After moving on to Masonville I halted and ordered up the wagon train for the purpose of furnishing Colonel Johnson's troops with ammunition and rations. About 10 o'clock at night I ordered the Twentieth Regiment Tennessee Cavalry, under the command of Lieut. Col. Jesse A. Forrest, and the Fourteenth Tennessee Cavalry, commanded by Lieutenant-Colonel White, of Kelley's brigade, to move during the night to McDonald's Station, between Decatur and Athens, and there capture a Government corral said to be located near that place, and also to destroy the railroad and telegraph line.

On the morning of the 23d the march toward Athens was resumed, which place was reached late in the evening. The enemy's pickets were developed about one mile from town and rapidly driven into the fort, when the enemy opened upon us with two pieces of artillery. The whistle of the locomotive was heard at the station, and I ordered the Second Tennessee, commanded by Colonel Barteau and Major Anderson, of my staff, to take my escort and move rapidly to the north side of town and cut the railroad and telegraph wires. This order was promptly executed, after which the same troops captured about 100 horses and some other property, then moved to the station, and returned and encamped upon the railroad during the night. At the same time I ordered Colonel Bell to move with his brigade on the right and occupy the eastern part of town. After some severe skirmishing Colonel Bell succeeded in driving the enemy into town, and rested during the night in the position to which he had been ordered. Colonel Kelley was ordered at a still later hour in the night to move round and occupy the southeast part of town, his left resting near the railroad, his right extending toward Colonel Bell's left. General Buford, with General Lyon's brigade, was ordered to remain on the west, his left on the Florence and Athens road, and his right on the Athens and Brown's Ferry road. Col. Jesse A. Forrest and Lieutenant-Colonel White, who were returning up the road from the duty assigned them the previous night, halted and occupied the ground between the Brown's Ferry road and the railroad. The town, fort, and block-houses were thus invested on the night of the 23d. The next morning Colonel Johnson, who had not previously been placed in position, was ordered to occupy the street leading from the court-house toward Florence.

During the night of the 23d and the morning of the 24th my artillery had been ordered in position bearing upon the fort. Hudson's battery, commanded by Lieut. E. S. Walton, was placed northeast of the fort; one section of Morton's battery, commanded by Lieut. Joe M. Mayson, on the west; the other section of Morton's battery, commanded by Lieut. J. W. Brown, on the north, all under the command of Capt. John W. Morton. About 7 o'clock, everything being in readiness, a general advance was ordered upon the fort and the artillery to open fire upon it. Colonel Bell's brigade, on the east, soon advanced across the railroad in full view of the fort. General Buford, with General Lyon's brigade, was moving forward on the west. Colonel Kelley was ordered to remain in his position, to throw out flankers, and to hold in check the re-enforcements reported to be advancing from the direction of Decatur. While my troops were steadily advancing upon the fort, and the artillery was pouring into it a concentrated fire, I ordered a halt and the artillery to cease firing. Knowing it would cost heavily to storm and capture the enemy's works, and wishing to prevent the effusion of blood that I knew would follow a successful assault, I determined to see if anything could be accomplished by negotiations. Accordingly, I sent Major Strange, of my staff, with a flag of truce, demanding the surrender of the fort and garrison. After much apparent hesitancy, [Union] Colonel [Wallace] Campbell refused to make the surrender. I returned to my command determined to renew the assault; but still desiring to spare my men and the massacre of the garrison, I sent another flag requesting an interview with Colonel Campbell at any place he might designate outside of the fort. The interview was granted. I assured Colonel Campbell that for the sake of humanity, I should do everything in my power to prevent a collision, and for that purpose I invited him to examine my troops for himself and judge of my ability to take his works. He accompanied me along my lines, and after witnessing the strength and enthusiasm of my troops he surrendered the fort with its entire garrison. Mean time heavy firing was heard down the road in the direction of Decatur. Dispatches informed me that re-enforcements were endeavoring to cut their way to the beleaguered fort. Colonel Kelley endeavored to intercept them with his brigade. The enemy took position behind a pile of cord wood where the railroad runs through a cut. The Fifteenth Tennessee, Col. Thomas H. Logwood commanding, with two companies of Forrest's regiment, charged them behind their breastworks, putting them to flight, killing several and capturing 8 prisoners. The re-enforcements then renewed their efforts to gain the fort and fought with great gallantry and desperation. They pressed on, but found the Twenty-first Tennessee, commanded by Lieutenant-Colonel Forrest, between them and the fort. This gallant regiment opened fire upon the advancing enemy, and it was during this engagement that Lieutenant-Colonel Forrest fell severely wounded. I ordered Colonel Nixon and Colonel Carter, with their respective commands (numbering about 150 men each), reporting to me, to move rapidly to the relief of Colonel Wilson. They did so, and after a short engagement the re-enforcements surrendered and marched up just in time to see the garrison march out of the fort and stack their arms. One block-house surrendered without the least hesitancy. The other defiantly refused. The artillery opened upon it. The second shot penetrated the walls, killing 2 negroes and wounding another, which caused the officer commanding to surrender. Everything of value being removed, the block-houses were burned and such parts of the fort as could be consumed by fire. Two locomotives and 2 trains of [railroad] cars were also burned. The enemy during the night destroyed many valuable stores of every description. Two pieces of artillery, a large amount of small-arms, 38 wagons, 2 ambulances, 300 horses, and a considerable amount of ordnance, quartermaster's, and commissary stores were captured. The prisoners and captured property were immediately started for Cherokee, under the command of Colonel Nixon.

In a few hours after the surrender of Athens I moved with my command toward Pulaski. Four miles north of Athens another block-house, with a garrison of 30 men, was surrounded and captured. The trestle railroad, and block-house at this point were all in blazing ruins twenty minutes after we reached them. I moved on and encamped eight miles from Athens at night.

The Sulphur Springs trestle was only two miles off, and on the morning of the 25th I moved upon that place, said to be the strongest on the road. The enemy's pickets were driven in with but little difficulty and the place soon invested. His defenses consisted of two block-houses and a large fort situated upon an eminence, but fortunately for us surrounded by hills still more elevated. I ordered the artillery to be placed at once in position. One section of Hudson's battery, commanded by Lieut. E. S. Walton, was placed on the southwest; one section, Ferrell's, commanded by Lieutenant Ozburn, on the southwest; one section of Morton's on the east, commanded by Lieut. J. W. Brown, the other section on the north, commanded by Lieut. J. M. Mayson, all under the direction of Captain Morton. The necessary disposition of troops being made, a general advance was ordered toward the fort. General Buford's division moved with alacrity and great promptitude. Colonel Kelley dashed across the field, followed by his brigade, and after reaching his desired position the enemy dared not raise his head above his own works. Colonel Johnson and his brave troops on this occasion acted within conspicuous gallantry in marching up and assaulting the enemy's works. Mean time the eight pieces of artillery from four different points poured a concentrated storm of shell into the fort. After two hours bombardment the enemy's guns were silenced and he exhibited no show of resistance. I deemed this an appropriate occasion to demand a surrender, and sent a flag of truce for that purpose. After a short parley with Col. J. B. Minnis, the commanding officer, who had expressed a desire for an interview, the fort surrendered. The enemy suffered severely in this assault. The colonel commanding was killed early in the fight. Almost every house was perforated with shell, and the dead lay thick along the works of the fort. The fruits of this victory consist, besides the prisoners, of 700 stand of small-arms, 2 pieces artillery, 3 ambulances, 16 wagons, 300 cavalry horses and equipments, medical, quartermaster's, and commissary stores. The trestle-work at this fort was 72 feet high and 300 feet long, and defended by two large block-houses, all of which were consumed by fire, and the prisoners turned over to Colonel Logwood, who started with them to the Tennessee River.

On the morning of the 26th the march toward Pulaski was renewed. With the horses captured at Athens and Sulphur Springs trestle I was now enabled to mount the troops that had been marching with my command on foot and to supply others whose horses had given out. I ordered General Buford to move along the dirt road parallel with the railroad. With the balance of my command I moved to Elkton. General Buford found the block-house at Elk River evacuated, which he destroyed, with the extensive bridge across the river and all the trestle-work on the opposite side. From Elkton I directed my course toward a Government corral at Brown's plantation, toward Pulaski. At this place I found about 2,000 negroes, consisting mostly of old men, women, and children, besides a large amount of commissary stores and medical supplies. General Buford having completed his work at Elk River joined me at this place, where I issued to my entire command several days rations, distributing among the troops as much sugar and coffee as they needed. The negroes were all ragged and dirty, and many seemed in absolute want. I ordered them to remove their clothing and bed clothes from the miserable hovels in which they lived and then burnt up this den of wretchedness. Near 200 houses were consumed.

From this corral I proceeded with my command to Richland Creek, six miles south of Pulaski, over which there was a long bridge defended by a block-house. The enemy returned to his works, from which he made a furious assault upon my troops, who were steadily advancing. With a part of my staff I crossed the creek and gained the rear of the enemy, from which point I sent a flag of truce, making the usual demand for surrender, which demand was promptly complied with, and fifty more prisoners yielded up their arms.

From Richland Creek I moved a part of my command across to the Pulaski and Elkton pike road, and encamped during the night ten miles from the former place.

On the morning of the 27th I ordered General Buford's division up the pike road toward Pulaski; Colonel Kelley's brigade and Johnson's command were ordered to advance on the road I had left the previous evening, running nearly parallel with the railroad. Six miles from Pulaski the enemy attacked my advance force and compelled them to fall back. General Buford hurried forward his division. I sent my escort to the extreme right, where they found the enemy strongly posted, and where seven of my escort were severely wounded in the engagement that occurred. The resistance of the enemy was most obstinate. He contested every inch of ground and grew more stubborn the nearer we approached town, but my troops drove them steadily back. Three miles from Pulaski he made a stand with seeming determination to yield no more ground. Colonel Kelley now occupied the extreme left, Colonel Johnson the center, and General Buford's division on the right. The engagement was becoming a general one. The enemy threw his right around for the purpose of making an enfilading fire upon my troops who had pushed far into his center. About this time my troops on the left advanced, and the artillery in that direction unexpectedly opened a destructive fire, which caused the enemy to make a hasty retreat. He was closely followed up and driven into town and into his fortifications. My command reached Pulaski about 1 o'clock, after seven hours constant fighting. With my escort I moved to the extreme right and succeeded in reaching the northern part of town. After making a careful reconnaissance I was fully satisfied that the enemy was strongly posted with a large force. I therefore determined to make no further assault, and returned to the left and ordered the entire command to be withdrawn. It was now nearly night, and I ordered camp-fires to be built along my entire lines for the purpose of deceiving the enemy. Pickets were thrown out in front of the fires to prevent him from discovering my real movements.

On leaving Pulaski I ordered Colonel Wheeler to proceed north of the town and to destroy the railroad and the telegraph line between Pulaski and Columbia. This duty was faithfully performed by Colonel Wheeler, who in addition burned a large wood-yard on the road. The night was exceedingly dark and the roads I was forced to travel almost impassable, and after marching eight miles from Pulaski I was forced to halt for the night.

On the 28th I reached Fayetteville. During the day I ordered Captain [Nathan] Boone, of my escort, to proceed with twenty men as rapidly as possible to the Nashville and Chattanooga Railroad and cut the same, with telegraph wires, at some point north of Tullahoma. At the same time I ordered Captain Kelleher, with thirty men of the Twelfth Kentucky, to move forward and strike the road and wires at some point south of Tullahoma. Both of these officers faithfully performed the work assigned them.

I encamped five miles from Fayetteville on the night of the 28th. The next morning I moved toward Tullahoma. About noon I halted my command near Mulberry. At this place I learned from my scouts, and from the concurrent testimony of reliable citizens, that the enemy was in strong force at Tullahoma, and at all other vulnerable points on the railroad in that direction. Re-enforcements from Atlanta, Chattanooga, and other points were being hurried forward. There were not less than 15,000 troops sent forward to intercept my movements. The severe engagements with the enemy at Athens, Sulphur Springs trestle, and Pulaski had exhausted nearly all my artillery ammunition. I had not over 100 rounds to the gun; besides, my forces had been greatly depleted by the large number necessarily sent back to guard prisoners and the captured property. Under these circumstances I deemned it hazardous and unwise to move upon the enemy, who was prepared to meet me with overwhelming numbers. Consequently I commenced disposing of my troops with a view of operating where there was a prospect of accomplishing some good. General Buford, with a portion of his division and parts of Kelley's and Johnson's troops, constituting a force of about 1,500 men, was ordered to proceed in the direction of Huntsville, to burn the bridge over Flint River at Brownsborough, to capture Huntsville if possible, and then destroy the Memphis and Charleston Railroad from Huntsville to Decatur. With the balance of my troops, consisting of parts of General Lyon's and Colonel Bell's brigades, the Seventh Tennessee, and Forrest's old regiment, I changed my course from toward Tullahomna to the Tennessee and Alabama Railroad. Leaving Shelbyville to the right I marched on an obscure, circuitous road to Lewisburg, which place I reached at 12 o'clock on the 30th. At night I camped on the north side of Duck River.

On the 1st of October I moved upon Spring Hill, capturing at that place and in the neighborhood several Government horses and wagons, besides the stage running from Columbia to Nashville. After proceeding four miles along the pike road toward Columbia I turned abruptly to the right, ordering Colonel Bell to send one regiment on the pike road to develop the enemy and to watch his movements. After leaving the pike road running from Spring Hill to Columbia I moved my command upon the railroad twelve miles from Columbia. Here I found four block-houses, four bridges, an unusual amount of wood, an extensive Government saw-mill, several wagons, and about twenty head of cattle. The enemy made a feeble resistance and retreated to his fortifications. The usual demand to surrender was made, and after much hesitancy the demand was reluctantly complied with. One hundred and twenty prisoners surrendered. Immense injury was inflicted upon the enemy at this point. Four block-houses, three railroad bridges, wood-yard, and saw-mill were all consumed by fire. One block-house refused to surrender. I had not a single piece of artillery with me and could not force a surrender; but at night Colonel Bell called for volunteers to burn the bridge commanded by the block-house. Ten gallant men were marched forward, and in the face of the murderous fire applied the torch, which burned the bridge enough to make it useless, and to make the construction of a new one indispensable. The night was dark, but my command marched by the light of the burning ruins, which illuminated the country for miles.

On the morning of the 2d I proceeded toward Columbia, eight miles distant from where I encamped the previous night. Six miles from town I ordered Colonel Wheeler to advance and drive in the enemy's pickets. I followed close upon his rear with my whole command. Colonel Bell's brigade was ordered to move upon the northern part of town, General Lyon was ordered to throw his brigade on the west, but south of the Mount Pleasant pike. The reasons that prevented my storming and capturing Pulaski now existed with redoubled force, for I had not a single piece of artillery, and only half of the troops I had with me at Pulaski. Not intending to make a formidable assault I did not press the enemy. My object in making this demonstration was to take observations for future operations. Satisfying myself of the strength and position of the forts and fortifications, I returned toward Mount Pleasant, at which place I camped during the night.

On the 3d I camped eleven miles from Lawrenceburg. On the 4th I halted eighteen miles from florence. On the 5th I reached Florence. Here I found the river, which my troops forded two weeks previous, swollen by recent rains. The enemy was reported advancing on the Athens road. I ordered Colonel Windes, of General Roddey's command, to Shoal Creek with his regiment, and to hold him in check while my troops were crossing. The boats at Bainbridge were ordered down to the mouth of Cypress, at which place many of my troops were ferried over; but the next morning, the enemy making his appearance in Florence, the boats were dropped still lower down the river. The winds had made the river so rough that it was hazardous to ferry it, but the boats made regular trips day and night. But the enemy were pressing upon my rear, which was greatly endangered. At this critical juncture I ordered all troops on the north side of the river, with the exception of one regiment, to mount their horses and swim them across a slough about seventy yards wide to a large island, which would afford them ample protection and from which they could ferry over at leisure. Colonel Wilson was ordered to remain with his regiment and to skirmish with the enemy, and thereby divert his attention until the other troops had reached the island. This strategy was successful. Every man reached the island in safety. Colonel Wilson is entitled to the commendation of his Government and the lasting gratitude for the faithful [manner] in which he performed this important and hazardous trust. Surrounded by 15,000 of the enemy for three days, he hung upon his flanks, assaulted him on every favorable occasion, and would retire to the hills when pushed. He subsisted upon supplies captured from the enemy. He made no effort to escape from his perilous situation, but faithfully remained in the discharge of his duty until every Confederate soldier was across the river and the enemy commenced his retreat, when, unmolested, he ferried over his regiment and joined his command. Colonel Wilson had only 2 men killed and 4 missing, while he killed and wounded about 75 of the enemy.

I reached Cherokee on the 6th of October, which place I left on the 21st of September. Apprehending that the enemy would make an effort to throw troops across the river, I ordered, on the 9th, Colonel Kelley, with his brigade and one section of Hudson's battery, commanded by Lieutenant Walton, to proceed to Eastport and prevent any advance in that direction. On the 10th the enemy moved up the river with two gun-boats and three transports. Colonel Kelley masked his forces until the enemy debarked a brigade of infantry and three pieces of artillery, when he opened fire upon them with his artillery. Two balls penetrated one gun-boat and a shell burst in one of the transports, causing it to be enveloped in steam and flame. The first fire from the artillery caused the boats to push off from shore. Many in attempting to reach the boat were drowned, 12 were killed on the bank, and a large number killed and wounded on the boat; about 30 prisoners captured, with 3 James rifled guns, 60 small-arms, 20 horses, 4 boat cables, with some artillery harness. It was evident that a preconcerted plan had been arranged to capture my command. At least 15,000 men had been thrown forward for this purpose. Troops from half a dozen different commands were at Florence, at which place the enemy expected to intercept my crossing. The cavalry, under the command of [Union] General Hatch, and infantry were sent from Memphis up the Tennessee to aid in my capture. They are still on the opposite bank of the river but prevented from crossing by my troops, who are watching their movements.

The official report of my provost-marshal shows that during the expedition I captured 86 commissioned officers, 67 Government employés, 1,274 non-commissioned officers and privates, 933 negroes, besides killing and wounding in the various engagements about 1,000 more, making an aggregate of 3,360, being an average of one to each man I had in the engagements. In addition to these I captured about 800 horses, 7 pieces of artillery, 2,000 stand small-arms, several hundred saddles, 50 wagons and ambulances, with a large amount of medical, commissary, and quartermaster's stores, all of which has been distributed to the different commands. The greatest damage, however, done to the enemy was in the complete destruction of the railroad from Decatur to

Spring Hill, with the exception of the Duck River bridge. It will require months to repair the injury done to the road, and may possibly be the means of forcing the evacuation of Pulaski and Columbia, and thus relieve the people from further oppression.

During the trip mny troops supplied themselves with boots, shoes, hats, blankets, overcoats, oil-cloths, and almost everything necessary for their comfort. The accompanying report from Dr. J. B. Cowan, my chief surgeon, shows that in all the engagements my loss was 47 killed, 293 wounded, making a total of 340 killed and wounded.

My troops during the expedition acted with their accustomed gallantry. In camp, on the march, in the battle they exhibited all the traits of the gallant soldier. I take pleasure in commending the steadiness, self-denial, and patriotism with which they bore the hardships and privations incident to such a campaign. General Buford's division fully sustained that reputation it has so nobly won. General Lyon and Colonel Bell added new laurels to the chaplet which their valor and patriotism has already won. Colonel Johnson, commanding General Roddey's troops, displayed every soldierly virtue. He was prompt in obeying orders. I regret to announce that while gallantly leading his troops he was severely wounded. I take pleasure also in calling the notice of the Government to the conduct of Colonel Kelley, commanding Colonel [Edmund Winchester] Rucker's brigade. He displayed all the dash, energy, and gallantry which has so long made him an efficient officer, and justly merits promotion by his Government. The conduct of Lieut. Col. Jesse A. Forrest at Athens, Ala., is worthy of mention. While the enemy was attempting to re-enforce the fort, at the head of his splendid regiment, Colonel Forrest made a gallant charge, driving the enemy from his position, but in this charge he received a severe wound in the thigh. The splendid discipline of Col. James M. Warren's troops, of General Roddey's command, attracted my attention and received my commendation on the field. They moved forward in perfect order and with the steadiness of veteran soldiers. Colonel Warren has few superiors in the service, and is entitled to special mention for his uniform gallantry.

In conclusion, I would return my acknowledgments to my personal staff—Maj. J. P. Strange, assistant adjutant-general; Maj. C. W. Anderson, acting assistant adjutant-general; Col. R. W. Pitman, assistant inspector-general; Maj. G. V. Rambaut, [commissary;] and [Colonel] M. C. Galloway, aide-de-camp. They cheerfully and promptly executed my orders, and their bearing throughout was highly commendable. My thanks are also due to Capt. Thomas Robins and Lieut. J. N. Davis, attached to my staff, for the efficient service they rendered me during the expedition. They displayed gallantry and alacrity in conveying all orders.

All of which is respectfully submitted.

N. B. Forrest, Major-General.[260]

On October 26, 1864, an angry Forrest wrote the following note to Union General Cadwallader Colden Washburn. It concerns the wanton October 4, 1864, murder—by a Yankee lieutenant—of one of Forrest's men (a prisoner at the time), Ben A. Berry of Colonel Neely's regiment. Accompanying Forrest's note to Washburn was a detailed account of the crime by Ben's brother, Thomas Berry:
☞ HEADQUARTERS FORREST'S CAVALRY, IN THE FIELD, OCTOBER 26, 1864.

[The inclosed letter by Thomas Berry] Respectfully referred to [Union] Maj. Gen. C. C. Washburn, commanding U. S. forces at Memphis, with the request that he will cause this affair to be thoroughly investigated, and if the officer be guilty of the murder, as within alleged, that he be punished accordingly.

N. B. Forrest, Major-General.[261]

Forrest to Confederate General Richard Taylor, November 3, 1864:
☞ REPORTS OF MAJ. GEN. NATHAN B. FORREST, C.S. ARMY, COMMANDING FORREST'S CAVALRY. HEADQUARTERS FORREST'S CAVALRY, NEAR JOHNSONVILLE, NOVEMBER 3, 1864. [TO: LIEUT. GEN. H. TAYLOR, COMDG. DEPT. OF ALA., MISS., AND EAST LA., SELMA, ALA.]

General: Having advised you, by previous dispatch, of the capture of U.S. gun-boat 55 and 3 transports and barges, and also of the damage to steamer *Anna*, which, in consequence of damage from our batteries, is reported to have sunk, I have now the honor to state that my command is in front of Johnsonville, at which place there are three gun-boats, seven transports, and quite a number of barges. I have batteries above and below the boats, and am to-night fortifying and placing a battery directly opposite them, and will to-morrow endeavor to sink or destroy them. Johnsonville is strongly fortified with heavy siege pieces in their works, and is garrisoned by a heavy force. There are several boats and barges yet unloaded for want of room; the landing and banks (several acres in extent) are piled with freight for Sherman's army; all the houses are full, and trains are running incessantly night and day in removing them. I regret to state that the transport *Venus* was recaptured by the enemy. In moving up from Fort Heiman orders were misunderstood and the boats got in advance of our land batteries, were come upon suddenly, and vigorously attacked by two gun-boats of the enemy; the transport was disabled and abandoned; the crew escaped. Having only my ordnance train and a few wagons for carrying cooking utensils with me, I found it impossible to remove the stores captured from steamer *Mazeppa*, at Fort Heirnan, and had them placed on transport *Venus*, with a view, if possible, of carrying them up the river by Johnsonville or hauling them out from Reynoldsburg to Camden. Owing, also, to the condition of the roads and the fact that the horses attached to the 20-pounder Parrott guns were worn out, the guns were also placed upon the *Venus* and have fallen into the hands of the enemy. We still have the gun-boat in possession but she is out of coal, and her furnaces being built for coal, and it being impossible to supply her or get her by Johnsonville, I may have to burn her. Will make the attack on the transports to-morrow at Johnsonville, and will, day after to-morrow, if necessary to do so, burn the gun-boat and move to join General Hood.

My command is coming in. Many having been absent for clothing, and the bad roads and worn-down condition of the horses compel me to move slowly. Have ordered that portion of my command at Jackson and Lexington to move at once to Perryville and arrange for crossing the river with all the commissary and quartermaster stores I have there. Have also ordered my wagon train, with one regiment and one company which were left at Corinth, to move to Cherokee, and written General Hood to give them such orders as may be necessary. A portion of my Kentucky troops, sent in the direction of Paducah to guard my flank, will also be here in time to move with me day after to-morrow. Will advise you again of the result of my operations to-morrow.

Have received an order from General Beauregard to move my command and report to General Hood, north of the Tennessee River, and will obey the order unless it is countermanded. I am of the opinion, however, that blockading the river here will be more detrimental to the enemy and advantageous to General Hood than to move my command into Middle Tennessee; nevertheless, I shall go there as soon as the scattered condition of my command and worn-out condition of my horses will permit.

I am, general, very respectfully, your obedient servant,

N. B. Forrest, Major-General.[262]

Forrest to Confederate General Richard Taylor, November 5, 1864:

☞ [NEAR JOHNSONVILLE, TENN., NOVEMBER 5, 1864. TO: GENERAL RICHARD TAYLOR:]

My forces under General's Chalmers and Buford attacked Johnsonville yesterday evening from south side of river, destroying the town and burning 3 gun-boats, 11 steamers, and 15 barges, a portion of the latter laden with quartermaster and commissary stores, also burnt most of the stores on the landing and in warehouses. The expedition thus far has resulted in a loss to the enemy of 4 gun-boats, 8 guns each, 14 steam-boats, and 17 barges, and quartermaster's stores estimated at from 75,000 to 120,000 tons. The quantity burned on the wharf and in buildings was immense. Fire still raging.

N. B. Forrest, Major-General.[263]

On November 12, 1864, having by then heard about the reelection of the treasonous, and treacherous, big government liberal Abraham Lincoln to a second term (on November 8), Forrest took a few moments to send a thank-you note to General Richard Taylor, one of the few Confederate officers the Tennessean actually respected. The missive reveals both the deeply personal relationship the two had forged and Forrest's undying devotion to the Confederate Cause:

☞ HEADQUARTERS FORREST'S CAVALRY, CORINTH, NOVEMBER 12, 1864. LIEUT. GEN. R. TAYLOR: GENERAL:

In a few days I will forward you a report of my recent operations on the Tennessee River, together with a report of my expedition to Memphis. These two documents will, I presume, for the present terminate my official connection with you, an event which I deeply deplore. Our intercourse has not been of long duration, but to me it has been most pleasant and agreeable, certainly of such a character as to render our separation a source of regret, but duty calls me elsewhere. I go to share in the toils and, I trust, in the victories of other fields, but in leaving you I shall carry with me a sincere friendship made so by your kindness and official courtesy. I congratulate you on leaving that so much of the territory under your jurisdiction has been rescued from the grasp of the invader. Twelve months ago I entered your department and found the people groaning under the most cruel and merciless oppression. They were despondent and traitors exultant. I leave the department in security and the people hopeful. The unprincipled, uncivilized, and destroying foe has been driven to other fields where the strong arms of patriots are still striving to chastise his atrocities. I know not how long we are to labor for that independence for which we have thus far struggled in vain, but this I do know that I will never weary in defending our cause, which must ultimately triumph. Faith is the duty of the hour. We will succeed. We have only to "work and wait." Be assured, my dear general, that wherever I may go, I shall deeply sympathize in all that concerns your interest and always exult in your success.

    With great respect, I am, general, your friend and obedient servant,

    N. B. Forrest, Major-General.[264]

Forrest to Union General Lovell Harrison Rousseau, December 16, 1864:
☛ HEADQUARTERS FORREST'S CAVALRY CORPS, IN FRONT OF MURFREESBOROUGH [TENN.], DECEMBER 16, 1864. MAJ. GEN. L. H. ROUSSEAU, COMMANDING U.S. FORCES, MURFREESBOROUGH:

    General: I have captured recently a good many Federal prisoners belonging to your command, and who, being unable to make the marches required to get them to a Southern prison, are very anxious for an exchange. I am informed, also, that you have some of my command as well as other soldiers of the Confederate Army, prisoners now in your hands. For the sake of humanity on behalf of both parties I now propose to exchange prisoners, man for man, rank for rank, as far as the prisoners you have may hold out. Any special officer or soldier whom you may desire exchanged in this way I will forward to you if they be under my control. I ask as a special favor that Mrs. Dave Spence, who is now in

Murfreesborough, be allowed to come through your lines to see her husband, who is now very ill and exceedingly desirous to see her. Mrs. Spence, if allowed to come out, will find her husband at Doctor Manson's.

    I am, general, very respectfully, &c.,

    N. B. Forrest, Major-General.[265]

Forrest to Confederate William Hicks "Red" Jackson, December 30, 1864:

☞ HEADQUARTERS FORREST'S CAVALRY CORPS, IUKA, DECEMBER 30, 1864. [GENERAL W. H. JACKSON:]

    General: You will leave Brigadier-General Ross at this place (Iuka) with his brigade, leaving one regiment at Bear Creek bridge, and send one regiment to Eastport to picket the Tennessee River from the mouth of Bear Creek to the mouth of Yellow Creek. You will bring General Ross' train to Burnsville, except commissary, with a sufficient [?] to procure forage from the country for the present. The regiment sent to the river must forage from the citizens until the road is opened. General Ross will report to me at Burnsville, for the present, any movements of the enemy. You will stop General Armstrong's train and General Ross', if you think best, up Bear Creek for the present. General Armstrong, with a portion of his brigade, has been ordered back to Tuscumbia, General Roddey being hard pressed by the enemy from Decatur. I desire you to take charge of Bell's brigade and Rucker's brigade, and proceed to Jackson, Tenn. You can make your arrangements accordingly. Bell's and Rucker's brigades have been ordered to Burnsville, where you meet them, and you can report to me in person at Burnsville. Harvey's scouts have been ordered on Tennessee River, in the vicinity of Eastport, and will scout and act in conjunction with the regiment that you may send over to Eastport.

    Yours, respectfully,

    N. B. Forrest, Major-General.[266]

SECTION FIVE

1865

1865

The year 1865 opens with Forrest's final promotion: on March 2 he rises to the rank of lieutenant general and is now in charge of 10,000 men, covering three states. There can be little doubt that if Lincoln's War had lasted even a few months longer, Forrest would have eventually been made a full general.

Though Confederate General Robert E. Lee surrendered his army on April 9, it was not until nearly a month later, on May 3, that the freedom-loving Forrest officially (and finally) accepted the defeat of his beloved country: the Confederate States of America. Six days later, on May 9, his official farewell speech is printed on flyers and handed out to his despondent troops: nearly all had wanted to keep the fight going under their awe-inspiring commander.

Financially destroyed by the War and nearly crippled by several battlefield wounds, on May 25 Forrest returns to his plantation "Green Grove" at Sunflower Landing, in Coahoma County, Mississippi. Here, he begins rebuilding his life under the illegal, purposefully humiliating, and unnecessarily harsh and cruel military despotism known as "Reconstruction."

Forrest to Confederate General Richard Taylor, January 2, 1865:
☛ HEADQUARTERS FORREST'S CAVALRY CORPS, CORINTH, MISS., JANUARY 2, 1865.   LIEUT. GEN. R. TAYLOR, COMMANDING DEPARTMENT:

General: I have the honor to state that I have just had an interview with [Confederate] General [John Bell] Hood, and am informed by him that the Army of Tennessee is ordered to Augusta, and that I will be left to defend as well as can be done this section of the country. I regret to say that the means at my disposal are not adequate to the task devolving upon me. My command is greatly reduced in numbers and efficiency by losses in battle and in the worn-down and unserviceable condition of animals. The Army of Tennessee was badly

252 ᴄᴧ⊚ Gɪᴠᴇ 'ᴇᴍ Hᴇʟʟ Bᴏʏs!

defeated and is greatly demoralized, and to save it during the retreat from Nashville I was compelled almost to sacrifice my command. Aside from the killed, wounded, and captured of my command, many were sent to the rear with barefooted, lame, and unserviceable horses, who have taken advantage of all the confusion and disorder attending the hasty retreat of a beaten army, and are now scattered through the country or have gone to their homes. The enemy have about 10,000 cavalry, finely equipped and recently mounted on the best of horses, and I ask that you will send McCulloch's brigade to me at once, with any other cavalry you can possibly spare. I am also greatly in need of artillery horses. I have four batteries of four guns each, but have not a sufficiency of serviceable horses to haul two of them. I desire to state further that my horses are suffering badly for forage, and are only getting one-third of a ration of corn per day (say four pounds to the horse), and if they remain much longer upon that allowance they will be worthless; in fact, from the hard service performed and want of forage, it will require at least six weeks to put them in condition for active service in the field. I shall remain in General Hood's rear until he moves off from here, and if the railroad can not supply me with forage in a short time will be compelled to leave a small force here and follow him down to the prairies and save my stock, if possible to do so. Our mules are also worn down and many of them unfit for service, and unless recruited will prove a total loss.

I assure you, general, that any assistance you may have it in your power to give me in fitting up my transportation and artillery will be appreciated, and, if in your power to do so, would be glad to see you up here, or have the privilege of visiting you myself, as I am anxious to see you personally in regard to changes, &c., in the cavalry of my command. Many regiments are greatly reduced, and it is absolutely necessary to reorganize it. As soon as the Army of Tennessee gets away, I will forward you full reports, giving the effective strength, &c., of my command. So much am I impressed with the necessity of reorganizing the cavalry, and never having visited Richmond, I would like much to visit the capital and urge upon the Department the adoption of such measures as will increase its efficiency and bring it under proper control and discipline. I am confident the trip would prove beneficial to the service and a recreation to myself, and the latter is much needed, as I have had no rest or relief from duty since I came into this department, and, whenever circumstances will allow it, I respectfully ask that Major-General Gardner or some other competent officer be placed in command of my troops and permission given me to make the visit proposed. There is a column of the enemy at Courtland and a large force of cavalry on the north bank of the river, with six gun-boats and seven transports in the Tennessee River between Eastport and Florence. My scouts also report thirty transports below Savannah, and I fear they will cross the river and follow up General Hood's army, or with their heavy force of cavalry cross at Decatur or Bainbridge and move on Selma. Should they move on us here, I shall (after the departure of General Hood's army) be compelled to fall back before them, as my force is not sufficient to meet and defeat them.

I am, general, very respectfully, your obedient servant,

N. B. Forrest, Major-General.[267]

Forrest to Union General Napoleon Jackson Tecumseh Dana, January 6, 1865:
☛ HEADQUARTERS FORREST'S CAVALRY CORPS, IN THE FIELD, JANUARY 6, 1865. MAJOR-GENERAL DANA, COMMANDING U.S. FORCES, MEMPHIS, TENN.:

General: I have the honor herewith to transmit copies of communications between [Union] Major-General Rousseau and myself relative to an exchange of prisoners. The arrangement or agreement failed on account of the defeat of our army at Nashville, and about 1,600 Federal prisoners captured by the cavalry of my command still remain in my possession. Accompanying his written communication I received a verbal message from Major-General Rousseau through Captain McConnell, of his staff, requesting "that [Union] Lieutenant-Colonel Grass, of the Sixty-first Illinois, be treated as kindly as circumstances would permit, as he was a high-toned gentleman, a brave soldier, and a magnanimous foe." Since his capture Colonel Grass has remained at my headquarters, and is now released upon parole and accompanies my adjutant-general, Maj. J. P. Strange, to Memphis under a flag of truce with these dispatches, for the purpose of effecting an exchange for [Confederate] Col. E[dmund]. W[inchester]. Rucker, of my command, who was captured and wounded during the recent engagement in front of Nashville. You are no doubt aware also of an agreement made between [Union] Major-General [C. C.] Washburn and myself for exchanging prisoners, which has been approved by [Confederate] General [John Bell] Hood and by Lieutenant-General Taylor, commanding this department, and under which a number of exchanges, both special and general, have been made. I am still willing to continue that arrangement; also to meet the expressed wishes of Major-General Rousseau in regard to Colonel Grass, by sending him on his parole of honor (a copy of which is herewith inclosed) to effect an exchange for Colonel Rucker. My adjutant-general, Major Strange, is fully anthorized to arrange for any further exchange of prisoners, man for man, rank for rank. And believing it to be the duty of every government to relieve their faithful soldiers, whether sick, wounded, or in prison, I shall, so long as permitted to do so, hold myself in readiness to exchange, as far as in my power to do so, all Federal prisoners falling into my hands for those of my own command first, and then for any others belonging to the C.S. Army in the hands of the enemy. Quite a number of your men recently captured are without sufficient clothing, shoes, and blankets. Should you desire to supply them with any articles necessary to their comfort, I will see that they are safely transmitted and issued to those of your army who most need them.

Assuring you of my desire, as far as practicable, to mitigate human suffering and lessen the privations of the soldiers,

I am, general, very respectfully, &c.,

N. B. Forrest, Major-General.[268]

Forrest to Confederate Lieutenant Colonel Eustace Surget, January 12, 1865, concerning the Battle of Johnsonville (fought November 3-5, 1864):

☞ HEADQUARTERS FORREST'S CAVALRY CORPS, VERONA, MISS., JANUARY 12, 1865. [TO: COL. E. SURGET, ASSISTANT ADJUTANT-GENERAL, MERIDIAN, MISS.]

Colonel: Continued active service in the field for two months has prevented me from reporting at an earlier day the action of my troops on the expedition along the Tennessee River. I avail myself; however, of the first leisure moment, and have the honor of submitting the following report:

On the 16th of October I ordered Colonel [Tyree H.] Bell to move with his brigade from Corinth and to form a camp at Lavinia. On the 18th Brigadier-General [Abe] Buford was ordered to move with the

Kentucky brigade to Lexington for the purpose of watching General [Edward] Hatch, who was reported to be in that direction. I moved from Corinth on the morning of the 19th, with my escort and [Edmund W.] Rucker's brigade, to Jackson, Tenn. At this place I was joined by Brigadier-General [James R.] Chalmers with about 250 men of McCulloch's brigade and 300 of Mabry's brigade, which, with Rucker's brigade, constituted his division. On the 29th I ordered him to proceed to the Tennessee River and there co-operate with Brigadier-General Buford, who was blockading the river at Fort Heiman and Paris Landing. On arriving at the river I found it most effectually blockaded by a judicious disposition of the troops and batteries sent for this purpose.

On the morning of the 29th the steamer *Mazeppa*, with two barges in tow, made her appearance. As she passed the battery at Fort Heiman, supported by Brigadier-General Lyon, she was fired upon by one section of Morton's battery and two 20-pounder Parrott guns. Every shot must have taken effect, as she made for the shore after the third fire and reached the opposite bank in a disabled condition, where she was abandoned by the crew and passengers, who fled to the woods. A hawser was erected on this side of the river and she was towed over, and on being boarded she was found to be heavily loaded with blankets, shoes, clothing, hard bread, &c. While her cargo was being removed to the shore three gun-boats made their appearance, and commenced shelling the men who were engaged in unloading the *Mazeppa*. They were forced to retire, and fearing the boat might be captured Brigadier-General Buford ordered her to be burned.

On the 30th the steamer *Anna* came down the river and succeeded in passing both the upper and lower batteries, but was so disabled that she sunk before she reached Paducah. The *Anna* was followed by two transports (*J. W. Cheeseman*, the *Venus*) and two barges under convoy of gun-boat *Undine*. In attempting to pass my batteries all the boats were disabled. They landed on the opposite side of the river and were abandoned by the crews, who left their dead and wounded. Lieutenant-Colonel Kelley, with two companies of his regiment, was thrown across the river and soon returned to Paris Landing with the boats. The steamer *J. W. Cheeseman* was so disabled that she was ordered, with the two barges, to be burned; the gun-boat was also burned while moving up the river to Johnsonville. The *Venus* was recaptured by the enemy on (November 2,) but was destroyed the next day (November 4) at Johnsonville by my batteries.

On the 1st of November I ordered my command to move in the direction of Johnsonville, which place I reached on the 3d. At this point Colonel Mabry joined General Chalmers with [James C.] Thrall's battery. The wharf at Johnsonville was lined with transports and gun-boats. An immense warehouse presented itself and was represented as being stored with the most valuable supplies, while several acres of the shore were covered with every description of army stores. The fort was situated on a high hill and in a commanding position, and defended by strong works.

All my troops having arrived, I commenced disposing of them with a view of bombarding the enemy. As he commanded the position I designed to occupy, I was necessarily compelled to act with great caution. I planted most of my guns during the night, and while completing the work the next morning my men worked behind ambuscades, which obscured everything from the enemy. Thrall's battery of howitzers was placed in position above Johnsonville, while Morton's and Hudson's batteries were placed nearly opposite and just below town.

I ordered a simultaneous assault to commence at 3 o'clock. All my movements for twenty-four hours had been so secretive the enemy seemed to think I had retired, and for the purpose of making a reconnaissance two gun-boats were lashed together and pushed out just before the attack opened. The bombardment commenced by the section of Morton's battery commanded by Lieutenant Brown. The other batteries joined promptly in the assault. The enemy returned the fire from twenty-eight guns on their gun-boats and fourteen guns on the hill. About fifty guns were thus engaged at the same time, and the firing was terrific. The gun-boats, in fifteen minutes after the engagement commenced, were set on fire, and made rapidly for the shore, where they were both consumed. My batteries next opened upon the transports, and in a short time they were in flames. The immense amount of stores were also set on fire, together with the huge warehouse above time landing. By night the wharf for nearly one mile up and down the river presented one solid sheet of flame. The enemy continued a furious cannonading on my batteries.

Having completed the work designed by the expedition, I moved my command six miles during the night by the light of the enemy's burning property. The roads were almost impassable, and the march to Corinth was slow and toilsome, but I reached there on November 10, after an absence of over two weeks, during which time I captured and destroyed 4 gun-boats, 14 transports, 20 barges, 26 pieces of artillery, $6,700,000 worth of property, and 150 prisoners. Brigadier-General Buford, after supplying his own command, turned over to my chief quartermaster about 9,000 pairs of shoes and 1,000 blankets.

My loss during the entire trip was 2 killed and 9 wounded; that of the enemy will probably reach 500 killed, wounded, and prisoners.

On this expedition my division commanders, Brigadier-Generals Chalmers and Buford, displayed the same prompt observance in obeying orders, the same skill, coolness, and undaunted courage which they have heretofore exhibited, and for which I thank them.

My brigade commanders, Colonels Bell, Rucker, Crossland, and Mabry, are deserving of the highest commendation for their conduct on this as on all former occasions.

Brigadier-General Lyon, who had been assigned to another department, reported to me on this expedition and rendered much valuable service at Johnsonville and Fort Heiman.

To Capt. John W. Morton, acting chief of artillery, and the brave troops under his command, my thanks are especially due for their efficiency and gallantry on this expedition. They fired with a rapidity and accuracy which extorted the commendation of even the enemy. The rammers were shot from the hands of the cannoneers, some of whom were nearly buried amid the dirt which was thrown upon them by the storm of shell which rained upon them by the enemy's batteries. All of which is respectfully submitted.

N. B. Forrest, Major-General.[269]

Forrest to Confederate General James Ronald Chalmers, January 18, 1865:
☞ VERONA, JANUARY 18, 1865. BRIGADIER-GENERAL CHALMERS:

Take command of General Wheeler's and all other cavalry at Pikeville, or that may be ordered there, and officers refusing to obey your orders you will arrest.

N. B. Forrest, Major-General.[270]

Forrest to Confederate General Frank Crawford Armstrong, January 19, 1865:
☞ VERONA [TENN.], JANUARY 19, 1865. BRIGADIER-GENERAL
ARMSTRONG, [at] OKOLONA [MISS.]:

Move at once with your brigade by nearest route to Saltillo.
Corn will sent up by train for you. Send cooking utensils by rail and
leave wagon train at camp. Do not send men east [of] Tombigbee [River]
as ordered. Courier at Okolona will take this out at once.

N. B. Forrest, Major-General.[271]

Forrest to Confederate General James Ronald Chalmers, January 20, 1865:
☞ VERONA, JANUARY 20, 1865. BRIGADIER-GENERAL
CHALMERS:

You will retain Holman's, Biffle's, and Russell's regiments, and
send Wheeler's and the Fourth Tennessee Regiment and all other parts
of regiments and detachments whose command may be in Georgia.

N. B. Forrest, Major-General.[272]

*Forrest to Confederate Lieutenant Colonel A. P. Mason, January 24, 1865. What
follows is Forrest's official report concerning the three battles that would alter both
Southern and American history: Spring Hill, Franklin II, and Nashville:*
☞ REPORT OF MAJ. GEN. NATHAN B. FORREST, C. S. ARMY,
COMMANDING CAVALRY, OF OPERATIONS NOVEMBER 16,
1864 TO JANUARY 23, 1865. HEADQUARTERS FORREST'S
CAVALRY CORPS, VERONA, MISS., JANUARY 24, 1865.

Colonel: I have the honor to submit the following report of the
operations of the troops under my command during the recent
movements in Middle Tennessee:

While in West Tennessee I received orders from General
Beauregard on the 30th of October, to report without delay to General
Hood at Florence, Ala. I was then actively operating against
Johnsonville, and so soon as I completed the destruction of the enemy's
fleet and stores at that place I commenced moving up the Tennessee
River. I halted my command at Perryville with a view of crossing the
river at that point, but being without facilities, and the river already high
and rising rapidly, I found it impossible to cross over. I succeeded,

however, in throwing across a portion of Rucker's brigade, while I moved to Corinth with the balance of my command. My men and horses were much jaded, but I moved at once to Florence and crossed the river on the 16th and 17th of November. On my arrival at Florence I was placed in command of the entire cavalry then with the Army of Tennessee, consisting of Brigadier-General Jackson's division and a portion of Dibrell's brigade, under command of Colonel Biffle, amounting to about 2,000 men, together with three brigades of my former command, making in all about 5,000 cavalry. I bivouacked my command at Shoal Creek until the morning of the 21st, when, in obedience to orders from General Hood, I commenced a forward movement. My command consisted of three divisions—Chalmers', Buford's, and Jackson's. I ordered Brigadier-General Chalmers to advance via West Point, Kelly's Forge, Henryville, and Mount Pleasant. Brigadier-Generals Buford and Jackson were ordered to move up the military road to Lawrenceburg, and thence southeastward in the direction of Pulaski. Both these divisions had several engagements with the enemy, and were almost constantly skirmishing with him, but drove him in every encounter.

At Henryville Brigadier-General Chalmers developed the enemy's cavalry and captured forty-five prisoners. At Fouché Springs the enemy made another stand. I ordered General Chalmers to throw forward Rucker's brigade and to keep up a slight skirmish with the enemy until I could gain his rear. I ordered Lieutenant-Colonel Kelley to move by the left flank and join me in rear of the enemy. Taking my escort with me I moved rapidly to the rear. Lieutenant-Colonel Kelley being prevented from joining me as I had expected, I made the charge upon the enemy with my escort alone, producing a perfect stampede, capturing about 50 prisoners, 20 horses, and 1 ambulance. It was now near night, and I placed my escort in ambush. Colonel Rucker pressed upon the enemy, and as they rushed into the ambuscade my escort fired into them, producing the wildest confusion. I ordered Colonel Rucker to rest his command until 1 a. m., when the march was renewed toward Mount Pleasant, where he captured 35,000 rounds of small-arm ammunition and the guard left in charge of it. Meantime Brigadier-Generals Buford and Jackson had proceeded from Lawrenceburg toward Pulaski and encountered Hatch's division of cavalry at Campbellsville, and routed him after a short but vigorous engagement, in which he lost about 100 prisoners and several in killed and wounded. Most of my troops having reached Columbia on the evening of the 24th I invested the town from Duck River to the extreme north, which position I held until the arrival of the infantry on the morning of the 27th, when I was relieved.

Columbia having been evacuated on the night of [November] the 28th [27th] I was ordered to move across Duck River on the morning of the 28th. Chalmers' division was ordered to cross at Carr's Mill, seven miles above Columbia, Jackson's, at Holland's Ford, while I crossed at Owen's Ford with a portion of Colonel Biffle's regiment. Before leaving Columbia I sent my escort to Shelbyville for the purpose of ascertaining the movements of the enemy and destroying the railroad, and I regret to announce that Captain Jackson was seriously wounded on this expedition. On the night of the 28th I was joined by Chalmers' division about eight miles from Columbia on the Spring Hill and Carr's Mill road. Jackson's division was ordered to proceed to the vicinity of Hurt's Cross Roads on the Lewisburg pike. At 11 o'clock at night I received a dispatch from General Buford informing me that the enemy had made such a stubborn resistance to his crossing that he could not join the command until the morning of the 29th. I ordered General Jackson to move along the Lewisburg pike toward Franklin until he developed the enemy. Brigadier-General Armstrong notified me that he had struck the enemy, when I ordered him not to press too vigorously until I reached his flank with Chalmers' division. The enemy gradually fell back, making resistance only at favorable positions. After waiting a short time for my troops to close up, I moved rapidly toward Spring Hill with my entire command. Two miles from town the enemy's pickets were encountered and heavy skirmishing ensued. I ordered General Armstrong to form his brigade in line of battle. I also ordered a portion of the Kentucky brigade and the Fourteenth Tennessee Regiment, under Colonel White, to form, which being done I ordered a charge upon the enemy, but he was so strongly posted upon the crest of a hill that my troops were compelled to fall back. I then dismounted my entire command amid moved upon the enemy. With a few men I moved to the left on a high hill, where I discovered the enemy hurriedly moving his wagon train up the Franklin pike. I ordered my command to push the enemy's right flank with all possible vigor. At the same time I ordered Brigadier-General Buford to send me a regiment mounted. He sent the Twenty-first Tennessee, Colonel Wilson commanding, which I ordered to charge upon the enemy. Colonel Wilson at the head of his splendid regiment made a gallant charge through an open field. He received three wounds, but refused to leave his command. About this time I received orders from General Hood to hold my position at all hazards, as the advance of his infantry column was only two miles distant and rapidly advancing. I ordered up my command, already dismounted. Colonel Bell's brigade was the first to reach me, when I immediately ordered it to the attack. Major-General Cleburne's division soon arrived, and, after some delay, was formed in line of battle and moved upon the enemy on my left. Colonel Bell reported that he had only four rounds of ammunition to the man when I ordered him to charge the enemy. This order was executed with a promptness and energy amid gallantry which I have never seen excelled. The enemy was driven from his rifle-pits, and fled toward Spring Hill. I then ordered Brigadier-General Jackson to move with his division in the direction of Thompson's Station and there intercept the enemy. He struck the road at Fitzgerald's, four miles from Spring Hill, at 11 o'clock, just as the front of the enemy's column had passed. This attack was a complete surprise, producing much panic and confusion. Brigadier-General Jackson had possession of the pike and fought the enemy until near daylight, but receiving no support, he was compelled to retire, after killing a large number of horses and mules and burning several wagons. Chalmers' and Buford's divisions being out of ammunition, I supplied them from the infantry (my ordnance being still at Columbia), when I ordered Brigadier-General Chalmers to move at daylight on the morning of the 30th to the Carter's Creek turnpike, between Columbia and Spring Hill, and there intercept a column of the enemy reported to be cut off. General Chalmers moved as ordered, but reported to me that the enemy had passed unmolested on the main pike during the night. Buford and Jackson were ordered to move forward with their divisions on the Franklin pike and to attack the enemy. They overtook his rear two miles from where General Jackson had cut his column the night previous and pushed him on to Winstead's Hill, where he was strongly posted. General Stewart's corps arriving upon the ground, I moved with Buford's and Jackson's divisions to the right, my right extending to Harpeth River, and ordered Brigadier-General Chalmers on the left. The enemy retired from Winstead's Hill toward their fortifications at Franklin. I ordered Brigadier-General Chalmers to advance on the left, which he did, charging and dislodging the enemy from every position he had taken. The enemy was posted on a strong hill on the opposite side of Harpeth River, from which position he was firing upon our troops on the Lewisburg pike. I ordered Brigadier-General Jackson to cross over and drive the enemy from this hill and to protect our right. I ordered Brigadier-General Buford to dismount his command and take position in line of battle on the right of Stewart's corps, covering the ground from the Lewisburg pike to Harpeth River. Skirmishing at once commenced, and Buford's division rapidly advancing drove the enemy across Harpeth River, where he joined the cavalry. Brigadier-General Jackson engaged the united forces of both infantry and cavalry, and held him in check until night, when he threw forward his pickets and retired across Harpeth for the purpose of replenishing his ammunition. The enemy held strong positions commanding all the fords. I ordered Brigadier-General Buford to remount his command and hold himself in readiness for action at a moment's warning. Brigadier-General Jackson's troops being out of ammunition, and my ordnance still in the rear, Captain Vanderford furnished me with the necessary supply.

At daylight on the 1st of December [1864] I moved across Harpeth River and advanced up the Wilson pike, and struck the enemy at Owen's Cross-Roads, in strong force. I ordered Captain Morton to open upon him with his battery. Soon afterward I ordered Brigadier-General Buford to charge, which order he executed by dislodging the enemy and capturing several prisoners. I then moved with Jackson's and Buford's divisions to Brentwood, where I was joined by Brigadier-General Chalmers. Ordering Chalmers to proceed with his division up the Franklin and Hillsborough pike, and to cross over and intercept, if possible, the enemy retreating toward Nashville, I moved with Buford's and Jackson's divisions toward the Nashville pike, and, learning the enemy had reached Nashville, I camped for the night.

On the following morning (the 2d) I ordered Brigadier-General Chalmers to move on the left and to guard the Hillsborough and Hardin pikes, while I proceeded to the right with Buford's and Jackson's divisions and took position in sight of the capitol at Nashville. I ordered Brigadier-General Buford to move with his division across to Mill Creek and to form line of battle near the lunatic asylum on the Murfreesborough pike. Jackson's division was ordered into position so as to cover the Nashville and Mill Creek pike. My command being relieved by the infantry I commenced operating upon the railroad, block-houses, and telegraph lines leading from Nashville to Murfreesborough. I ordered Buford's division on the Nashville and Chattanooga Railroad for the purpose of destroying stockades and block-houses.

On the 3d of December stockade No.2 surrendered, with 80 prisoners, 10 men killed, and 20 wounded in the attack by Morton's battery. On the day previous, while assaulting stockade No. 2, a train of cars came from Chattanooga loaded with negro troops. The train was captured, but most of the troops made their escape.

On the 4th I ordered Brigadier-General Buford to attack block-house No. 3, but the demand for surrender was complied with, and the garrison of thirty-two men made prisoners. An assault was also ordered on stockade No. 1, on Mill Creek, but the garrison unhesitatingly surrendered. I ordered the destruction of the block-house and two stockades, in which were captured 150 prisoners.

On the morning of the 4th I received orders to move with Buford's and Jackson's divisions to Murfreesborough, and to leave 250 men on the right to picket from the Nashville and Murfreesborough pike to the Cumberland River. Colonel Nixon, of Bell's brigade, was left for this purpose.

On the morning of the 5th I moved, as ordered, toward Murfreesborough. At La Vergne I ordered Brigadier-General Jackson to move on the right of town and invest the fort on the bill, while I moved with Buford's division to block-house No. 4. The usual demand for surrender was sent under flag of truce and a surrender made. The garrison on the hill, consisting of 80 men, 2 pieces of artillery, several wagons, and a considerable supply of stores, also surrendered to Brigadier-General Jackson. A large number of houses, built and occupied by the enemy, were ordered to be burned.

Four miles front La Vergne I formed a junction with Major-General Bate, who had been ordered to report to me with his division for the purpose of operating against Murfreesborough. I ordered Brigadier General Jackson to send a brigade across to the Wilson [Wilkinson] Pike, and moving on both pikes the enemy was driven into his works at Murfreesborough. After ordering General Buford to picket from the Nashville and Murfreesborough to the Lebanon pikes on the left, and Jackson to picket on the right to the Salem pike, I encamped for the night.

The infantry arrived on the morning of [December] the 6th, when I immediately ordered it in line of battle and to move upon the enemy's works. After skirmishing for two hours the enemy ceased firing, and showed no disposition to give battle. I ordered a regiment from Brigadier-General Armstrong's brigade, with which I made a careful reconnaissance of the enemy's position and works. On the evening of the 6th I was re-enforced by Sears' and Palmer's brigades of infantry. I ordered Colonel Palmer in position on the right upon a hill, and to fortify during the night.

On the morning of the 7th I discovered from the position occupied by Colonel Palmer the enemy moving out in strong force on the Salem pike, with infantry, cavalry, and artillery. Being fully satisfied that his object was to make battle, I withdrew my forces to the Wilkinson pike, and formed a new line on a more favorable position. The enemy moved boldly forward, driving in my pickets, when the infantry, with the exception of Smith's brigade, from some cause which I cannot explain, made a shameful retreat, losing two pieces of artillery. I seized the colors of the retreating troops and endeavored to rally them, but they could not be moved by any entreaty or appeal to their patriotism. Major-General Bate did the same thing, but was equally as unsuccessful as myself. I hurriedly sent Major Strange, of my staff, to Brigadier-Generals Armstrong and Ross, of Jackson's division, with orders to say to them that everything depended on their cavalry. They proved themselves equal to the emergency by charging on the enemy, thereby checking his farther advance. I ordered the infantry to retire to Stewart's Creek, while my cavalry encamped during the night at Overall's Creek. The enemy returning to Murfreesborough, I ordered my cavalry to resume its former position.

It is proper to state here that I ordered Brigadier-General Buford to protect my left flank, but he was so remote the order never reached him. While the fight was going on, however, he made a demonstration on Murfreesborough, and succeeded in reaching the center of town, but was soon compelled to retire.

On the 9th General Hood sent to my support Smith's brigade, commanded by Colonel Olmstead, and ordered Bate's division to report back to his headquarters. On the 11th I ordered Brigadier-General Buford to proceed to the Hermitage, and to picket the Cumberland River, so as to prevent any flank movement in that direction. On the 12th I ordered the infantry to destroy the railroad from La Vergne to Murfreesborough, which was most effectually done. Brigadier-General Jackson, who had been previously ordered to operate south of Murfreesborough, captured, on [December] the 13th, a train of seventeen cars and the Sixty-first Illinois Regiment of Infantry, commanded by Lieutenant-Colonel Grass. The train was loaded with supplies of 60,000 rations, sent from Stevenson to Murfreesborongh, all of which were consumed by fire, after which the prisoners, about 200 in number, were sent to the rear.

On the 14th I moved with Colonels Olmstead's and Palmer's brigades across Stone's River and east of Murfreesborough, with a view of capturing the enemy's forage train, but on the evening of the 15th I received notice from General Hood that a general engagement was then going on at Nashville, and to hold myself in readiness to move at any moment. Accordingly, on the 16th I moved my entire command to the Wilkinson Cross-Roads, at the terminus of the Wilkinson pike, six miles from Murfreesborough. On the night of the 16th one of General Hood's staff officers arrived, informing me of the disaster at Nashville and ordering me to fall back via Shelbyville and Pulaski. I immediately dispatched orders to Brigadier-General Buford to fall back from the Cumberland River, via La Vergne, to the Nashville pike, and to protect my rear until I could move my artillery and wagon train. From this position General Buford was ordered across to the Nashville and Columbia pike, for the purpose of protecting the rear of General Hood's retreating army. My sick, wounded, and wagon train being at Triune, I did not retreat via Shelbyville, but moved in the direction of Lillard's Mills, on Duck River. I ordered Brigadier-General Armstrong to the Nashville and Columbia pike. Most of the infantry under my command were barefooted and in a disabled condition, and being encumbered with several hundred head of hogs and cattle, my march along the almost impassable roads was unavoidably slow. On reaching Duck River at Lillard's Mills I ordered everything to be hurried across, as the stream was rapidly rising. After putting over a part of my wagon train the stream became unfordable. I was therefore compelled to change my direction to Columbia, which place I reached on the evening of the 18th.

On the morning of [December] the 19th the enemy was reported at Rutherford's Creek in strong force. I immediately commenced disposing of my troops for the purpose of preventing his crossing. Everything being across Duck River I was ordered by General Hood to withdraw my command at 3 o'clock, which I did, and went into camp at Columbia. Chalmers' division having been sent to the right, I am unable to state anything from personal knowledge as to his operations from the 3d to the 19th; but I learn from his official report that his line extended from the Hillsborough pike, on the right, across the Hardin and Charlotte pikes to the river, on the left; that he captured two transports laden with horses and mules; that the transports were recaptured, but leaving on his hands 56 prisoners and 197 horses and mules; that the enemy made several attempts with his monitors and gun-boats to silence his river batteries, all of which were unsuccessful; that he maintained a strict blockade of the river and his position until Ector's brigade of infantry fell back; that he prevented Hatch from gaining the rear of our army; and that he was constantly and severely engaged every day while protecting the rear of General Hood's army until he crossed Rutherford's Creek.

On the 20th General Hood, on leaving Columbia, gave me orders to hold the town as long as possible, and when compelled to retire to move in the direction of Florence, Ala., via Pulaski, protecting and guarding his rear. To aid me in this object he ordered Major-General Walthall to report to me with about 1,900 infantry, 400 of whom were unserviceable for want of shoes. The enemy appeared in front of Columbia on the evening of the 20th and commenced a furious shelling upon the town. Under a flag of truce I proceeded to the river and asked an interview with General Hatch, who I informed by verbal communication across the river that there were no Confederate troops in town, and that his shelling would only result in injury to the women and children and his own wounded, after which interview the shelling was discontinued.

The enemy succeeded in crossing Duck River on the morning of the 22d. I at once ordered my troops to fall back in the direction of Pulaski. Brigadier-General Chalmers was ordered on the right down the Bigbyville pike toward Bigbyville. The infantry moved down the main pike from Columbia to Pulaski, the rear protected by both Buford's and Jackson's divisions of cavalry, while a few scouts were thrown out on the left flank. The enemy made his first demonstration on my rear pickets near Warfield's, three miles south of Columbia. He opened upon us with artillery, which forced us to retire farther down the road in a gap made by two high hills on each side of the road; where he was held in check for some time. On the night of the 23d I halted my command at and near Lynnville, in order to hold the enemy in check and to prevent any pressure upon my wagon train and the stock then being driven out.

On the morning of [December] the 24th I ordered the infantry back toward Columbia on the main pike and my cavalry on the right and left flanks. After advancing about three miles the enemy was met, where a severe engagement occurred and the enemy was held in check for two hours. I retreated two miles, where I took position at Richland Creek. Brigadier-General Armstrong was thrown forward in front and General Ross on the right flank. Chalmers and Buford formed a junction, and were ordered on the left flank. Brigadier-General Armstrong was ordered to the support of six pieces of my artillery, which were placed in position immediately on the main pike and on a line with Buford's and Chalmer's divisions and Ross' brigade, of Jackson's division. After severe artillery firing on both sides two pieces of the enemy's artillery were dismounted. The enemy then flanked to the right and left and crossed Richland Creek on my right, with the view of gaining my rear. I immediately ordered Armstrong and Ross, of Jackson's division, to cross the bridge on the main pike and move around and engage the enemy, who were crossing the creek. Both Buford and Chalmers were heavily pressed on the left, and after an engagement of two hours I ordered them to fall back across Richland Creek. I lost 1 killed and 6 wounded in this engagement. The enemy lost heavily. Brigadier-General Buford was wounded in this engagement, and I ordered Brigadier-General Chalmers to assume command of Brigadier-General Buford's division together with his own. I reached

Pulaski without further molestation.

On the morning of the 25th, after destroying all the ammunition which could not be removed from Pulaski by General Hood and two trains of cars, I ordered General Jackson to remain in town as long as possible and to destroy the bridge at Richland Creek after everything had passed over. The enemy soon pressed General Jackson, but he held him in check for some time, killing and wounding several before retiring. Seven miles from Pulaski I took position on King's Hill, and awaiting the advance of the enemy, repulsed him, with a loss of 150 killed and wounded, besides capturing many prisoners and one piece of artillery. The enemy made no further demonstrations during the day. I halted my command at Sugar Creek, where it encamped during the night.

On the morning of [December] the 26th the enemy commenced advancing, driving back General Ross' pickets. Owing to the dense fog he could not see the temporary fortifications which the infantry had thrown up and behind which they were secreted. The enemy therefore advanced to within fifty paces of these works, when a volley was opened upon him, causing the wildest confusion. Two mounted regiments of Ross' brigade and Ector's and Granbury's brigades of infantry were ordered to charge upon the discomfited foe, which was done, producing a complete rout. The enemy was pursued for two miles, but showing no disposition to give battle my troops were ordered back. In this engagement he sustained a loss of about 150 in killed and wounded; many prisoners and horses were captured and about 400 horses killed. I held this position for two hours, but the enemy showing no disposition to renew the attack, and fearing he might attempt a flank movement in the dense fog, I resumed the march, after leaving a picket with orders to remain until 4 o'clock. The enemy made no further attack between Sugar Creek and Tennessee River, which stream I crossed on the evening of the 27th of December. The infantry were ordered to report back to their respective corps, and I moved with my cavalry to Corinth.

The campaign was full of trial and suffering, but the troops under my command, both cavalry and infantry, submitted to every hardship with an uncomplaining patriotism; with a single exception, they behaved with commendable gallantry.

From the day I left Florence, on the 21st of November, to the 27th of December my cavalry were engaged every day with the enemy.

My loss in killed and wounded has been heavy. I brought out of the campaign three pieces of artillery more than I started with.

My command captured and destroyed 16 block-houses and stockades, 20 bridges, several hundred horses and mules, 20 yoke of oxen, 4 locomotives, and 100 cars and 10 miles of railroad, while I have turned over to the provost-marshal-general about 1,600 prisoners.

To my division commanders—Brigadier-Generals Chalmers, Buford, and Jackson—I take pleasure in acknowledging the promptitude with which they obeyed and executed all orders. If I have failed to do justice in this report it is because they have not furnished me with a detailed report of the operations of their respective commands.

I am also indebted to Major-General Walthall for much valuable service rendered during the retreat from Columbia. He exhibited the highest soldierly qualities. Many of his men were without shoes, but they bore their sufferings without murmur and were ever ready to meet the enemy.

I am again under obligations to my staff for their efficient aid during the campaign.

All of which is respectfully submitted.

N. B. Forrest, Major-General.[273]

Addenda [attached to above January 24, 1865, report]: Address of Maj. Gen. N. B. Forrest to his troops:

☞ Soldiers: The old campaign is ended, and your commanding general deems this an appropriate occasion to speak of the steadiness, self-denial, and patriotism with which you have borne the hardships of the past year. The marches and labors you have performed during that period will find no parallel in the history of this war.

On the 24th day of December there were 3,000 of you, unorganized and undisciplined, at Jackson, Tenn., only 400 of whom were armed. You were surrounded by 15,000 of the enemy, who were congratulating themselves on your certain capture. You started out with your artillery, wagon trains, and a large number of cattle, which you succeeded in bringing through, since which time you have fought and won the following battles—battles which will enshrine your names in the hearts of your countrymen, and live in history an imperishable monument to your prowess: Jack's Creek, Estenaula, Somerville,

Okolona, Union City, Paducah, Fort Pillow, Bolivar, Tishomingo Creek, Harrisburg, Hurricane Creek, Memphis, Athens, Sulphur Springs, Pulaski, Carter's Creek, Columbia, and Johnsonville are the fields upon which you have won fadeless immortality. In the recent campaign in Middle Tennessee you sustained the reputation so nobly won. For twenty-six days, from the time you left Florence, on the 21st of November to the 26th of December you were constantly engaged with the enemy, and endured the hunger, cold, and labor incident to that arduous campaign without murmur. To sum up, in brief, your triumphs during the past year, you have fought fifty battles, killed and captured 16,000 of the enemy, captured 2,000 horses and mules, 67 pieces of artillery, 4 gun-boats, 14 transports, 20 barges, 300 wagons, 50 ambulances, 10,000 stand of small-arms, 40 block-houses, destroyed 36 railroad bridges, 200 miles of railroad, 6 engines, 100 cars, and $15,000,000 worth of property.

In the accomplishment of this great work you were occasionally sustained by other troops, who joined you in the fight, but your regular number never exceeded 5,000, 2,000 of whom have been killed or wounded, while in prisons you have lost about 200.

If your course has been marked by the graves of patriotic heroes who have fallen by your side, it has, at the same time, been more plainly marked by the blood of the invader. While you sympathize with the friends of the fallen, your sorrows should be appeased by the knowledge that they fell as brave men battling for all that makes life worth living for.

Soldiers! you now rest for a short time from your labors. During the respite prepare for future action. Your commanding general is ready to lead you again to the defense of the common cause, and he appeals to you, by a remembrance of the glories of your past career; your desolated homes; your insulted women and suffering children; and, above all, by the memory of your dead comrades, to yield a ready obedience to discipline, and to buckle on your armor anew for the fight. Bring with you the soldier's safest armor—a determination to fight while the enemy pollutes your soil; to fight as long as he denies your rights; to fight until independence shall have been achieved; to fight for home, children, liberty, and all you hold dear. Show to the world the superhuman and sublime spirit with which a people may be inspired when fighting for the inestimable boon of liberty. Be not allured by the siren song of peace, for there can be no peace save upon your separate independent nationality. You can never again unite with those who have murdered your sons, outraged your helpless families, and with demoniac malice wantonly destroyed your property, and now seek to make slaves of you. A proposition of reunion with a people who have avowed their purpose to appropriate the property and to subjugate or annihilate the freemen of the South would stamp with infamy the names of your gallant dead and the living heroes of this war. Be patient, obedient, and earnest, and the day is not far distant when you can return to your homes and live in the full fruition of freemen around the old family altar.

N. B. Forrest, Major-General, Comdg. District of Mississippi and East Louisiana.[274]

Forrest had the following circular distributed to his men, January 24, 1865:
☞ HDQRS. CAV., DEPT. OF ALA., MISS., AND EAST LA., VERONA, JANUARY 24, 1865.

In obedience to orders from department headquarters I hereby assume command of the district of Mississippi, East Louisiana, and Tennessee. In doing so it is due, both to myself and the troops thus placed under my command, to say that every effort will be made to render them thoroughly effective. To do this, strict obedience to all orders must be rigidly enforced by subordinate commanders, and prompt punishment inflicted for all violations of law and of orders. The rights and property of citizens must be respected and protected, and the illegal organizations of cavalry prowling through the country under various authorities, not recognized as legitimate, or which have been by the proper authorities revoked, must be placed regularly and properly in the service or driven from the country. They are in many instances nothing more nor less than roving bands of deserters, absentees, stragglers, horse-thieves, and robbers, who consume the substance and appropriate the property of citizens without remuneration, and whose acts of lawlessness and crime demand a remedy, which I shall not hesitate to apply, even to extermination. The maxim that kindness to bad men is cruelty to the good, is peculiarly applicable to soldiers, for all agree that without obedience and strict discipline troops cannot be made effective, and kindness to a bad soldier does great injustice to those who are faithful and true, and it is but justice to those who discharge their

272 ᠭ GIVE 'EM HELL BOYS!

duties with promptness and fidelity that others who are disobedient, turbulent and mutinous, or who desert or straggle from their commands, should be promptly and effectively dealt with, as the law directs. I sincerely hope, therefore, while in the discharge of the arduous duties devolving upon me, and in all the efforts necessary to render the troops of this command available and effective to suppress lawlessness and defend the country, I shall have the hearty co-operation of all subordinate commanders, and the unqualified support of every brave and faithful soldier. [N. B. FORREST.][275]

Forrest to Confederate General James Ronald Chalmers, January 27, 1865:
☞ VERONA, JANUARY 27, 1865. BRIG. GEN. J. R. CHALMERS:
    After you establish your headquarters at West Point establish courier-lines from West Point to Grenada direct and not via Houston.
    N. B. Forrest, Major-General.[276]

Forrest to Confederate General Richard Taylor, January 28, 1865:
☞ VERONA, MISS., JANUARY 28, 1865. [TO: GENERAL RICHARD TAYLOR:]
    Scouts just from Nashville report [Union General] Thomas with his army gone into winter quarters at Waterloo and Clifton. Nine transports, loaded with infantry, passed down Tennessee River on 21ˢᵗ.
    N. B. Forrest, Major-General.[277]

Forrest to Confederate General William Hicks "Red" Jackson, February 1, 1865:
☞ MERIDIAN [MISS.], FEBRUARY 1, 1865. BRIG. GEN. W. H. JACKSON, COLUMBUS, MISS.:
    You are assigned to command of Ross' and two Tennessee brigades for your division. Order Ross immediately with wagon train and everything to Canton. He will receive orders temporarily through General Adams, commanding sub-district.
    N. B. Forrest, Major-General.[278]

Forrest to Confederate General James Ronald Chalmers, February 19, 1865:
☞ WEST POINT [MISS.], FEBRUARY 19, 1865. BRIG. GEN. J. R. CHALMERS:
    Spare no time, hasten to reorganize, and fit up your command.

We have no time to lose.

N. B. Forrest, Major-General.[279]

Forrest to Confederate General James Ronald Chalmers, February 20, 1865:
☛ WEST POINT, MISS., FEBRUARY 20, 1865.

General Chalmers: Order Colonel Russell with the Fourth and Seventh Alabama to camp in vicinity of Columbus until further orders. As soon as Armstrong can cross, dispose of him as directed. I go to Meridian to-day.

N. B. Forrest, Major-General.[280]

Forrest to Confederate General Richard Taylor, February 22, 1865:
☛ HEADQUARTERS CAVALRY, DEPARTMENT OF ALA., MISS., AND EAST LA. WEST POINT, MISS., FEBRUARY 22, 1865. LIEUT. GEN. R. TAYLOR, COMMANDING DEPARTMENT, &C., [AT] MERIDIAN:

General: I have the honor to acknowledge receipt of your favor of yesterday, inclosing copy of instructions to Brigadier-General Adams. I sent you a special messenger this morning asking instructions, also to get your views as to the proper disposition of my troops. Have already ordered Brigadier-General Adams to retain all the troops he had and to withdraw everything from the bottom and prepare to meet the enemy. McGuirk's regiment, of Gholson's brigade, was also ordered to report to him, and orders are sent him to-day to carry out your instructions. Brigadier-General Chalmers has also been ordered to move Armstrong's brigade across the Tombigbee, to supply him at once with everything needed, and put it in motion for Selma. I send my ordnance officer, Capt. C. S. Hill, down to-day to hurry forward supplies now on the way, and hope he may be able to get arms, &c. Have been getting up all the arms I can find scattered through the country, but will require 2,000 stand. Have both written and telegraphed in regard to the horses for artillery, and feel some uneasiness on that score, for unless I get them will only be able to move with one battery.

I am, general, very respectfully, your obedient servant,

N. B. Forrest, Major-General.[281]

Forrest to Confederate General James Ronald Chalmers, February 22, 1865:

☞ WEST POINT, MISS., FEBRUARY 22, 1865. BRIG. GEN. J. R. CHALMERS:

Prepare Armstrong's brigade to move to Selma. Move him across the Tombigbee and make requisitions for everything he needs so as to supply him before he gets below Pickensville.

N. B. Forrest, Major-General.[282]

Forrest to Union Colonel John. G. Parkhurst, February 23, 1865:

☞ WEST POINT [MISS.], FEBRUARY 23, 1865. COLONEL PARKHURST, [AT] RIENZI:

Will be on train this evening.

N. B. Forrest, Major-General.[283]

Forrest to Union General George Henry Thomas, February 23, 1865:

☞ HDQRS. CAVALRY, DEPT. OF ALA., MISS., AND EAST LA., RIENZI, MISS., FEBRUARY 23, 1865. MAJ. GEN. G. H. THOMAS, COMDG. DEPARTMENT OF THE CUMBERLAND, NASHVILLE, TENN.:

General: I have the honor to acknowledge the receipt of your favor of the 17th instant per [Union] Colonel Parkhurst.

Your proposition to exchange prisoners is accepted, subject, however, to the approval of the lieutenant-general commanding this department, which I have no hesitation in saying will be readily given. Will inform you by flag of truce at the earliest possible moment of his approval, and think the prisoners now in our hands can be delivered at Iuka by the 3d or 4th of March.

The trains also for supplying the destitute citizens along the line of the Mobile and Ohio and the Memphis and Charleston railroads will be run subject to the conditions named in your letter. No Confederate soldiers or officers will be authorized or allowed to go upon those trains. At the same time you are fully aware that the border is infested by lawless bands of deserters from both armies, and in case they should force themselves upon the train I hope you will not act hastily in the matter. To prevent such an occurrence was my reason for proposing to place a sufficient guard upon the trains to enforce a strict observance of the agreement. At any rate, every effort will be made to carry out the agreement in good faith.

I will place in the hands of the conductors operating the train or trains a safeguard, enumerating and naming each man upon the train, with orders to run them under a "white flag" as often as may be necessary for the purpose as agreed.

The people here are compelled to have corn until they can raise a crop. The trains will be run exclusively to supply them, and [on] no condition whatever are they to be used for military purposes by either Federal or Confederate authority.

As to the prisoners of General [Philip D.] Roddey's command, as well as all others belonging to our Army which it may be desired or desirable to deliver in this department, I request them sent to Iuka or any point which may be agreed upon or designated by [Confederate] Lieutenant-General [Richard] Taylor for the delivery of all prisoners now in this department belonging to the Federal Army.

In regard to the murder of Federal soldiers by guerrillas and the threatened execution of a number of Ferguson's brigade in retaliation, I have nothing to say. I know nothing of the facts and can only forward the papers to [Confederate] General Beauregard, commanding the Military District of the West, for his consideration and action.

The communications in regard to [Confederate] Major Smith, captured at or near Murfreesborough, will receive attention. If retained as a prisoner of war he was doubtless sent forward by General Hood in advance of my command. The papers will be forwarded, and if he is in this department he will be sent to Iuka. All citizens captured by me were released, and although I am not cognizant of any charges against Major Smith, he will either be returned or copies of charges against him forwarded to you, provided there are any.

Assuring you, general, of my willingness and desire to relieve the suffering and alleviate the condition of the soldier in captivity and the wants of the destitute and dependent women and children of the country,

I am, yours, very respectfully,

N. B. Forrest, Major-General.[284]

Forrest to Union Colonel John G. Parkhurst, February 26, 1865:
☞ LAUDERDALE, FEBRUARY 26, 1865. COLONEL PARKHURST, U.S. ARMY:

Owing to heavy rains and washing of track I have not seen General Taylor. Will do so to-day and telegraph you from Meridian.
N. B. Forrest, Major-General.[285]

Forrest to Union Colonel John G. Parkhurst, February 26, 1865:
☛ MERIDIAN [MISS.], FEBRUARY 26, 1865. COLONEL PARKHURST, U.S. ARMY:
Col. N. G. Watts, assistant to Col. Robert Ould, has been sent for by [Confederate] Lieutenant-General [Richard] Taylor. As soon as he arrives he will be sent to Iuka to perfect the exchange of prisoners as agreed upon and to deliver them. It will not be necessary for you to remain longer at Rienzi.
N. B. Forrest, Major-General.[286]

Forrest to Union Colonel John G. Parkhurst, March 2, 1865:
☛ HDQRS. DEPT. OF MISSISSIPPI AND EAST LOUISIANA, WEST POINT, MISS., MARCH 2, 1865. COL. J. G. PARKHURST, PROVOST-MARSHALL-GENERAL DEPT. OF THE CUMBERLAND, U.S. ARMY:
It will be the 10th at least before we can send prisoners to Iuka. High water and bad condition of roads render it impossible to do so earlier.
N. B. Forrest, Major-General.[287]

Forrest to Confederate General Richard Taylor, March 6, 1865:
☛ HEADQUARTERS FORREST'S CAVALRY CORPS, WEST POINT [MISS.], MARCH 6, 1865. LIEUT. GEN. R. TAYLOR, [AT] MERIDIAN [MISS.]:
General: I have the honor to state that everything in my power is being done to have the troops in readiness for the field. It has rained almost every other day and the country is flooded with water. Tombigbee River is a mile wide. A part of Armstrong's brigade is on one side and a part on the other of that stream, with no chance or way of getting it together until the water falls. Tibbee River is over the whole country and several bridges and water-gaps washed out of the railroad between this place and Verona. To move with troops, wagons, or artillery until the streams run down is utterly impossible. I think,

however, in the course of four or five days it can be done. Have sent competent men with a force of negroes to repair the roads to Tuscaloosa and rebuild the bridges in that direction which have been washed away. Am also rebuilding the bridges on the railroad above this place. As soon as the waters recede can place Jackson's division in the field with about 2,500 effective men. The high water has prevented many men from reaching their commands, and I have written General Roddey almost daily directing him to use all possible expedition in getting to Montevallo with his command, to consolidate and reorganize it, and have ordered General Buford to move there at once with two regiments of Alabama cavalry—Fourth and Seventh—for the purpose of expediting and superintending the reorganization of those troops. An inspector leaves to-day for Jackson to inspect and assist General Adams in organizing and fitting up his brigade, and to hurry him up. Another also goes to Columbus ou similar duty, and as soon as Armstrong's brigade is supplied with guns and the streams get within their banks, he will be in condition for duty in the field and for any movement desired. I am of opinion that the cavalry should (as much as possible) be kept together and in readiness to concentrate and effectually resist the movements of the enemy from some of the directions in which he is anticipated, or will doubtless move as soon as the weather will permit him to do so. Colonel McCulloch's regiment is here, but a third of it is dismounted, having lost their horses by disease around Mobile. I have given the dismounted men ten days leave in which to procure horses, and think most or nearly all of them can do so in that time. Will send McCulloch to Grenada to report to General Wright, unless some move of the enemy renders it unnecessary to do so. I look for no assistance from State troops, as none of them have as yet reported at Macon. Lieutenant-Colonel Hyams, who bears you this and is on his way to Jackson, will communicate to you verbally instructions which are given him, as well as those he is authorized and instructed to make to you.

I am, general, very respectfully, your obedient servant,

N. B. Forrest, Major-General.[288]

Forrest to Confederate General James Ronald Chalmers, March 6, 1865:
☞ WEST POINT, MISS., MARCH 6, 1865. GENERAL J. R. CHALMERS:

I would recommend that you collect your command in vicinity of Pickensville, if you can procure forage. Have your command in readiness for a thorough inspection without delay, and notify me. Send a man to see that the road from Columbus to Selma by the direct stage road, and by the way of Tuscaloosa, is put in order. I think you will move in direction of Selma.

N. B. Forrest, Major-General.[289]

Forrest to Confederate General James Ronald Chalmers, March 6, 1865:
☛ WEST POINT, MISS. MARCH 6, 1865. BRIG. GEN. J. R. CHALMERS:

Prepare your command to move at once and be in readiness to move on twenty-four hours' notice.

N. B. Forrest, Major-General.[290]

Forrest to Confederate General W. F. Bullock, Jr., March 6, 1865:
☛ [WEST POINT, MISS.?] MARCH 6, 1865. [TO: W. F. BULLOCK, JR. ASSISTANT ADJUTANT-GENERAL.

Move Ross down so as to get his brigade together. Instruct him to keep in front of enemy should they attempt to cross from Clinton toward Mobile. Only Griffith's regiment and Willis' battalion to report to General Ross. Keep your Mississippi command in front of Vicksburg. Order General Hodge to such a point below as will enable him to join Ross or yourself.

N. B. Forrest, Major-General.[291]

Forrest to Confederate General James Ronald Chalmers, March 7, 1865:
☛ WEST POINT, MISS. MARCH 7, 1865. BRIGADIER-GENERAL CHALMERS:

Have 2,000 men with four days' cooked rations ready in their camps to move by railroad if necessary. Bring all your wagons and artillery west of river if you have to move. Enemy reported at Rienzi.

N. B. Forrest, Major-General.[292]

Forrest to Confederate General James Ronald Chalmers, March 7, 1865:
☛ WEST POINT, MISS, MARCH 7, 1865. BRIGADIER-GENERAL CHALMERS:

The enemy's advance reached Ripley yesterday at 5 P.M.; supposed to be 5,000. Hold your troops in readiness to move by railroad, leaving their horses. Cook four days rations from to-morrow morning. Answer how many troops you can have ready.

N. B. Forrest, Major-General.[293]

Forrest to Confederate General James Ronald Chalmers, March 7, 1865:

☛ WEST POINT, MARCH 7, 1865. BRIG. GEN. J. R. CHALMERS:

Have 1,800 men and officers, with five days cooked rations and forty rounds of ammunition to the man, on the railroad to-morrow morning between Columbus and Artesia by 9 o'clock to take the cars on arrival. Order telegraph office to open at 7 o'clock in the morning so as to receive instructions whether you will move or not.

N. B. Forrest, Major-General.[294]

Forrest to Confederate General James Ronald Chalmers, March 12, 1865:

☛ WEST POINT, MARCH 12, 1865. BRIGADIER-GENERAL CHALMERS:

Send a company of scouts to Fulton. Enemy reported moving from Eastport in that direction. Prepare Armstrong's brigade at once to cross the river to meet the enemy in the event they move on. Work day and night to get your command in order.

N. B. Forrest, Major-General.[295]

Forrest to Confederate General James Ronald Chalmers, March 13, 1865:

☛ WEST POINT, MISS., MARCH 13, 1865. BRIGADIER-GENERAL CHALMERS:

Brigadier-General Adams' brigade ordered to Macon. Make preparations to supply him at that place. He probably left Jackson to-day.

N. B. Forrest, Major-General.[296]

Forrest to Confederate Colonel Eustace Surget, March 13, 1865:

☛ HEADQUARTERS FORREST'S CAVALRY CORPS, WEST POINT [MISS.], MARCH 13, 1865. COL. E. SURGET, ASSISTANT ADJUTANT-GENERAL:

Colonel: I telegraphed the lieutenant-general commanding

to-day and repeat the substance of that dispatch. My scouts report the enemy as having withdrawn their pickets from Iuka, and at 7 o'clock yesterday evening their pickets were stationed three miles from Eastport; their lines are closed and no one is permitted to come out. Citizens report them moving down the river on opposite side. I have sent two flags of truce up to them; besides have thrown out sufficient scouts to ascertain their real movements. Captain Henderson has been ordered to send men across the Tennessee at several points, and I expect early and reliable information from them. The division of Brigadier-General Jackson has arrived here, and the bridge across the Bigbee at Waverly is ready. Have also ordered 20,000 rations of corn to Columbus and five days rations for the men, so that everything will he ready in the event of any movement of the enemy. Have established the courier-line from Moulton to Montevallo, or ordered it done; also, from Montevallo to Columbus, still keeping up a line from Verona across to Moulton. With the country well scouted on the river and the above means of communication, I do not fear any movement of the enemy will be made without my knowing it in time to meet them.

I am, colonel, very respectfully, your obedient servant,

N. B. Forrest, Major-General.[297]

Forrest to Confederate General James Ronald Chalmers, March 14, 1865:
☛ WEST POINT, MISS., MARCH 14, 1865. BRIGADIER-GENERAL CHALMERS:

Can you be ready to move with your command day after to-morrow morning to Montevallo with four days' cooked rations and two days' forage? Answer immediately.

N. B. Forrest, Major-General.[298]

Forrest to Confederate General W. F. Bullock, Jr., March 15, 1865:
☛ HEADQUARTERS FORREST'S CAVALRY CORPS, WEST POINT [MISS.], MARCH 15, 1865. CAPT. W. F. BULLOCK, JR., ASSISTANT ADJUTANT-GENERAL:

Captain: I have the honor to acknowledge receipt of papers relative to the situation of affairs at Natchez. Should the lieutenant-general commanding think it advisable to do so, he can order Colonel Mabry, in command of Ross brigade, to attempt the capture of the place, but do not think it necessary to turn General Adams back for that purpose. General Adams reported to me a short time since that he had 2,000 effective for duty, and now that he is ordered in this direction, reports only 700 men. He doubtless included Powers' and the Fourth and Sixth Mississippi in the estimate, but (without these) in the Third Mississippi Regiment and Moorman's battalion he should have more than he now reports. Colonel Scott telegraphs me that ninety of his men ran away night before last. I know Colonel Scott to be a disorganizer, and if things cannot be changed his whole command ought to be dismounted. If Cockrell's Missouri brigade were mounted upon their horses and the Louisiana troops placed in Gibson's brigade, with the addition of McCulloch's regiment, a good Missouri brigade could be made which, if sent to scour the Southern District of Missisippi and East Louisiana, would, by arresting stragglers, deserters, and illegal squads and companies of cavalry now infesting that region, in a short [time], add 1,500 men to our army. It is useless to send men from Scott's or Adams' command to get out these men. A command from some other section who knows no one can alone accomplish it. Whatever can be gotten to Macon of the commands above referred to I will endeavor to fit up and equip for the field.

I am, very respectfully, your obedient servant,

N. B. Forrest, Major-General.[299]

Forrest to Confederate General James Ronald Chalmers, March 18, 1865:
☛ WEST POINT, MISS., MARCH 18, 1865. BRIGADIER-GENERAL CHALMERS:

Order all Mississippi cavalry you have around Jackson, Vicksburg, and elsewhere on outpost duty to report at Macon, Miss. Send officer to have their transportation brought. Also General Starke telegraphs that Major Mims is at Clinton with fourteen wagons belonging to Mabry's brigade awaiting orders. Why don't he bring wagons over? What [city named] Clinton does Starke allude to?

N. B. Forrest, Major-General.[300]

Forrest to Confederate Colonel Eustace Surget, March 18, 1865:
☛ HEADQUARTERS FORREST'S CAVALRY CORPS, WEST POINT, MISS., MARCH 18, 1865. COL. E. SURGET, ASSISTANT

ADJUTANT-GENERAL:

Colonel: I have the honor to state that a few days since I directed Brigadier-General Wright to order out of West Tennessee a number of officers purporting to have authorities to raise troops between the ages of eighteen and forty-five years. In reply I received from General Wright a letter, an extract from which I respectfully inclose. I of course was not aware that Colonel Looney or any one else held authority from the lieutenant-general commanding to raise new commands in West Tennessee, and from a conversation had with him am not yet satisfied that they have such orders from department headquarters. In regard to Colonel Looney, I desire to say that he was a friend and fellow-townsman of mine before the war, a lawyer, and an out-and-out war man. He raised a regiment, fell out with General Bragg at Shiloh, got out of his command, and has done nothing since. He has been ostensibly engaged since 1862 in raising a regiment. He has not succeeded, nor do 1 believe, even under the most favorable circumstances, he ever will succeed. I hope, therefore, that all such officers may be ordered to report to department headquarters, that the authorities given them may be revoked, and they be put in the service. Colonel L. is a stout, able man, has played around long enough, and it is due to himself, his family, and the country that he should go into the Army, and into the ranks, if he can do no better. I herewith inclose a letter to the honorable Secretary of War [see below], which I hope the lieutenant-general commanding will indorse and forward. If all men engaged in raising commands were ordered into the ranks, and all squads and unattached companies not regularly in the service were outlawed, we would get ten men to fill up our old commands to where we now get one. Those we could not run down and catch the Federals would drive out to us. At any rate, we would rid ourselves of the odium attached to their paternity, and would not by the people be held responsible for their acts of lawlessness and crime. I do not for a moment question the motives of the honorable Secretary of War or the lieutenant-general commanding in giving these authorities, for every one is naturally desirous of increasing our strength, and willing to do almost anything to accomplish that end. It is not the authority itself but the abuse of it which is complained of, and in giving them the benefit of my experience and observation as to practical results, I hope I shall not be deemed officious or as assuming to myself superior judgment in such matters; but I speak truly when I say that whenever a paper of the kind is presented to me I can but regard it as an exemption from duty for the war, a license to plunder, and a nest-egg of desertion, all of which is chargeable not to the measures adopted to increase the strength of our Army, but to the men, who not only fail to make good their representations and promises in raising additional troops for the Army, but are actually creating uncontrollable currents of desertion, which are rapidly depleting commands already in the field.

    I am, colonel, very respectfully, your obedient servant,

    N. B. Forrest, Major-General.[301]

[INCLOSURE ATTACHED TO PREVIOUS LETTER]

☞ Colonel Looney was sent to me while in West Tennessee by Lieutenant-General Taylor with written authority from department headquarters to raise and organize a regiment of men between the ages of eighteen and forty-five years. Subsequently, under General Taylor's orders, three or four officers were sent to report to Colonel Looney. I showed Colonel Looney orders from the Adjutant and Inspector Generals Office, Richmond, prohibiting the organization of new commands of men between the ages of eighteen and forty-five years, but I of course felt bound to obey Lieutenant-General Taylor's orders.

    [N. B. Forrest.][302]

Forrest to Confederate Secretary of War John Cabell Breckinridge, March 18, 1865:

☞ HEADQUARTERS FORREST'S CAVALRY CORPS, WEST POINT, MISS., MARCH 18, 1865. HON. JOHN C. BRECKINRIDGE, SECRETARY OF WAR, RICHMOND, VA.:

    General: I take the liberty of addressing you relative to the state of affairs in the District of Southern Kentucky, and to bring to your notice and knowledge existing evils, which can alone be corrected by yourself as the chief of the War Department. It is due to myself to state that I disclaim all desire or intention to dictate. So far from it, I hesitate even now to make known the facts or to suggest the remedies to be applied. No other motive than the "good of the service" prompts me to address you. A military district was formed in Southern Kentucky, including a small portion of West Tennessee, and Brig. Gen. A. R. Johnson assigned to the command of it. The object in creating this district was doubtless for the purpose of raising and organizing troops for our army. Its permanent occupation by any force raised within its limits was not expected or calculated upon. If it was, the sequel shows that both in raising troops or holding the territory the experiment is a complete failure. General Johnson was often reported to have from 1,200 to 1,800 men, was finally wounded and captured, and his men scattered to the four winds. Brigadier-General Lyon then succeeded him and was driven across the Tennessee River into North Alabama, with only a handful of men. Nothing has been added to our army, for while the men flock to and remain with General Johnson or General Lyon as long as they can stay in Kentucky, as soon as the enemy presses and they turn southward the men scatter, and my opinion is that they can never be brought out or organized until we send troops there in sufficient numbers to bring them out by force. So far from gaining any strength for the army, the Kentucky brigade now in my command has only about 300 men in camps (Third, Seventh, and Eighth Kentucky Regiments). They have deserted and attached themselves to the roving bands of guerrillas, jayhawkers, and plunderers who are the natural offspring of authorities given to parties to raise troops within the enemy's lines. The authorities given to would-be colonels, and by them delegated to would-be captains and lieutenants, have created squads of men who are dodging from pillar to post, preying upon the people, robbing them of their horses and other property, to the manifest injury of the country and our cause.

The same state of affairs exists in West Tennessee and along the Mississippi River. The country is filled with deserters and stragglers, who run away and attach themselves to the commands of those who have the authorities referred to. They never organize, report to nobody, are responsible to no one, and exist by plunder and robbery. There may, perhaps, be a few exceptions, but as a general thing men who besiege the Department for such authorities are officers without position or command, who by flattering representations, recommendations, and influential friends avoid the ranks by obtaining authorities to raise troops within the enemy's lines. I venture the assertion that where one succeeds and organizes a command ninety-nine fail, and that they take twenty men out of the army to one placed in it. I therefore unhesitatingly recommend that all parties holding such authorities or are acting under orders from those who do hold them be ordered to report with what men they have to the nearest department commander within a limited period for consolidation and organization, and those failing so to report to have their authorities revoked and themselves subjected to conscription whenever caught. Do not understand me as reflecting on General Johnson or General Lyon. They did all they could no doubt to carry out the objects of the Department in their district. They have failed, and the fact to my mind is demonstrated most clearly that the conscripts and deserters in West Tennessee and Kentucky will never come out until brought out by force. If all authorities to raise troops in enemy's lines are revoked and the mustering officers ordered out, troops can be occasionally sent in under good and reliable officers to arrest and bring out deserters and break up the bands of lawless men who not only rob the citizens themselves, but whose presence in the country gives a pretext to Federal authority for oppressing the people.

I am, general, very respectfully, your obedient servant,

N. B. Forrest, Major-General.[303]

Forrest to Confederate General Richard Taylor, April 13, 1865:

☞ HEADQUARTERS FORREST'S CAVALRY CORPS, GAINESVILLE, APRIL 13, 1865. LIEUT. GEN. B. TAYLOR:

General: I have ordered Lieutenant Moore, in charge of ordnance stores at this place, to turn over to Captain Hill, my ordnance officer, some few spare traces for the use of the Hudson battery, which could not be moved without them; also some few cartridge and cap boxes, not waiting to send the requisition to you for approval, from the fact that the steamer was on the eve of leaving with ordnance for Jackson's division, to be delivered at Finch's Ferry, and it was the only immediate opportunity I had of sending them, as the bridges were washed away and the wagons ordered to this point after stores could not get here. Not having time to telegraph you and get a reply before the departure of the boat, I presume under the circumstances (as I am ordered to be ready to move at a moments notice) that it will make no difference and this explanation will be satisfactory.

I remain, general, your obedient servant,

N. B. Forrest, Lieutenant-General.[304]

Forrest to Confederate Colonel Eustace Surget, April 16, 1865:
☛ HEADQUARTERS FORREST'S CAVALRY CORPS, GAINESVILLE, APRIL 16, 1865. COL. E. SURGET:

Colonel: General Starke with his command and a portion of General Jackson's wagon train are on this side of the Warrior [River], and General Jackson's division on the east side and in consequence of high water will not be able to reach here until the evening of the 18th instant. I have sent a steamer to Finch's Ferry to cross General Jackson's command. The pontoon bridge was removed on account of high water. I have also ordered General [Philip D.] Roddey's wagon train, with the exception of a sufficient number to transport cooking utensils, to move to this place. There are some several pieces of artillery and about fifty caissons, and I should like to have the privilege of exchanging the caissons, as some that I have are somewhat dilapidated. I will order General Starke on his arrival to move as ordered in the direction of Livingston. Some dispatches have been received from Captains Henderson and Harvey, via Selma, and I presume you have received them, as I gave orders for all information to be given you. General Adams will strike the Byler road about thirty miles north of Tuscaloosa, and the latest information I have of Croxton was that he was moving in direction of Decatur, on Tennessee River. I find General Adams wagon train is in a very bad condition, and I will endeavor to fit it up if you think we will have any use for it. The larger portion of the forage in this country has been consumed by beef cattle, and I find it is in a greater abundance in the vicinity [of] Sumterville. In one of your dispatches you mentioned our former plan. I do not know which you alluded to, as there were two directions spoken of—north and west.

I am, colonel, your obedient servant,
N. B. Forrest, Lieutenant-General.[305]

Forrest to Confederate General William Hicks "Red" Jackson, April 21, 1865:
☛ GAINESVILLE, APRIL 21, 1865. BRIGADIER-GENERAL JACKSON, [AT] GREENSBOROUGH:

Send all your cooking utensils, &c., by boat. Move with your command at once to Demopolis. Withdraw courier-line to Eutaw and this place, and establish it from Greensborough to Demopolis. Leave Roddey's troops at Greensborough to carry out former instructions.

N. B. Forrest, Lieutenant-General.[306]

Forrest to Confederate Colonel Sam Jones, April 22, 1865:
☞ MERIDIAN, APRIL 22, 1865. [TO: LIEUTENANT-COLONEL S. JONES, COMMANDING POST.

It is reported many men represented to belong to my command are illegally impressing stock in the vicinity of Demopolis. You will arrest, iron [shackle], and keep in close confinement all men found impressing without proper authority, and report facts to me.

N. B. Forrest, Lieutenant-General.[307]

Though, on April 9, 1865, Lincoln's War had finally come to an end, Forrest, a natural-born warrior who loved the manly, open-air life of the soldier, could not bear to put his weapons down. There was something in him that simply could not accept defeat or offer capitulation, and for a few days, in vain hope, he considered the story of Lee's surrender nothing more than Yankee disinformation, as his April 25, 1865, general order to his men indicates:
☞ HEADQUARTERS FORREST'S CAVALRY CORPS, IN THE FIELD, APRIL 25, 1865.

Soldiers: the enemy have originated and sent through our lines various and conflicting dispatches indicating the surrender of General Robert E. Lee and the Army of Northern Virginia. A morbid appetite for news and sensation rumors has magnified a simple flag of truce from Lieutenant General Taylor to General Canby at Mobile into a mission for negotiating the terms of surrender of the troops of his department. Your commanding general desires to say to you that no credence should be given to such reports; nor should they for a moment control the actions or influence the feelings, sentiments, or conduct of the troops of this command. On the contrary, from Southern sources and now published in our papers, it is reported that General Lee has not surrendered; that a cessation of hostilities has been agreed upon between Generals Johnston and Sherman for the purpose of adjusting the difficulties and differences now existing between the Confederate and the United States of America. Also that since the evacuation of Richmond and the death of Abraham Lincoln, Grant has lost in battle and by desertion 100,000 men. As your commander he further assures you that at this time, above all others, it is the duty of every man to stand firm at his post and true to his colors. Your past services, your gallant and heroic conduct on many victorious fields, forbid the thought that you will ever ground your arms except with honor. Duty to your country, to yourselves, and the gallant dead who have fallen in this great struggle for liberty and independence, demand that every man should continue to do his whole duty. With undiminished confidence in your courage and fortitude, and knowing you now will not disregard the claims of honor, patriotism, and manhood, and those of the women and children of the country, so long defended by your strong arms and willing hearts, he announces his determination to stand by you, stay with you, and lead you to the end. A few days more will determine the truth or falsity of all the reports now in circulation. In the meantime let those who are now absent from their commands for the purpose of mounting themselves, or otherwise, return without delay. In conclusion, be firm and unwavering, discharging promptly and faithfully every duty devolving upon you. Preserve untarnished the reputation you have so nobly won, and leave results to Him who in wisdom controls and governs all things.

N. B. Forrest, Lieutenant- General.[308]

In Gainesville, Alabama, on May 9, 1865, the General bid farewell to his soldiers as only a man like Forrest could. His last known official military writing, it is one of the War's most sublime speeches:[309]

☞ HEADQUARTERS FORREST'S CAVALRY CORPS, GAINESVILLE, ALA., MAY 9, 1865.

Soldiers, by an agreement made between [Confederate] Lieutenant-General [Richard] Taylor, commanding the Department of Alabama, Mississippi, and East Louisiana, and [Union] Major-General [Edward R. S.] Canby, commanding United States forces, the troops of this department have been surrendered.

I do not think it proper or necessary at this time to refer to causes which have reduced us to this extremity; nor is it now a matter of material consequence to us how such results were brought about. That we are beaten is a self-evident fact, and any further resistance on our part would justly be regarded as the very height of folly and rashness.

The armies of Generals Lee and Johnson having surrendered,

you are the last of all the troops of the Confederate States Army east of the Mississippi River to lay down your arms.

The Cause for which you have so long and so manfully struggled, and for which you have braved dangers, endured privations, and sufferings, and made so many sacrifices, is today hopeless. The government which we sought to establish and perpetuate, is at an end. Reason dictates and humanity demands that no more blood be shed. Fully realizing and feeling that such is the case, it is your duty and mine to lay down our arms, submit to the "powers that be," and to aid in restoring peace and establishing law and order throughout the land.

The terms upon which you were surrendered are favorable, and should be satisfactory and acceptable to all. They manifest a spirit of magnanimity and liberality, on the part of the Federal authorities, which should be met, on our part, by a faithful compliance with all the stipulations and conditions therein expressed. As your Commander, I sincerely hope that every officer and soldier of my command will cheerfully obey the orders given, and carry out in good faith all the terms of the cartel.

Those who neglect the terms and refuse to be paroled, may assuredly expect, when arrested, to be sent North and imprisoned. Let those who are absent from their commands, from whatever cause, report at once to this place, or to Jackson, Mississippi; or, if too remote from either, to the nearest United States post or garrison, for parole.

Civil war, such as you have just passed through naturally engenders feelings of animosity, hatred, and revenge. It is our duty to divest ourselves of all such feelings; and as far as it is in our power to do so, to cultivate friendly feelings towards those with whom we have so long contended, and heretofore so widely, but honestly, differed. Neighborhood feuds, personal animosities, and private differences should be blotted out; and, when you return home, a manly, straightforward course of conduct will secure the respect of your enemies. Whatever your responsibilities may be to Government, to society, or to individuals, meet them like men.

The attempt made to establish a separate and independent Confederation has failed; but the consciousness of having done your duty faithfully, and to the end, will, in some measure, repay for the hardships you have undergone.

In bidding you farewell, rest assured that you carry with you my best wishes for your future welfare and happiness. Without, in any way, referring to the merits of the Cause in which we have been engaged, your courage and determination, as exhibited on many hard-fought fields, has elicited the respect and admiration of friend and foe. And I now cheerfully and gratefully acknowledge my indebtedness to the officers and men of my command whose zeal, fidelity and unflinching bravery have been the great source of my past success in arms.

I have never, on the field of battle, sent you where I was unwilling to go myself; nor would I now advise you to a course which I felt myself unwilling to pursue. You have been good soldiers, you can be good citizens. Obey the laws, preserve your honor, and the Government to which you have surrendered can afford to be, and will be, magnanimous.

N. B. Forrest, Lieutenant- General.[310]

Sadly, General Forrest spent the remainder of his days under so-called "Reconstruction" as a "prisoner on parole," allegedly guilty of the crime of "treason against the United States Government."

On October 29, 1877, the year "Reconstruction" ends, Forrest passes into the Better World at age fifty-six, a premature death brought on by the inhuman stresses of Lincoln's War. On October 31 he is buried at Elmwood Cemetery, Memphis, Tennessee, with full military honors. His beautiful Equestrian Statue marks the site to this day.

APPENDIX A

Forrest's Engagements
(From Seabrook's *A Rebel Born*)

- Includes battles, skirmishes, & raids -

November 1861-February 1862: raids from Hopkinsville, KY

December 28, 1861: Battle of Sacramento, KY

February 11-15, 1862: Ft. Henry, TN

February 11-16, 1862: Battle of Fort Donelson, Dover, TN

February 18-22, 1862: Nashville, TN

April 6-7, 1862: Battle of Shiloh, TN (Pittsburg Landing to Yanks)

July 13, 1862: Battle of Murfreesboro, TN

July 13-August 30, 1862: Middle TN and KY

December 10, 1862-January 6, 1863: West TN

December 18, 1862: Battle of Lexington, TN

December 31, 1862: Battle of Parker's Crossroads, TN

February 3, 1863: Battle of Dover (or Battle of Fort Donelson II), TN

March 5, 1863: Battle of Thompson's Station, TN

March 25, 1863: Battle of Brentwood, TN

April 10, 1863: Battle of Franklin I, TN

April 30, 1863: Battle of Day's Gap (Sand Mountain), AL

June 4, 1863: Triune, TN

June 10, 1863: Triune, TN

June 27, 1863: Rearguard, Tullahoma, TN

June 30, 1863: Cowan Pass-Chattanooga, TN

September 18-20, 1863: Battle of Chickamauga, GA

December 1-29, 1863: West TN

February 21, 1864: Battle of West Point, MS

February 22, 1864: Battle of Okolona, MS

March 15-May 5, 1864: West TN

March 25, 1864: Battle of Paducah, KY

April 12, 1864: Battle of Fort Pillow, TN

June 10, 1864: Battle of Brice's Cross Roads, MS

June 11, 1864: Battle of Tallahatchie, MS

June 11, 1864: Battle of Ripley, MS

July 14-15, 1864: Battle of Tupelo (Harrisburg), MS

July 15, 1864: Battle of Old Town Creek, MS

August 16, 1864: Battle of Hurricane Creek, MS

August 21, 1864: Forrest's Raid on Memphis, TN

September 21-October 6, 1864: Northern AL-Middle TN

September 25, 1864: Battle of Sulphur Branch Trestle, Elkmont, AL

September 27, 1864: Battle of Pulaski, TN

October 16-November 16, 1864: West TN

November 3-5, 1864: Battle of Johnsonville, TN

November 24-29, 1864: Battle of Columbia, TN

November 29, 1864: Battle of Spring Hill, TN

November 30, 1864: Battle of Franklin II, TN

December 15-16, 1865: Battle of Nashville (not present at actual battle, but defended the rearguard of the Army of Tennessee on its retreat south through TN, from Dec. 19 on)

December 25, 1864: Anthony's Hill, TN

December 26, 1864: Sugar Creek, TN

April 2, 1865: Battle of Selma, AL (Forrest's only loss as commander)

May 9, 1865: surrender at Gainesville, AL[311]

APPENDIX B

THE CONFEDERATE CONGRESS
RECOGNIZES FORREST

On May 1, 1863, the Confederate Congress gave special thanks to Forrest for his role at the Battle of Murfreesboro:
"RESOLVED BY THE CONGRESS OF THE CONFEDERATE STATES OF AMERICA,

"That the thanks of Congress are eminently due, and are hereby cordially given, to Brigadier-General N. B. Forrest and the officers and men under his command for gallantry and successful enterprise during the present war, and especially for the daring and skill exhibited the capture of Murfreesboro on the 13th of July last, and in subsequent brilliant achievements. Approved, May 1, 1863."[312]

On February 17, 1864, the Confederate Congress gave special thanks to Forrest for his role at the Battle of Chickamauga:
"THANKS OF THE CONFEDERATE CONGRESS TO GENERAL NATHAN B. FORREST AND THE OFFICERS AND MEN OF HIS COMMAND.

"Resolved by the Congress of the Confederate States of America, That the thanks of Congress are again due, and are hereby tendered, to General N. B. Forrest and the officers and men of his command, for meritorious service in the field, and especially for the daring, skill, and perseverance exhibited in the pursuit and capture of the largely superior forces of the enemy, near Rome, Ga., in May last; for gallant conduct at Chickamauga, and for his recent brilliant services in West Tennessee. Approved, February 17, 1864."[313]

On May 23, 1864, the Confederate Congress gave special thanks to Forrest for his role at the Battle of Fort Pillow:
"JOINT RESOLUTION OF THANKS TO MAJ. GEN. N. B. FORREST AND THE OFFICERS AND MEN OF HIS COMMAND, FOR THEIR

CAMPAIGN IN MISSISSIPPI, WEST TENNESSEE, AND KENTUCKY.
"Resolved by the Congress of the Confederate States of America,
That the thanks of Congress are eminently due, and are hereby cordially
tendered, to Maj. Gen. N. B. Forrest, and the officers and men of his
command, for their late brilliant and successful campaign in Mississippi,
West Tennessee, and Kentucky—a campaign which has conferred upon
its authors fame as enduring as the records of the struggle which they
have so brilliantly illustrated. Approved, May 23, 1864."[314]

*On December 6, 1864, Forrest was given his fourth and final official thanks from
the Confederate Congress.*

NOTES

1. Seabrook, ARB, p. 552.
2. Seabrook, ARB, p. 8.
3. Seabrook, NBF, p. 71.
4. Seabrook, ARB, pp. 560-580.
5. ORA, Ser. 1, Vol. 4, p. 551.
6. ORA, Ser. 1, Vol. 7, pp. 4-6.
7. ORA, Ser. 1, Vol. 7, pp. 64-66.
8. ORA, Ser. 1, Vol. 7, pp. 383-387.
9. ORA, Ser. 1, Vol. 7, pp. 295-296.
10. ORA, Ser. 1, Vol. 7, pp. 429-431.
11. ORA, Ser. 1, Vol. 16, Pt. 1, pp. 809-811.
12. ORA, Ser. 1, Vol. 16, Pt., 1, p. 805.
13. ORA, Ser. 1, Vol. 16, Pt. 1, p. 809.
14. ORA, Ser. 1, Vol. 16, Pt. 2, p. 735.
15. ORA, Ser. 1, Vol. 16, Pt. 1, pp. 818-819.
16. ORA, Ser. 1, Vol. 52, Pt. 2, p. 338.
17. ORA, Ser. 1, Vol. 52, Pt. 2, p. 348.
18. ORA, Ser. 1, Vol. 52, Pt. 2, p. 349.
19. ORA, Ser. 1, Vol. 16, Pt. 2, p. 837.
20. ORA, Ser. 1, Vol. 16, Pt. 2, pp. 837-838.
21. ORA, Ser. 1, Vol. 16, Pt. 2, pp. 863-864.
22. ORA, Ser. 1, Vol. 16, Pt. 2, p. 868.
23. ORA, Ser. 1, Vol. 16, Pt. 2, p. 952.
24. ORA, Ser. 1, Vol. 16, Pt. 2, pp. 970-971.
25. ORA, Ser. 1, Vol. 20, Pt. 1, pp. 6-7.
26. ORA, Ser. 1, Vol. 7, p. 387.
27. ORA, Ser. 1, Vol. 20, Pt. 2, p. 411.
28. ORA, Ser. 1, Vol. 20, Pt. 2, pp. 435-436.
29. ORA, Ser. 1, Vol. 17, Pt. 1, pp. 593-595.
30. ORA, Ser. 1, Vol. 17, Pt. 1, pp. 595-597.
31. ORA, Ser. 2, Vol. 5, p. 262.
32. ORA, Ser. 1, Vol. 23, Pt. 2, pp. 637-638.
33. ORA, Ser. 1, Vol. 23, Pt. 2, p. 638.
34. ORA, Ser. 1, Vol. 23, Pt. 2, p. 641.
35. ORA, Ser. 1, Vol. 23, Pt. 1, pp. 120-121.
36. ORA, Ser. 1, Vol. 23, Pt. 2, p. 669.
37. ORA, Ser. 1, Vol. 23, Pt. 1, pp. 187-189.
38. ORA, Ser. 1, Vol. 23, Pt. 2, p. 856.
39. ORA, Ser. 1, Vol. 23, Pt. 2, p. 856.
40. ORA, Ser. 1, Vol. 23, Pt. 2, p. 940.
41. Sheppard, pp. 306-307.
42. Wyeth, LGNBF, p. 641.
43. Lytle, p. 194.
44. ORA, Ser. 1, Vol. 23, Pt. 2, pp. 955-956; ORA, Ser. 1, Vol. 30, Pt. 4, pp. 508-509.
45. ORA, Ser. 1, Vol. 30, Pt. 4, p. 507.
46. ORA, Ser. 1, Vol. 30, Pt. 4, p. 615.
47. ORA, Ser. 1, Vol. 30, Pt. 4, p. 628.
48. ORA, Ser. 1, Vol. 30, Pt. 4, p. 675.
49. ORA, Ser. 1, Vol. 30, Pt. 4, p. 681.
50. ORA, Ser. 1, Vol. 30, Pt. 4, p. 711.

51. ORA, Ser. 1, Vol. 30, Pt. 4, p. 711.
52. ORA, Ser. 2, Vol. 6, pp. 414-415.
53. ORA, Ser. 1, Vol. 30, Pt. 2, pp. 523-526.
54. ORA, Ser. 1, Vol. 31, Pt. 3, pp. 645-646.
55. ORA, Ser. 1, Vol. 31, Pt. 3, p. 730.
56. ORA, Ser. 1, Vol. 31, Pt. 3, p. 751.
57. ORA, Ser. 1, Vol. 31, Pt. 3, pp. 789-790.
58. ORA, Ser. 1, Vol. 31, Pt. 3, p. 798.
59. ORA, Ser. 1, Vol. 31, Pt. 3, p. 797.
60. ORA, Ser. 1, Vol. 31, Pt. 3, p. 799.
61. ORA, Ser. 2, Vol. 6, pp. 691-693.
62. ORA, Ser. 1, Vol. 31, Pt. 3, p. 817.
63. ORA, Ser. 1, Vol. 31, Pt. 3, pp. 844-845.
64. ORA, Ser. 1, Vol. 31, Pt. 3, p. 846.
65. ORA, Ser. 1, Vol. 31, Pt. 3, pp. 853-854.
66. ORA, Ser. 1, Vol. 31, Pt. 3, pp. 858-859.
67. ORA, Ser. 1, Vol. 31, Pt. 3, pp. 876-877.
68. ORA, Ser. 1, Vol. 31, Pt. 1, pp. 620-621.
69. ORA, Ser. 1, Vol. 31, Pt. 1, p. 621.
70. ORA, Ser. 2, Vol. 6, p. 800.
71. ORA, Ser. 1, Vol. 32, Pt. 2, pp. 512-513.
72. ORA, Ser. 2, Vol. 6, p. 813.
73. ORA, Ser. 2, Vol. 6, p. 811.
74. ORA, Ser. 1, Vol. 32, Pt. 2, p. 579.
75. ORA, Ser. 1, Vol. 32, Pt. 2, p. 617.
76. ORA, Ser. 1, Vol. 32, Pt. 2, p. 648.
77. ORA, Ser. 1, Vol. 32, Pt. 2, p. 650.
78. ORA, Ser. 1, Vol. 32, Pt. 2, p. 673.
79. ORA, Ser. 1, Vol. 32, Pt. 2, p. 673.
80. ORA, Ser. 1, Vol. 32, Pt. 2, p. 680.
81. ORA, Ser. 1, Vol. 32, Pt. 2, p. 680.
82. ORA, Ser. 1, Vol. 32, Pt. 1, pp. 346-347.
83. ORA, Ser. 1, Vol. 32, Pt. 2, p. 685.
84. ORA, Ser. 1, Vol. 32, Pt. 2, p. 685.
85. ORA, Ser. 1, Vol. 32, Pt. 2, p. 691.
86. ORA, Ser. 1, Vol. 32, Pt. 2, p. 691.
87. ORA, Ser. 1, Vol. 32, Pt. 2, p. 691.
88. ORA, Ser. 1, Vol. 32, Pt. 2, p. 696.
89. ORA, Ser. 1, Vol. 32, Pt. 2, p. 696.
90. ORA, Ser. 1, Vol. 32, Pt. 2, p. 703.
91. ORA, Ser. 1, Vol. 32, Pt. 2, p. 703.
92. ORA, Ser. 1, Vol. 32, Pt. 2, p. 703.
93. ORA, Ser. 1, Vol. 32, Pt. 2, p. 707.
94. ORA, Ser. 1, Vol. 32, Pt. 2, p. 707.
95. ORA, Ser. 1, Vol. 32, Pt. 1, p. 347.
96. ORA, Ser. 1, Vol. 32, Pt. 2, p. 722.
97. ORA, Ser. 1, Vol. 32, Pt. 1, p. 348.
98. ORA, Ser. 1, Vol. 32, Pt. 1, p. 348.
99. ORA, Ser. 1, Vol. 32, Pt. 1, p. 348.
100. ORA, Ser. 1, Vol. 32, Pt. 2, p. 737.
101. ORA, Ser. 1, Vol. 32, Pt. 1, pp. 348-349.
102. ORA, Ser. 1, Vol. 32, Pt. 1, p. 349.
103. ORA, Ser. 1, Vol. 32, Pt. 2, p. 740.
104. ORA, Ser. 1, Vol. 32, Pt. 1, p. 349.

105. ORA, Ser. 1, Vol. 32, Pt. 2, p. 758.
106. ORA, Ser. 1, Vol. 32, Pt. 1, pp. 349-350.
107. ORA, Ser. 1, Vol. 32, Pt. 2, pp. 770-771.
108. ORA, Ser. 1, Vol. 32, Pt. 2, p. 771.
109. ORA, Ser. 1, Vol. 32, Pt. 2, p. 787.
110. ORA, Ser. 1, Vol. 32, Pt. 2, p. 788.
111. ORA, Ser. 1, Vol. 32, Pt. 2, p. 795.
112. ORA, Ser. 1, Vol. 32, Pt. 1, pp. 350-351.
113. ORA, Ser. 1, Vol. 32, Pt. 3, p. 588.
114. ORA, Ser. 1, Vol. 32, Pt. 1, pp. 351-355.
115. ORA, Ser. 1, Vol. 32, Pt. 3, p. 609.
116. ORA, Ser. 1, Vol. 32, Pt. 3, pp. 609-610.
117. Seabrook, ARB, pp. 310-311.
118. ORA, Ser. 1, Vol. 32, Pt. 1, pp. 365-357.
119. ORA, Ser. 1, Vol. 32, Pt. 3, p. 616.
120. ORA, Ser. 1, Vol. 32, Pt. 3, p. 651.
121. ORA, Ser. 1, Vol. 32, Pt. 3, p. 650.
122. ORA, Ser. 1, Vol. 32, Pt. 3, pp. 663-665.
123. ORA, Ser. 1, Vol. 32, Pt. 3, p. 117.
124. ORA, Ser. 1, Vol. 32, Pt. 3, p. 119.
125. ORA, Ser. 1, Vol. 32, Pt. 1, p. 545.
126. ORA, Ser. 1, Vol. 32, Pt. 1, p. 547.
127. ORA, Ser. 1, Vol. 32, Pt. 1, p. 548.
128. ORA, Ser. 1, Vol. 32, Pt. 1, p. 607.
129. ORA, Ser. 1. Vol. 32, Pt. 3, p. 733.
130. ORA, Ser. 1, Vol. 32, Pt. 1, pp. 608-609.
131. ORA, Ser. 1, Vol. 52, Pt. 2, p. 653.
132. ORA, Ser. 1, Vol. 32, Pt. 3, pp. 769-770.
133. ORA, Ser. 1, Vol. 32, Pt. 3, p. 770.
134. ORA, Ser. 1, Vol. 32, Pt. 1, p. 596. See also p. 560. See also Jordan and Pryor, p. 431.
135. ORA, Ser. 1, Vol. 32, Pt. 1, p. 596. See also p. 561.
136. ORA, Ser. 1, Vol. 32, Pt. 1, p. 597.
137. ORA, Ser. 1, Vol. 32, Pt. 3, p. 778.
138. ORA, Ser. 1, Vol. 32, Pt. 1, p. 609.
139. Seabrook, ARB, pp. 361-363.
140. ORA, Ser. 1, Vol. 32, Pt. 1, pp. 609-611.
141. ORA, Ser. 1, Vol. 32, Pt. 1, pp. 611-613.
142. ORA, Ser. 1, Vol. 32, Pt. 3, pp. 786-787.
143. ORA, Ser. 1, Vol. 32, Pt. 3, p. 798.
144. ORA, Ser. 1, Vol. 32, Pt. 3, pp. 798-799.
145. ORA, Ser. 1, Vol. 32, Pt. 3, p. 809.
146. ORA, Ser. 1, Vol. 32, Pt. 3, p. 807.
147. ORA, Ser. 1, Vol. 32, Pt. 3, pp. 821-822.
148. ORA, Ser. 1, Vol. 32, Pt. 3, p. 822.
149. ORA, Ser. 1, Vol. 32, Pt. 1, pp. 613-617.
150. ORA, Ser. 1, Vol. 32, Pt. 3, p. 837.
151. ORA, Ser. 1, Vol. 32, Pt. 3, p. 854.
152. ORA, Ser. 1, Vol. 39, Pt. 2, p. 594.
153. ORA, Ser. 1, Vol. 39, Pt. 2, p. 595.
154. ORA, Ser. 1, Vol. 39, Pt. 2, p. 595.
155. ORA, Ser. 1, Vol. 39, Pt. 2, p. 597.
156. ORA, Ser. 1, Vol. 39, Pt. 2, p. 597.
157. ORA, Ser. 1, Vol. 39, Pt. 2, p. 601.
158. ORA, Ser. 1, Vol. 39, Pt. 2, p. 601.

159. ORA, Ser. 1, Vol. 39, Pt. 2, pp. 601-602.
160. ORA, Ser. 1, Vol. 39, Pt. 2, p. 603.
161. ORA, Ser. 1, Vol. 32, Pt. 1, pp. 617-618.
162. ORA, Ser. 1, Vol. 39, Pt. 2, p. 605.
163. ORA, Ser. 1, Vol. 39, Pt. 2, p. 606.
164. ORA, Ser. 1, Vol. 38, Pt. 4, pp. 723-724.
165. ORA, Ser. 1, Vol. 39, Pt. 2, p. 608.
166. ORA, Ser. 1, Vol. 39, Pt. 2, pp. 613-614.
167. ORA, Ser. 1, Vol. 38, Pt. 4, p. 734.
168. ORA, Ser. 1, Vol. 39, Pt. 1, p. 17.
169. ORA, Ser. 1, Vol. 39, Pt. 2, pp. 617-618.
170. ORA, Ser. 1, Vol. 38, Pt. 4, pp. 740-741.
171. ORA, Ser. 1, Vol. 39, Pt. 2, p. 625.
172. ORA, Ser. 1, Vol. 38, Pt. 4, p. 747.
173. ORA, Ser. 1, Vol. 38, Pt. 4, pp. 747-748.
174. ORA, Ser. 1, Vol. 38, Pt. 4, p. 748.
175. ORA, Ser. 1, Vol. 38, Pt. 4, p. 750.
176. ORA, Ser. 1, Vol. 38, Pt. 4, pp. 750-751.
177. ORA, Ser. 1, Vol. 39, Pt. 2, p. 645.
178. ORA, Ser. 1, Vol. 39, Pt. 2, p. 652.
179. ORA, Ser. 1, Vol. 39, Pt. 2, p. 652.
180. ORA, Ser. 1, Vol. 32, Pt. 1, pp. 586-587.
181. ORA, Ser. 1, Vol. 39, Pt. 2, p. 651.
182. ORA, Ser. 1, Vol. 39, Pt. 2, p. 659.
183. ORA, Ser. 1, Vol. 32, Pt. 1, pp. 591-593.
184. ORA, Ser. 1, Vol. 32, Pt. 1, p. 618.
185. Warner, GB, s.v. "Cadwallader Colden Washburn."
186. ORA, Ser. I, Vol. 32, Pt. 1, pp. 590-591.
187. ORA, Ser. 1, Vol. 39, Pt. 2, p. 666.
188. ORA, Ser. 1, Vol. 39, Pt. 2, p. 666.
189. ORA, Ser. 1, Vol. 39, Pt. 2, p. 665.
190. ORA, Ser. 1, Vol. 39, Pt. 2, p. 667.
191. ORA, Ser. 1, Vol. 39, Pt. 2, p. 647.
192. ORA, Ser. 1, Vol. 39, Pt. 2, p. 668.
193. ORA, Ser. 1, Vol. 39, Pt. 2, p. 671.
194. ORA, Ser. 1, Vol. 39, Pt. 2, p. 671.
195. ORA, Ser. 1, Vol. 39, Pt. 2, p. 671.
196. ORA, Ser. 1, Vol. 39, Pt. 1, pp. 228-230.
197. ORA, Ser. 1, Vol. 39, Pt. 2, p. 672.
198. ORA, Ser. 1, Vol. 39, Pt. 2, p. 672.
199. ORA, Ser. 1, Vol. 39, Pt. 2, p. 674.
200. ORA, Ser. 1, Vol. 39, Pt. 2, p. 674.
201. ORA, Ser. 1, Vol. 39, Pt. 2, p. 675.
202. ORA, Ser. 1, Vol. 39, Pt. 2, p. 155.
203. ORA, Ser. 1, Vol. 39, Pt. 1, pp. 221-226.
204. ORA, Ser. 1, Vol. 39, Pt. 2, p. 682.
205. ORA, Ser. 1, Vol. 39, Pt. 2, pp. 683-684.
206. ORA, Ser. 1, Vol. 39, Pt. 2, p. 696.
207. ORA, Ser. 1, Vol. 39, Pt. 2, pp. 715-716.
208. ORA, Ser. 1, Vol. 39, Pt. 2, p. 717.
209. ORA, Ser. 1, Vol. 39, Pt. 2, p. 733.
210. ORA, Ser. 1, Vol. 39, Pt. 1, pp. 320-324.
211. ORA, Ser. 1, Vol. 39, Pt. 2, pp. 756-757.
212. ORA, Ser. 1, Vol. 39, Pt. 2, p. 763.

213. ORA, Ser. 1, Vol. 39, Pt. 2, p. 764.
214. ORA, Ser. 1, Vol. 39, Pt. 2, pp. 760-761.
215. ORA, Ser. 1, Vol. 39, Pt. 2, p. 765.
216. ORA, Ser. 1, Vol. 39, Pt. 2, p. 765.
217. ORA, Ser. 1, Vol. 39, Pt. 2, p. 765.
218. ORA, Ser. 1, Vol. 39, Pt. 2, p. 766.
219. ORA, Ser. 1, Vol. 39, Pt. 2, p. 766.
220. ORA, Ser. 1, Vol. 39, Pt. 2, p. 779.
221. ORA, Ser. 1, Vol. 39, Pt. 2, p. 783.
222. ORA, Ser. 1, Vol. 39, Pt. 2, p. 783.
223. ORA, Ser. 1, Vol. 39, Pt. 2, p. 788.
224. ORA, Ser. 1, Vol. 39, Pt. 1, p. 484.
225. ORA, Ser. 2, Vol. 7, p. 663.
226. ORA, Ser. 1, Vol. 39, Pt. 2, p. 792.
227. ORA, Ser. 1, Vol. 39, Pt. 2, p. 793.
228. ORA, Ser. 1, Vol. 39, Pt. 2, p. 795.
229. ORA, Ser. 1, Vol. 39, Pt. 2, p. 797.
230. ORA, Ser. 1, Vol. 39, Pt. 2, p. 797.
231. ORA, Ser. 1, Vol. 39, Pt. 2, p. 798.
232. ORA, Ser. 1, Vol. 39, Pt. 2, p. 798.
233. ORA, Ser. 1, Vol. 39, Pt. 2, p. 799.
234. ORA, Ser. 1, Vol. 39, Pt. 2, pp. 800-801.
235. ORA, Ser. 1, Vol. 39, Pt. 2, p. 801.
236. ORA, Ser. 1, Vol. 39, Pt. 2, p. 804.
237. ORA, Ser. 1, Vol. 39, Pt. 2, p. 805.
238. ORA, Ser. 1, Vol. 39, Pt. 2, pp. 805-806.
239. ORA, Ser. 1, Vol. 39, Pt. 2, p. 806.
240. ORA, Ser. 1, Vol. 39, Pt. 2, p. 813.
241. ORA, Ser. 1, Vol. 39, Pt. 2, p. 813.
242. ORA, Ser. 2, Vol. 7, pp. 715-716.
243. ORA, Ser. 1, Vol. 52, Pt. 2, p. 731.
244. ORA, Ser. 1, Vol. 39, Pt. 2, p. 819.
245. ORA, Ser. 1, Vol. 39, Pt. 2, p. 819.
246. ORA, Ser. 1, Vol. 39, Pt. 2, p. 819.
247. ORA, Ser. 1, Vol. 39, Pt. 2, pp. 845-846.
248. ORA, Ser. 1, Vol. 39, Pt. 2, p. 846.
249. ORA, Ser. 1, Vol. 39, Pt. 2, p. 859.
250. ORA, Ser. 1, Vol. 39, Pt. 2, p. 870.
251. ORA, Ser. 1, Vol. 39, Pt. 1, p. 521.
252. ORA, Ser. 1, Vol. 39, Pt. 1, p. 522.
253. ORA, Ser. 1, Vol. 39, Pt. 1, pp. 522-523.
254. ORA, Ser. 1, Vol. 39, Pt. 2, p. 874.
255. ORA, Ser. 2, Vol. 7, p. 1154.
256. ORA, Ser. 1, Vol. 39, Pt. 2, p. 878.
257. ORA, Ser. 1, Vol. 39, Pt. 2, p. 879.
258. ORA, Ser. 1, Vol. 39, Pt. 1, pp. 516-517.
259. ORA, Ser. 1, Vol. 39, Pt. 3, p. 807.
260. ORA, Ser. 1, Vol. 39, Pt. 1, pp. 542-549.
261. ORA, Ser. 1, Vol. 41, Pt. 4, p. 537.
262. ORA, Ser. 1, Vol. 39, Pt. 1, pp. 868-869.
263. ORA, Ser. 1, Vol. 52, Pt. 2, p. 777.
264. ORA, Ser. 1, Vol. 39, Pt. 3, p. 915.
265. ORA, Ser. 2, Vol. 7, p. 1233.
266. ORA, Ser. 1, Vol. 45, Pt. 2, p. 748.

267. ORA, Ser. 1, Vol. 45, Pt. 2, pp. 756-757.
268. ORA, Ser. 2, Vol. 8, pp. 31-32.
269. ORA, Ser. 1, Vol. 39, Pt. 1, pp. 870-872.
270. ORA, Ser. 1, Vol. 45, Pt. 2, p. 794.
271. ORA, Ser. 1, Vol. 52, Pt. 2, pp. 809-810.
272. ORA, Ser. 1, Vol. 45, Pt. 2, p. 800.
273. ORA, Ser. 1, Vol. 45, Pt. 1, pp. 751-759.
274. ORA, Ser. 1, Vol. 45, Pt. 1, pp. 759-760.
275. ORA, Ser. 1, Vol. 49, Pt. 1, pp. 930-931.
276. ORA, Ser. 1, Vol. 49, Pt. 1, p. 938.
277. ORA, Ser. 1, Vol. 49, Pt. 1, p. 940.
278. ORA, Ser. 1, Vol. 49, Pt. 1, p. 952.
279. ORA, Ser. 1, Vol. 49, Pt. 1, p. 994.
280. ORA, Ser. 1, Vol. 49, Pt. 1, p. 997.
281. ORA, Ser. 1, Vol. 49, Pt. 1, pp. 1004-1005.
282. ORA, Ser. 1, Vol. 49, Pt. 1, p. 1005.
283. ORA, Ser. 2, Vol. 8, p. 325.
284. ORA, Ser. 2, Vol. 8, pp. 327-328.
285. ORA, Ser. 2, Vol. 8, p. 326.
286. ORA, Ser. 2, Vol. 8, p. 326.
287. ORA, Ser. 2, Vol. 8, p. 335.
288. ORA, Ser. 1, Vol. 49, Pt. 1, pp. 1030-1031.
289. ORA, Ser. 1, Vol. 49, Pt. 1, p. 1032.
290. ORA, Ser. 1, Vol. 49, Pt. 1, p. 1032.
291. ORA, Ser. 1, Vol. 49, Pt. 1, p. 1033.
292. ORA, Ser. 1, Vol. 49, Pt. 1, p. 1036.
293. ORA, Ser. 1, Vol. 49, Pt. 1, p. 1037.
294. ORA, Ser. 1, Vol. 49, Pt. 1, p. 1037.
295. ORA, Ser. 1, Vol. 49, Pt. 1, p. 1051.
296. ORA, Ser. 1, Vol. 49, Pt. 1, p. 1058.
297. ORA, Ser. 1, Vol. 49, Pt. 1, p. 1057.
298. ORA, Ser. 1, Vol. 49, Pt. 1, p. 1060.
299. ORA, Ser. 1, Vol. 49, Pt. 1, p. 1061.
300. ORA, Ser. 1, Vol. 49, Pt. 2, p. 1127.
301. ORA, Ser. 1, Vol. 49, Pt. 2, pp. 1225-1226.
302. ORA, Ser. 1, Vol. 49, Pt. 2, p. 1226.
303. ORA, Ser. 1, Vol. 49, Pt. 2, pp. 1124-1125.
304. ORA, Ser. 1, Vol. 49, Pt. 2, p. 1134.
305. ORA, Ser. 1, Vol. 49, Pt. 2, p. 1247.
306. ORA, Ser. 1, Vol. 49, Pt. 2, p. 1258.
307. ORA, Ser. 1, Vol. 49, Pt. 2, p. 1258.
308. ORA, Ser. 1, Vol. 49, Pt. 2, pp. 1263-1264.
309. Forrest's speech was not actually given, but was handed out on flyers. Morton, p. 317.
310. ORA, Ser. 1, Vol. 49, Pt. 2, pp. 1289-1290.
311. Seabrook, ARB, pp. 558-559.
312. ORA, Ser. 2, Vol. 3, p. 143.
313. ORA, Ser. 1, Vol. 23, Pt. 1, p. 295.
314. ORA, Ser. 1, Vol. 32, Pt. 1, p. 619.

BIBLIOGRAPHY

Jordan, Thomas, and John P. Pryor. *The Campaigns of General Nathan Bedford Forrest and of Forrest's Cavalry.* New Orleans, LA: Blelock and Co., 1868.

Lytle, Andrew Nelson. *Bedford Forrest and His Critter Company.* New York, NY: G. P. Putnam's Sons, 1931.

Morton, John Watson. *The Artillery of Nathan Bedford Forrest's Cavalry.* Nashville, TN: The M. E. Church, 1909.

ORA (full title: *The War of the Rebellion: A Compilation of the Official Records of the Union and Confederate Armies.* (Multiple volumes.) Washington, D.C.: Government Printing Office, 1880.

Seabrook, Lochlainn. *Nathan Bedford Forrest: Southern Hero, American Patriot: Honoring a Confederate Hero and the Old South.* 2007. Franklin, TN: Sea Raven Press, 2010 ed.

——. *Abraham Lincoln: The Southern View - Demythologizing America's Sixteenth President.* 2007. Franklin, TN: Sea Raven Press, 2010 ed.

——. *Everything You Were Taught About the Civil War is Wrong, Ask a Southerner! - Correcting the Errors of Yankee "History."* Franklin, TN: Sea Raven Press, 2010.

——. *A Rebel Born: A Defense of Nathan Bedford Forrest.* 2010. Franklin, TN: Sea Raven Press, 2011 ed.

——. *The Quotable Nathan Bedford Forrest: Selections From the Writings and Speeches of the Confederacy's Most Brilliant Cavalryman.* 2012. Franklin, TN: Sea Raven Press.

Sheppard, Eric William. *Bedford Forrest, The Confederacy's Greatest Cavalryman.* 1930. Dayton, OH: Morningside House, 1981 ed.

Warner, Ezra J. *Generals in Gray: Lives of the Confederate Commanders.* 1959. Baton Rouge, LA: Louisiana State University Press, 1989 ed.

——. *Generals in Blue: Lives of the Union Commanders.* 1964. Baton Rouge, LA: Louisiana State University Press, 2006 ed.

Wyeth, John Allan. *Life of General Nathan Bedford Forrest.* New York, NY: Harper and Brothers, 1899.

INDEX

MEET THE AUTHOR

LOCHLAINN SEABROOK, winner of the prestigious Jefferson Davis Historical Gold Medal for his "masterpiece," *A Rebel Born: A Defense of Nathan Bedford Forrest,* is an unreconstructed Southern historian, award-winning author, Forrest scholar, and traditional Southern Agrarian of Scottish, English, Irish, Welsh, German, and Italian extraction. An encyclopedist, lexicographer, musician, artist, graphic designer, genealogist, and photographer,

(Illustration © Tracy Latham)

as well as an award-winning poet, songwriter, and screenwriter, he has a thirty year background in historical nonfiction writing and is a member of the Sons of Confederate Veterans, the Civil War Trust, and the Grange.

Due to similarities in their writing styles, ideas, and literary works, Seabrook is referred to as the "American ROBERT GRAVES," after his cousin, the prolific English writer, historian, mythographer, poet, and author of the classic tomes *The White Goddess* and *The Greek Myths.*

The grandson of an Appalachian coal-mining family, Seabrook is a seventh-generation Kentuckian, co-chair of the Jent/Gent Family Committee (Kentucky), founder and director of the Blakeney Family Tree Project, and a board member of the Friends of Colonel Benjamin E. Caudill. Seabrook's literary works have been endorsed by leading authorities, museum curators, award-winning historians, bestselling authors, celebrities, noted scientists, well respected educators, renown military artists, esteemed Southern organizations, and distinguished academicians from around the world.

As a writer, Seabrook has authored some thirty popular adult books specializing in the following topics: the American Civil War, pro-South studies, Confederate biography and history, the anthropology of religion, genealogical monographs, Goddess-worship (thealogy), ghost stories, the paranormal, family histories, military encyclopedias, etymological dictionaries, ufology, social issues, comparative analysis of the origins of Christmas, and cross-cultural studies of the family and marriage.

Seabrook's eight children's titles include a pro-South book on Lincoln's War, a dictionary of religion and myth, a rewriting of the King Arthur legend (which reinstates the original pre-Christian motifs), two bedtime stories for preschoolers, a naturalist's guidebook to owls, a worldwide look at the family, and an examination of the Near-Death Experience.

Of blue-blooded Southern stock through his Kentucky, Tennessee, Virginia, West Virginia, and North Carolina ancestors, he is a direct descendant of European royalty via his 6th great-grandfather, the EARL OF OXFORD, after which London's famous Harley Street is named. Among his celebrated male Celtic ancestors is ROBERT THE BRUCE, King of Scotland, Seabrook's 22nd great-grandfather. The 21st great-grandson of EDWARD I "LONGSHANKS" PLANTAGENET), King of England, Seabrook is a thirteenth-generation Southerner through his descent from the colonists of Jamestown, Virginia (1607).

The 2nd, 3rd, and 4th great-grandson of dozens of Confederate soldiers, one of his closest connections to the War for Southern Independence is through his 3rd great-grandfather, ELIAS JENT, SR., who fought for the Confederacy in the Thirteenth Cavalry Kentucky under Seabrook's 2nd cousin, Colonel BENJAMIN E. CAUDILL. The Thirteenth, also known as "Caudill's Army," fought in numerous conflicts, including the Battles of Saltville, Gladsville, Mill Cliff, Poor Fork, Whitesburg, and Leatherwood.

Seabrook is also related to the following Confederates and other 19th-Century luminaries: ROBERT E. LEE, STEPHEN DILL LEE, JOHN SINGLETON MOSBY, STONEWALL JACKSON, NATHAN BEDFORD FORREST, JAMES LONGSTREET, JOHN HUNT MORGAN, JEB STUART, P. G. T. BEAUREGARD (designed the Confederate Battle Flag), JOHN BELL HOOD, ALEXANDER PETER STEWART, ARTHUR M. MANIGAULT, JOSEPH MANIGAULT, CHARLES SCOTT VENABLE, THORNTON A. WASHINGTON, JOHN A. WASHINGTON, ABRAHAM BUFORD, EDMUND W. PETTUS, THEODRICK "TOD" CARTER, JOHN B. WOMACK, JOHN H. WINDER, GIDEON J. PILLOW, STATES RIGHTS GIST, EDMUND WINCHESTER RUCKER, HENRY R. JACKSON, JOHN C.

(Photo © Lochlainn Seabrook)

BRECKINRIDGE, LEONIDAS POLK, ZACHARY TAYLOR, SARAH KNOX TAYLOR (the first wife of JEFFERSON DAVIS), RICHARD TAYLOR, DAVY CROCKETT, DANIEL BOONE, MERIWETHER LEWIS (of the Lewis and Clark Expedition) ANDREW JACKSON, JAMES K. POLK, ABRAM POINDEXTER MAURY (founder of Franklin, TN), WILLIAM GILES HARDING, ZEBULON VANCE, THOMAS JEFFERSON, GEORGE WYTHE RANDOLPH (grandson of Jefferson), FELIX K. ZOLLICOFFER, FITZHUGH LEE, NATHANIEL F. CHEAIRS, JESSE JAMES, FRANK JAMES, ROBERT BRANK VANCE, CHARLES SIDNEY WINDER, JOHN W. MCGAVOCK, CARRIE (WINDER) MCGAVOCK, DAVID HARDING MCGAVOCK, LYSANDER MCGAVOCK, JAMES

RANDAL MCGAVOCK, RANDAL WILLIAM MCGAVOCK, FRANCIS MCGAVOCK, EMILY MCGAVOCK, WILLIAM HENRY F. LEE, LUCIUS E. POLK, MINOR MERIWETHER (husband of noted pro-South author Elizabeth Avery Meriwether), ELLEN BOURNE TYNES (wife of Forrest's chief of artillery, Captain John W. Morton), South Carolina Senators PRESTON SMITH BROOKS and ANDREW PICKENS BUTLER, and famed South Carolina diarist MARY CHESNUT.

Seabrook's modern day cousins include: PATRICK J. BUCHANAN (conservative author), REBECCA GAYHEART (Kentucky-born actress), SHELBY LEE ADAMS (Letcher County, Kentucky, portrait photographer), BERTRAM THOMAS

COMBS (Kentucky's fiftieth governor), EDITH BOLLING (wife of President Woodrow Wilson), and actors ROBERT DUVALL, REESE WITHERSPOON, LEE MARVIN, and TOM CRUISE.

Born with music in his blood, Seabrook is an award-winning, multi-genre, BMI-Nashville songwriter and lyricist who has composed some 3,000 songs (250 albums), and whose original music has been heard on TV and radio worldwide. A musician, producer, multi-instrumentalist, and renown performer—whose keyboard work has been variously compared to pianists from HARGUS ROBBINS and VINCE GUARALDI to ELTON JOHN and LEONARD BERNSTEIN—Seabrook has opened for groups such as the EARL SCRUGGS REVIEW, TED NUGENT, and BOB SEGER, and has performed privately for such public figures as President RONALD REAGAN, BURT REYNOLDS, and Senator EDWARD W. BROOKE.

Seabrook's cousins in the music business include: JOHNNY CASH, ELVIS PRESLEY, BILLY RAY and MILEY CYRUS, PATTY LOVELESS, TIM MCGRAW, LEE ANN WOMACK, DOLLY PARTON, PAT BOONE, NAOMI, WYNONNA, and ASHLEY JUDD, RICKY SKAGGS, the SUNSHINE SISTERS, MARTHA CARSON, and CHET ATKINS.

Seabrook lives with his wife and family in historic Middle Tennessee, the heart of Forrest country and the Confederacy, where his conservative Southern ancestors fought valiantly against liberal Lincoln and the progressive North in defense of Jeffersonianism, constitutional government, and personal liberty.

LOCHLAINNSEABROOK.COM

MEET THE COVER ARTIST

For over 30 years American artist JOHN PAUL STRAIN has been amazing art collectors with his unique talent of capturing moments in time from the early days of the American Frontier, the glory and pageantry of the American Civil War, to contemporary scenic and romantic locations across the world. From the early age of twenty-one, Mr. Strain's paintings were represented by Trailside Galleries, America's most prestigious western art gallery. For fifteen years his beautiful landscapes, wild life paintings, and depictions of Indian life were represented by most every major western art gallery and top art auctions in the United States.

In 1991 Mr. Strain broadened his subjects to include historical art of the American Civil War. During the next seventeen years he focused his work on the world of daring horseback raids and epic battles with great armies and leaders, capturing and preserving a unique era in history. Over a period of years, Mr. Strain became known as America's leading historical artist, with over fifty magazine covers featuring his paintings.

His work is featured in books, movies, and film. Mr. Strain's book, *A Witness to the Civil War*, released in November 2002, was a best seller for his publisher and quickly sold out of its first printing. The book is unusual among art books in that it is written by the artist. The Scholastic Resources Company purchased over 3,000 copies of the edition for school libraries across the US. His newest book was released in 2009.

Strain's paintings have helped to raise funds for many historical restoration projects and battlefield preservation organizations. The National Park Service uses his images in their publications and at battlefield sites. A number of historical private institutions have on site displays featuring his work such as General JEB Stuart's home and estate, and General Jubal Early's boyhood home.

Mr. Strain and his paintings were also featured on the television shows of C-Span's Washington Journal, The History Channel, and Extreme Makeover Home Edition. Throughout his career he has won many awards for his art. Reproductions of his work have won numerous first place awards and "Best of

Show" honors, such as the PICA Awards, The Printing Industry of the Carolinas, and just recently at the PIAG 2008 Awards in Georgia, he won the Top Gold Award for his painting "New Year's Wish," and Best Of Category Giclée for "Fire In the Sky."

Strain is also a featured artist for internationally know collector art companies the Bradford Exchange and the Franklin Mint, where he has created a Civil War Chess Set, several limited edition plate series, sculptures, and many other collectable items featuring his paintings. Mr. Strain has also completed a number of commissioned works for the United States Army, which are on permanent display at Fort Leavenworth, Kansas, Fort McNair, Washington, D.C., and the battlefield visitor's center at Normandy, France.

Today, Mr. Strain's original paintings can be found in many noted museums such as the Museum of Fredericksburg, South Georgia Relics Museum, and at Thomas Jefferson's home, Monticello. His work is included in many private fine art collections, corporate collections, and is owned by dignitaries such as United States Senators, Congressmen and a number of State Governors.

If you enjoyed Mr. Seabrook's *Give 'Em Hell Boys!*
you will be interested in his excellent companion works:

A REBEL BORN: A DEFENSE OF NATHAN BEDFORD FORREST
NATHAN BEDFORD FORREST: SOUTHERN HERO, AMERICAN PATRIOT
THE QUOTABLE NATHAN BEDFORD FORREST

Available from Sea Raven Press and wherever fine books are sold.

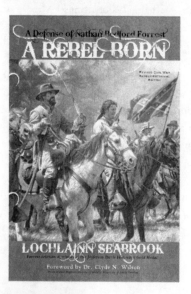

CPSIA information can be obtained at www.ICGtesting.com
Printed in the USA
LVOW05s0359090114

368620LV00001B/29/P

9 780983 818564